OSCAR ROMERO

MEMORIES IN MOSAIC

By
MARÍA LÓPEZ VIGIL

Translated by
KATHY OGLE

Published by
EPICA
Ecumenical Program on Central America & the Caribbean
Washington, DC, USA
&
CAFOD
Catholic Fund for Overseas Development
London, England, UK
&
DARTON, LONGMAN AND TODD, LTD.
London, England, UK

First edition (in Spanish), 1993, UCA Editores, Universidad Centroamericana José Simeón Cañas, Apartado 01-575, San Salvador, El Salvador, under ISBN 84-8405-109-9 (ES)

Catholic Fund for Overseas Development (CAFOD)
2 Romero Close, Stockwell Road, London SW9 9TY England

Darton, Longman and Todd, Ltd.
1 Spencer Court, 140-142 Wandsworth High Street,
London SW18 4JJ England

Cost: $19.95 plus $3.50 postage and handling (USA)

Cover art by Rae Johnson
Book and cover design by Ann Butwell
Photos courtesy of Equipo MAIZ and Octavio Durán

Library of Congress Cataloging-in-Publication Data
López Vigil, María
    [Piezas para un retrato, English]
    Oscar Romero: memories in mosaic / by María López
       Vigil ; translated by Kathy Ogle. p. cm.
    ISBN 0-918346-24-X (USA)
    ISBN 0 232 52371 1 (UK)
     1. Romero, Oscar A. (Oscar Arnulfo), 1917-1980. 2.
    Catholic Church--El Salvador--Bishops--Biography. I. Title.
BX4705.R669 L6613 2000
282'.092--dc21
  [B]   99-462256

ACKNOWLEDGMENTS

Oscar Romero once said, "I've often been accused of consulting with too many people. But that's the nicest thing anyone could accuse me of, and I don't intend to mend my ways!" In this way, perhaps the translation of this book has been a fitting tribute to Romero. It was truly a collective process, and the book is undoubtedly the richer for it. As colorful Salvadoran expressions and slang rendered dictionaries useless, I relied on a team of Salvadoran friends near and far to describe phrases in enough detail to help me choose worthy English equivalents. These consultations always generated moments of laughter and discussion—due appreciation for the linguistic creativity of the Salvadoran people. I am especially grateful to Zoila Elías, for whom no moment was inopportune to discuss the intricacies of Salvadoran *caliche*. Thanks also to Adoneth Landaverde, Carlos García, Federico Talavera and Sonia Umanzor.

On the English side, an even larger team of people helped to polish and shape the rough translations as I chiseled them out. Gene Palumbo, who has long been an advocate for the translation of this book, poured over the text with loving scrutiny, while Marilu MacCarthy, who fell in love with the book as she read, also dedicated hundreds of hours to making it shine. I am indebted to Irene Hodgson and Andrés Thomas Conteris for their thorough readings, and to Julian Filochowski and Damian Conlin of CAFOD for the same. Hats off also to Gus Bono, John Schmitt, Sarah Gammage, and Deb Delavan for their essential contributions. And thank God for proofreaders, especially Erin Yost and Siobhán Dugan!

Above all, my co-workers at EPICA—Ann, Scott, Zoila, Carlos and Marilu—made this translation possible by giving me the time and encouragement necessary to take it on. It was Ann Butwell's idea from the beginning after all, and she was always there with back-rubs and pep-talks. Ann also did all the layout and design, working with artist Rae Johnson on the beautiful cover. Scott Wright provided the space for lunchtime readings and helped make EPICA a place where we could laugh and cry over the stories and share our appreciation for this wonderful work.

It's hard to believe that I could have enjoyed the translation of a 400-page book, but this one really was a joy and an inspiration from beginning to end. As I worked, I realized more fully what it had taken for María López Vigil to write it: the hundreds of hours of taping and transcribing, the editing and arranging of vignettes, the imaginative transformations of diary excerpts into dialogue, the creative bridges of "rumors" and "news flashes," and the moving images of Romero's final moments. María's own writing is the glue that holds the stories together, making this a unique mosaic masterpiece, a collective portrait of Oscar Romero.

Finally, it was Monseñor Romero who, through the simple and courageous consistency of his life, inspired us all to contribute to this remembrance for him on the 20th anniversary of his death and resurrection. Every time I go back to El Salvador, I make a pilgrimage to the little house where Monseñor Romero lived on the grounds of the Divine Providence Hospital. It's a place that reminds me that it's possible to live according to our beliefs. Hundreds of people still go there each year to pay tribute. The last time I was there, a Salvadoran couple came in with their four-day-old son, Oscar. They were there to give thanks for their child, and to say, "We have not forgotten." And so his memory lives on in so many different ways. We will not forget.

Kathy Ogle
Washington, DC

TABLE OF CONTENTS

FOREWORD

One only needs to open this book by María López Vigil to finish reading it in one sitting. The author's remarkable talents combine with the compelling figure of Monseñor Romero in a book that is truly splendid, one that needs no introduction. I will focus my comments, then, on Monseñor Romero himself, in the hope that my reflections may help to place him in context 20 years after his death.

Monseñor Romero loved the poor. He didn't just help them, he defended them. To do that he vehemently denounced their oppressors: the economic elite, the armed forces, governments, political parties, the media, the justice system . . . Like Amos, Isaiah and Jeremiah, he was the people's great prophet.

Monseñor Romero was a guiding light for his people. His long homilies—some even an hour and a half long—put the reality of the country and God's reality into words. His pastoral letters and talks analyzed the structures, the idols and the sin that existed in the country, as well as the rights of the campesinos and the hope that justice was possible. He was the people's great teacher.

Monseñor Romero visited peasant farmers in the most remote villages. He listened to the suffering of mothers and wives when their children disappeared and when the tortured bodies were found. He said once, "It's my job to retrieve the dead." He was the people's great consolation.

Monseñor Romero loved to be with people. In his visits to parishes, he stood in line, plate in hand, to receive his food just like everyone else. And he sat among the children, the young people, women and the old folks. Being with his people gave him strength and joy for living. "With a people like this, it's not hard to be a good shepherd," he said. He was the people's great pastor.

Monseñor Romero suffered defamation, persecution and threats. When the government hypocritically offered him protection, he responded, "I don't want protection as long as my people are not given protection.

With them, I want to run all of the risks that my vocation demands of me." Monseñor Romero was firm and faithful. He was a brother in solidarity with his people.

Monseñor Romero placed his confidence and his joy in God. He prayed even in moments of darkness and fear. Enveloped in that mystery of light coexisting with darkness, he walked humbly with God and towards God, as Micah says. Romero was the people's great example of faithfulness.

On one March 24, the day after he denounced repression and begged for it to stop "in the name of God and of this suffering people whose cries rise up to heaven," he offered bread and wine at the altar, and he offered himself along with those elements. As he did so, he ended his life with these words, "May this immolated body and this blood sacrificed for all people nourish us so that we may also be able to give our body and our blood to suffering and pain, like Christ, not for ourselves, but in order to give justice and peace to our people." Monseñor Romero was the great martyr of the Salvadoran people.

The people of El Salvador and of many other countries know all of these things very well. They give thanks and praise to Monseñor Romero, but as they do so, they see in him the Salvadoran people and all of the suffering people of this world. Monseñor Romero was truly a great person, but at the same time, he is a symbol that expresses more than what he was in life. In his own words, he represents the "suffering servant of Yahweh." In the words of Ignacio Ellacuría he represents "the crucified people." This is why many people in many places see the relationship between Monseñor Romero and the victims of their countries' own tragedies.

Therein lies the deepest universality of Monseñor Romero. A few days after his assassination, Pedro Casaldáliga wrote the poem "Saint Romero of the Americas." At that time many were struck by the evangelical audacity of calling him a "saint," but the deeper truth is that Monseñor had already become a symbol of the crucified Americas. This includes both Latin America and North America. Eight months after Monseñor Romero's blood was shed, so was that of Ita, Maura, Dorothy and Jean, three religious sisters and a lay missioner from the United States. And like them, there are other North Americans who have given their lives on this continent. It is fitting that on the front wall of Westminster Abbey the figures of Monseñor Romero and Martin Luther King are side by side, forever engraved.

Now that we are in the process of Monseñor's beatification, we would like two things. The first is that the Monseñor who is beatified be the real Monseñor—not a watered down version of a priest who is pious but distant from his people. The second is that Monseñor Romero be canonized along with all of the Salvadoran martyrs, all of the martyrs of the Americas, and indeed, all of the martyrs of the Reign of God.

Monseñor Romero cannot be separated from his people. He gave everything to his people, even his very being. And the Salvadoran people, with the best of their faith, hope and love made him what he was. "The people are my prophet," he used to say. His identification with the people was total and complete in his death. It gives us chills even today to hear the words with which he expressed this identification. "Brothers and sisters, I'm glad that the Church is being persecuted. In a country where so many horrendous murders are occurring, it would be very sad to think that there were no priests among the victims. Their deaths are a symbol that the Church has incarnated itself among the poor." This prophetic statement was fulfilled in his own death.

Monseñor Romero's identification with the people continues even after his death. "If they kill me, I will rise again in the Salvadoran people," he said, and even today there are many for whom the memory of Monseñor Romero is a source of strength and encouragement.

And like Jesus, Monseñor has not wanted to infantilize his people, to tie them or enslave them to himself. Rather, he liberated his people so that they could do great things themselves, even after his own death. That was certainly his desire. In the midst of the persecution of the Church, he said, "If one day, they took our radio station away from us, closed the newspaper or didn't let us speak; if they killed off all of our priests and the bishop too, and you were left as a people without priests; then each one of you would have to be a microphone for God. Each one of you would have to be a messenger, a prophet. As long as there is one baptized person left, the Church will continue to exist!" And a few days before his death, he said simply, "I hope they will be convinced that it would be waste of their time. A bishop would die, but the Church of God, which is the people, will never perish."

Jon Sobrino
San Salvador, El Salvador

INTRODUCTION

By now he could have been a cardinal of the Catholic Church, preaching his sermons at assemblies and conferences, a red biretta on his head. With his history of faithful orthodoxy, he had just about paid the necessary dues to be awarded that kind of position.

Instead, he's buried in the basement of the rickety Cathedral of a poor Central American country in the forgotten South, with a bullet in his heart.

There aren't many human beings who pull the rug out from under themselves when they are getting on in their years. Trading security for danger and hard-earned truths for new uncertainties are adventures for the youngest of us. Old people don't change; it's one of life's rules.

And it's one of history's rules that the more power you have, the more distanced you become from people and the less your heart is touched by their troubles. You move up in the world, and other people get left behind. Power makes you drunk. It isolates you.

Oscar Romero broke both of these rules. He experienced "conversion" when he was 60 years old. It was when he was ascending to the highest levels of the Church hierarchy in his country that he truly moved closer to the people and their everyday reality. And it was when he was at the height of his career, when his years began to ask him for rest, that he decided to understand that there is no greater ascension than to move towards the earth.

So he journeyed downward toward the reality of life on earth.

In that eleventh hour, he chose to open himself to compassion and even to put his life on the line. And so he lost his life. That doesn't happen to many.

For this and many other reasons, I believe Oscar Romero's story is worth telling. I first thought of doing this book in 1981. At that time, more than 30 dead bodies were turning up every morning on the roads and back streets of El Salvador. And every Salvadoran I ran into spoke to me passionately about his or her personal connection with Monseñor Romero.

It seemed to me that the Archbishop of San Salvador had left as big a mark on his country as he had in the hearts of so many of its people. So it became a challenge for me to find the social relevance in these scattered memories, to put these well-told anecdotes into the common arena and transform them into pieces of a mosaic that would yield a portrait of Oscar Romero. In the end, would it be a portrait of the real Monseñor Romero? It would be a portrait, in any case; one made as a collective effort.

I dreamt about this book during the time of the worst repression, when the memory of Monseñor was still fresh and when the destiny of poor peoples' struggle for liberation caused the world to feel the pain of that struggle. At that time, "solidarity" was practically a sacred word.

I wrote the book, and now it's being published in another time. All of the bloodshed and the stubborn hope of the Salvadorans managed to force open the doors to another era, to the beginning of peace and the end of the armed conflict. Monseñor Romero is already a legend in the collective memory, but there is a whole new generation of Salvadorans that doesn't know him very well.

It's another time in the world, too. Dreams, ideas and projects have been devalued quickly, and in the midst of a confusing wave of changes, we have to keep looking in the direction of solidarity even though our compasses are half broken.

The world has taken a sharp, screwed-up turn for the worse. Perhaps other, more encouraging times will come. But in spite of all the changes yesterday, today and tomorrow, I believe it's still worthwhile and necessary to tell the story of this good man, Oscar Romero.

Among other things, his story reveals how God acts, and how compassion keeps winning out over ideology. We need good leaders, today and at all times in this world. We need people with power—in the Church, among other places—who call things by their true names and look at reality itself, not at some representation of reality; people who feel compassion and take action. There is so much life half-lived, so much avoidable pain.

This is a book of personal stories, not a collection of documents or even a biography. There is no chronological rigor in the order of the stories, and there are a lot of holes and empty spaces. In the end, after talking with some 200 people for nearly 1,000 hours, I found myself at many crossroads where I had to choose. It wasn't easy. And perhaps I've been partial in my choices. The names of the witnesses are there, camouflaged only occasionally. In trying to reconstruct the portrait of Oscar Romero, the most universal of Salvadorans, the truth of all these testimonies came to me laden with love or already altered in some way by the golden aura of the icon and the legend. Each one gave me one or more pieces for the portrait. It was up to me to re-create them, shape them, bring out their shine, accent their colors here or there. I also wanted to include a measure of veneration from my own pen.

This is an incomplete book, and it's open to growing and maturing with the contributions of many more witnesses—those I was not able to reach.

It is dedicated to the Salvadoran people, the people who made Monseñor Romero.

María López Vigil
Managua, Nicaragua

SECTION ONE

What is the way to the place where lightning is dispersed?
Who has cleft a channel for the torrents of rain . . .
to bring rain to the desert?

—Job 38: 24-26

"My brother always turned inward, thought too much."

CIUDAD BARRIOS AWOKE from its peasant slumber as soon as the sun raised its head above the horizon in the usual place.

"The bishop is coming!"

San Miguel's very first bishop, Juan Antonio Dueñas y Argumedo, was coming to visit.

"Mamá," said Oscar, who was still a little boy, "Why don't you buy me a new shirt and a pair of pants so I can go see him?"

Niña Guadalupe de Jesús got the new clothes ready so her son would be neat and presentable. So the boy went about, here, there and everywhere, accompanying the bishop on all his rounds. The bishop was quite impressed with him.

"The bishop is leaving!"

And all of Ciudad Barrios got together to see him off.

"Oscar, come over here!" the bishop called to him in front of his townspeople.

"Yes, Monseñor?"

"Tell me, boy, what do you want to be when you grow up?"

"Well, I . . . I would like to be a priest!"

Then the bishop raised his hefty finger and pointed it straight at Oscar's forehead.

"You are going to be a bishop."

After marking the destiny of the boy, he went back to his mansion in San Miguel. And Ciudad Barrios went back to its drowsy sleep.

Fifty years later, Monseñor Romero touched that place on his forehead and told me, "I can still feel the touch of his finger right here."

(Carmen Chacón)

AS A BOY HE SEEMED A LITTLE SAD. My brother always turned inward, thought too much.

What games did he play? Well, he seemed to get the most fun out of doing processions. He'd put one of mother's aprons over the top of him and go around on the streets calling out to the other kids, pretending he was already a priest.

Oh, and the circus! He would die to go to the circus. He never missed one! You know, the tightrope walkers doing those balancing acts way up there on the wire . . . And the clowns! Circuses were his greatest joy.

Let's see, there was Gustavo, then Oscar, Zaida, Aminta, who died when she was little, Rómulo, who died when he was older, Mamerto, Arnoldo and Gaspar. That was our order as sisters and brothers. Oscar was born on August 15, 1917.

Of all of us, he was probably the one who prayed the most. Our father, Santos, had him apprenticed to Juan Leiva, the best carpenter in Ciudad Barrios, so Oscar worked alongside him and made doors, tables, china cabinets and even coffins. But more than anything else, he prayed. "I never saw a kid pray so much," Leiva would say. Because Oscar would go running out after his time in the carpentry shop and go straight to church for his prayers. Who knows? Maybe some day they'll make a national monument out of that place where he used to pray as a kid.

And at night, he'd jump out of the bed he shared with Mamerto to kneel on the floor and say a few more prayers, wouldn't he? That destiny given by God was already a part of him.

We scraped by. Mother had to rent out the upper part of the house, so the laundry area got moved to the downstairs patio where there was no roof. When it rained everything got soaked. She got wet one too many times working out there. Her body started to go into paralysis, and she ended up crippled. And to top it all off the tenants were these cheap-skates that didn't even pay! We had bad luck because our father also lost some coffee lands to an unscrupulous moneylender. So we barely managed to put food on the table for everyone.

When he was 13, Oscar was still determined to be a priest. So mother got his clothes ready, and he headed off to seminary in San Miguel. From there he went even farther away—to Rome, no less!—to finish his studies as a priest. He was living there during World War II. In any case, many years went by in which our brother was away from our family and from Ciudad Barrios.

(Zaida Romero/Tiberio Arnoldo Romero)

CIUDAD BARRIOS WAS ON MY WAY when I was walking one day to visit my grandmother who lived in Morazán. I was a vagabond of a kid—only 10 years old—but already I liked to go all over getting to know new places. I arrived and saw that Ciudad Barrios was all deco-rated up with coffee flowers and paper flags, and that they'd even brought in a marimba band. "Hmmm," I thought, "maybe I'll stay."

"A priest from here is going to say his first Mass in this church."

Everyone knew about it except me, since I wasn't from there. But when I found out, I went into the church to check it out and see everything from beginning to end with my own eyes.

I entered the church about an hour before this great Mass was sup-posed to start. My leather sandals were all covered with dust from my wanderings, and since it was really hot that day, I was sweating the whole time. It was embarrassing because the sweat was running down my body to my sandals and turning the dust into mud. Soon I had little trickles of mud dripping down and splattering on the bricks below me. But I didn't move an inch because I really liked that Mass with the new priest making his debut and all.

I arrived at my grandmother's house pretty late at night, all disheveled. She was one of these really religious women.

"Why are you coming in so late, young man?"

"I was at the Mass celebrated by a new priest."

"What priest . . ?"

I gave my grandmother the little prayer card they'd given out during the Mass. I couldn't read it, but his name was written there: *Oscar Arnulfo Romero. First Solemn Mass. Ciudad Barrios, January 11, 1944.*

"I have a feeling that priest is going to be a bishop," I told her.

"Oh, so you're a fortune-teller, are you? What do you know about being a bishop?"

"I don't know about it, but I can imagine."

(Moisés González)

"If they had given him a little wolf with fangs and all,
he would have received it in just the same way."

SHEPHERD OF SHEEP AND WOLVES
Parish Priest in San Miguel (1944-1967)

HE WAS ON THE GO AT ALL HOURS of the day and night. Hearing confessions the whole blessed day or the whole never-ending night after a rosary. That takes patience, now that I think about it! It was a constant effort because in San Francisco there was a rosary every night. And Father Romero was not one to let a rosary go by without a homily. He never wasted an opportunity! One day—he told us sacristans—he was almost finished hearing confessions when . . .

"Father, what penance should I do?" a woman asked him.

"You should pray five pesos," he mumbled.

He had fallen asleep! That's the way he was. He would work without stopping, until he was totally burned out.

(Raúl Romero)

FATHER RAFAEL VALLADARES was his best friend among the priests. He was a pal from seminary days, and they worked together for many years in San Miguel. The two were very different, but they complemented each other. Valladares was more of a writer, and Romero was the talker. Since Father Romero was so strict about how priests should behave, it was hard for him to accept the kinds of liberties that some priests took—for example, not wearing their cassocks. That, and other things like that, bothered him a lot. When Valladares would see him so upset, he would tease him:

"This guy stresses himself out by getting so angry! He blows his top so easily he's going to spend his entire life suffering from one sickness or another. Now, I, on the other hand, never get upset . . ."

Valladares would turn everything into a joke. But Romero wouldn't. He would just burn up on the inside, and we'd often see him ill at ease, nervous or depressed.

(Doris Osegueda)

THE BIG COFFEE PLANTATION OWNERS of San Miguel were very close to him. They'd give him money for charity and invite him to their farms, and he'd celebrate special masses in their plantation homes or go at Christmas time and help them hand out little presents to the poor workers there. Everyone knew that.

I was a little girl when a group of rich women friends of his—the Ladies of such-and-such a Charity—dreamed up an idea and called us school-girls to help them.

"We're going to fix up Father Romero's room the way he deserves."

They bought a new bed and put in these elegant curtains—really fancy ones. They changed everything! They took advantage of the fact that he was away on a trip. And they got enthusiastic about it because his little room at the parish house of the convent in Santo Domingo was pretty much nothing—really poor.

When Father Romero returned he was furious. He tore down the curtains and gave them to the first person he saw passing by. He gave away his new bedspread, the sheets—everything went out! Then he returned his cot and his old chair to their old places, and put everything back in his room just the way it was before.

"I may be their friend, but they're not going to start manipulating me, no matter how much money they have!"

The women really resented this.

(Nelly Rodríguez)

THE DRUNKS WERE THE ONES who sought him out the most. They say his brother Gustavo had drinking problems and died of it, and that he had gone staggering drunk around the streets of San Miguel and that everybody knew it. They say he would come to the parish looking for his brother, Father Romero, and that Romero would scold him, but that he also had a lot of patience with him. And with drunks you have to have a lot of patience because they'll drive you crazy!

We saw his patience with my brother Angelito. If Romero were there when Angelito came home after a big drinking spree, he wouldn't let any of us reproach him or hassle him.

"Come here, Angelito," he would say, "Sit down next to me and play the flute for me."

So he'd play Mexican and Guatemalan folk songs, which he could do really nicely, and the music would calm Angelito down. So you see, Father Romero always had a soft spot for drunks and for the downtrodden in life.

(Elvira Chacón)

HE LOVED US SEMINARIANS, and sometimes he even spoiled us. Besides everything else he had to do, Father Romero was also the head of the minor seminary in San Miguel.

Efraín, a buddy of ours who had been a seminarian since he was a little kid, didn't have a father or a mother or any money.

"I don't believe I have a vocation," he told Father Romero when he finished his twelfth grade studies, "I've fallen in love."

Disappointed, Romero watched him leave the seminary.

After some time, Efraín returned.

"I've come to ask you a favor, Father Romero."

"What is it?" he asked, thinking he was coming back to the fold.

"I'd like it if you would be the one to go to ask for my girlfriend's hand in marriage . . ."

"Me?"

"It's because I don't have anyone else. I'm working as a chauffeur, and she has a better job than I do. You know those families and how demanding they are. It'll only work if you put in a good word for me . . ."

"You really take the cake! You want to have it both ways!"

But he agreed, and he went to the girl's parents' house and played the role of the father who asks for the bride's hand for his son. And sure enough, they said yes. Only because Romero was the one backing him up.

"The priesthood is not for everyone," he started telling us from that day on, "but the seminary can help to form and educate all of you. Some of you will leave here to become priests, and some will go on to other things . . ."

And he looked at each one of us, as if he were trying to guess.

(Miguel Ventura)

MY GRANDFATHER Secundino's stories held our attention like magnets. He would tell us about Noah's ark and all the animals inside it, about Abraham, about Sarah who gave birth when she was already an old lady, and about Jonah and the whale, all in great detail. Around those parts in Cacaopera, he was the only one who had a Bible, but he kept it hidden away, and I had never even been able to hold it in my hands. I had a huge desire to know if all of those stories my grandfather was telling us at night were true.

In 1952, around Christmas time, I wove three hammocks that were each about eight feet long and I told my wife:

"I'm going to go to San Miguel to sell them, and with what I make, I'm going to buy a Bible."

Since I was going on my own business, I travelled alone. When I arrived, I went straight to the market where hammocks are sold. I got 10 *colones* for each one and with that, I was sure I'd have enough to buy myself a Bible. I went running to the church of San Francisco, and there I was allowed to see Father Romero.

"You know what? I don't have any Bibles here right now," he told me, "but I'm going to make a telephone call to San Salvador so they'll send me some on the afternoon truck. We'll have them by tomorrow, if you want to wait . . ."

"I'd be happy to wait, Father, but where would I stay the night?"

"No problem. You can do what you need to in the city, look around, and later on you can come back and sleep here in the convent."

I felt so welcomed even though I was just a poor *campesino*, a peasant farmer . . . When it was already late, I went back and I saw that other people were sleeping there too—other poor people. He had given them all a place.

My Bible had arrived in the afternoon so I finally had a way to read the stories first hand. As I was leaving, Father Romero gave me some advice.

"It's good to read the Bible by yourself, but it's even better if you read it together with other people. It's like when you go to gather *nance* fruits with a group. The more people that go, the more you pick up, and the better the harvest."

I went back home. And from then on I always listened to Father Romero on *Radio Chaparrastique*, where he was on every day talking about Bible passages. You had to be on the ball to figure out what book, what chapter and what verse he was reading from and not miss anything. I was there with other people, listening to him, harvesting. It was like having your own teacher.

(Alejandro Ortiz)

THE DRUNKS OF SAN MIGUEL knew that he gave out alms every day, but they also knew that he liked to have order and that he didn't like things to get chaotic. They started making a line early in the morning.

"Is there also something for me, Father . . ?

"Sure. And why not, woman? The rule is that everyone who asks receives."

"Even the hookers?" a lame man challenged.

Even them. The prostitutes, the drunks and the panhandlers lined up around the wall of the church, sure that each one would have a coin coming to them, even if it were just a quarter of one *colón*, because Father Romero never said no and because he always had coins in the pocket of his big black cassock. They would do their best to be still and quiet in line, and they would receive.

"Be good," he'd reproach them when the wretched line of beggars started to fall apart.

"What does it matter, Father? Good or bad, we're still coming back tomorrow!"

And the next day they'd return and the same line would appear, only longer. For latecomers, there might be lunch, or dinner, or a place to stay the night. And if *campesinos* came in from the countryside, he'd give them the bus fare for their return. He also took drunks into the convent. And old folks. And shoe shine boys. Romero was like St. Vincent de Paul—a mass of poor people always followed him around. Of course, with his way of thinking, he always got the rich people to pay alms so that he could give them to the poor. That way the poor could have some relief for their problems and the rich could relieve their consciences.

(Rutilio Sánchez)

IN THE PLACE WHERE THE CHAPARRASTIQUE volcano erupted, who knows when, there were some empty fields covered with lava rock that didn't belong to anybody. Not even weeds grew on those fields, and that's where the most desperately poor people would put up their little huts made of tin and boards. That place was called La Curruncha.

"That place is a den of thieves!"

"They'll cut you up and make soup out of you there!"

But really it wasn't that way, because when I was a young nun I went out there to teach catechism, and they always treated me with respect.

When one of those poor people there was at the end of his or her rope and knew their days were numbered, it was always the same thing.

"Do you want some medicine?"

"We want to speak with Father Romero."

They wanted to see him so they could make their last confession before they died. He never told them no, whether it was during those chilly wee hours of the morning or during the hours when La Curruncha burned like a pot on the fire.

(Angela Panameño)

HE WAS ALWAYS ASKING FOR DONATIONS to make improvements on the cathedral. It was his job to rebuild it, put up the ceilings, bells, and who knows how many other things that are still there, even today.

"I don't have money for the wages, Raúl! Go over to Niña Chabe Carmona's place. Tell her that I need a little money to pay the workers!" he'd say impatiently.

I would go, and they would give me whatever bit of money that Father Romero might have asked for. He was a friend of the García Prietos, the Bustamantes, the Estradas, the Canales . . . They all gave alms for his poor people. They all invited him to their plantations for lunches or to say Mass. But the closest friend he had in San Miguel was Don Ernesto Campos, the owner of La Roca brick factory.

"Father, how are you? Are you free? Let's go!"

He would come looking for Romero at the convent to take him out to El Cuco Beach—sheer leisure outings. They were great friends. And besides, he donated the bricks for the cathedral!

(Raúl Romero)

IT WASN'T JUST IN SAN MIGUEL. All of us in the eastern part of the country knew about him because of his programs on *Radio Chaparrastique*. I was a second grader in La Unión, and I never missed an opportunity to listen to him.

Laudetur Jesus Christus. Those were the closing words of his much-listened-to Morning Prayer and Evening Prayer. I liked hearing those Latin words so much, I would recite them by memory. There were also some great programs on *El Padre Vicente*, where they would tell real-life stories. All those things I heard on the radio really opened my mind. I learned from them.

A lot of people would write him letters asking about certain topics, asking for advice or financial help, or volunteering for his charities. And he would read that whole mess of letters on the radio. I loved that program because there was so much participation.

But for me, the most impressive things were the bells. You see, when he travelled to Rome and visited places that touched his soul, he would do a summary of his trip when he returned and tell the listeners his impressions. One day he even played a recording of the bells at Saint Peter's Basilica in Rome so that all of us could hear them as he had. The ringing of those bells from so far away, those chords, that sound . . . I was lost in it. It wasn't even like I was dreaming of travelling there. It was like I was there with him.

(Miguel Vázquez)

"HE'S A STICKLER, THAT PRIEST! You have to walk around on eggshells with him!"

Father Romero was a stickler, a *güishte*. Like one of those sharp slivers of glass that will cut you. Very, very strict. But then, how could he have been any different when the Diocese of San Miguel was such a disaster?!

"Those sloppy priests that go around without their cassocks!" he would agonize.

"Better that they go without their cassocks since they're just chasing after prostitutes anyway!"

And he'd agonize more. It was true. There were womanizing priests. And liquor flowed faster than communion wine among them. Pastoral plans? They all went up in smoke. There was no interest. There was no effort. And the bishop? Bishop Machado didn't give orders and he didn't give advice. What he gave were loans at outrageous interest rates. Everybody knew those stories, and Father Romero knew them best because he saw all the drama from the inside.

Since the clergy in San Miguel did whatever they pleased, it was up to Romero to do what they didn't do. He took responsibility for everything and more. He handled several parishes, all of the religious organizations, all of the movements, the work in the schools, the files, the jails, and, on top of all of that, he had to give the irresponsible priests a good chewing out. That *güishte*, as they called him, bothered them so much that they tried to marginalize him.

He would get depressed. I started to become aware of the difficulty of his situation. One day we were coming back from the plantation of a coffee-growing friend of his. Maybe because he'd been able to rest a little there, he confided in me, because he hardly ever did.

"They talk about me behind my back. They complain about me . . ."

"Well, if I were you, I wouldn't let it get to you. The people don't complain about you. When push comes to shove, when they need some advice or they're going through hard times, people don't go looking for those two-faced priests. They look for you. Don't they?"

He looked at me. I don't know if he shared my certainty.

(*Manuel Vergara*)

WE WERE DEVELOPING A FRIENDSHIP, getting to know each other in those glorious times of the Christian *Cursillo* Movement.[1] We were at a gathering in Mexico, and one night he came into my room, all discouraged and hanging his head.

"Father Chencho, tell me. Do you think I'm crazy?"

He sat down, and it was apparent that he had come for a heart-to-heart, even though that wasn't his style.

"What do you think?" he asked again.

I'd known him for years and knew about all of the various things he was involved in.

"Look, I don't believe any such thing. What I know is that you're the parish priest in San Francisco and Santo Domingo *and* at the cathedral, which is the brotherhood of all brotherhoods. I know that not a day goes by that you're not giving several sermons, that there wouldn't have been a Festival for the Virgin of Peace if it weren't for you, that now you're working with Alcoholics Anonymous, and that you hardly sleep . . ."

"So . . ."

"So, what you are is exhausted!"

I also knew that some priests in San Miguel were spreading the rumor that Father Romero had mental problems in order to undermine his

---

[1]Christian *Cursillo* Movement—A Catholic movement of Bible study and reflection through weekend retreat experiences.

credibility. And since Valladares, his best priest friend had died, Romero was feeling alone. Alone and isolated.

"Hey, don't let it get to you, man," I encouraged him, "Is it possible that they call exhaustion madness in San Miguel?"

We talked for about three hours, and gradually, he calmed down.

"Don't go back to El Salvador. Stay in Cuernavaca a while. Don't put off until tomorrow what you can do today. Put it off until the day *after* tomorrow! Give yourself a rest."

He listened to my advice.

(Inocencio Alas)

DOÑA GUADALUPE DE JESÚS GALDÁMEZ, his mother, or Niña Jesús as we called her, died in 1961. She had lived near her son, Father Romero, since he'd been assigned his priestly duties here in San Miguel. By the time he got here, her arm was already paralyzed by disease, and there was practically no feeling left in it. She was very quiet.

Every week Father Romero would go to visit her in the neighborhood of San Francisco where she lived. You could look at her face and see that mother and son looked exactly alike. Her face was his face. Her hands were his hands. You could see that the way she gestured with her hand, was the same way he moved his. Maybe his jaw was more pronounced than his mother's, but even that trait he got from her.

She died, and we buried her in San Miguel. And since Father Romero had relationships with the upper class families of San Miguel—from the García Prietos on down—people from the aristocracy went to the funeral. Coffee plantation owners showed up, and even a famous pianist from there. But since he also had friends like us who loved him, we went too. Nuns went, and children went. His whole family also arrived in San Miguel on that sad occasion, and we saw what they were like—of humble bearing. On the way to the cemetery after the funeral Mass, who do you think he walked with? He didn't go with the upper crust, he walked alongside the ones in simple dress, in country clothes—us!

"I was born with them. I'll go with them," he said quietly.

And that was what the whole way was like—him alongside the casket and alongside the crowds of the poor.

(Antonia Novoa)

HE WAS LYING IN A HAMMOCK on one of the trips to the beach that some of us priests from different dioceses went on. I didn't know him personally yet.

In order to start a conversation, I mentioned the speech on family planning that Pope Paul VI had directed to the Latin American bishops at the end of the Second Vatican Council. It was one speech among many. I started to make some comments on what I remembered the pope having said. Suddenly, Father Romero interrupted me.

"You're wrong. That's not what the Holy Father said."

"It's not?"

He started to correct me up and down. He seemed so sure that I didn't want to argue with him. Which one of us was right? I kept going back and forth in my head about this when I went in the ocean for a dip.

When I got back to San Salvador, I ran to look for the text of the pope's speech just to settle the matter. He was right! He'd remembered it exactly. He practically knew it by heart.

(Ricardo Urioste)

I DON'T KNOW IF I WAS HIS BEST FRIEND. Maybe I was. We began our friendship when he was just about to be transferred from San Miguel to San Salvador. I was working then, driving a huge truck. And Juan Salinas came looking for me.

"Do you think you could help Father Romero out?"

It was an enormous collection of books. I'd never seen so many in my life!

"That truck of yours is the only thing they'll all fit in."

Romero was always a human library. I knew him pretty well from those San Miguel days—his mannerisms, how he was with people. And I'd heard people say that he surrounded himself with rich people. But what can I say? I never saw him be a better friend to anyone than he was to the shoe shine boys in San Miguel. He even founded a Shoe Shiner's Association to bring them together, and he arranged for a space in the cathedral where they could sleep when they needed to. He was always talking and joking with them. And when they shined his shoes, he always said,

"See if you can make them so shiny they squeak!"

He liked his shoes to be smooth, all polished up, and with that last little squeak.

(Salvador Barraza)

WE THOUGHT HE WOULD BE THE NEW BISHOP of San Miguel. Pretty much everyone thought so. Who would it be if it wasn't Father Romero? He was the priest that everyone knew, the one in charge of everything. He'd be the one to be named, right?

But he wasn't made a bishop, and they didn't let him stay in San Miguel either. We never knew why, just that he'd received an order instructing him to go to San Salvador to work as a secretary for all the rest of the bishops.

There was a going away party for him at the movie theater in San Miguel. A huge crowd arrived and they couldn't even all fit inside. Rich, poor, kind-of-rich, kind-of-poor—we all showed up at the gathering. Everybody was there! I was all dressed up in my best outfit—a blue dress I had—but inside I was feeling pretty insecure because there were so many rich, fancy women around.

What I remember most about the event was that a little kid got up on stage with Romero to give him a lamb as a gift. Father Romero received it.

When we saw him holding the little animal in his arms, we all started applauding. I myself applauded and so did my *comadre*.[2] All the important women that had gathered to honor him applauded too. And amidst all the festivities and everyone applauding, I just kept looking at Father Romero . . .

Do you want me to be frank? Father Romero? He was a friend of the poor and a friend of the rich. To the rich he would say, "Love the poor." And to us poor he would tell us to love God, and that God knew what He was doing by putting us last in line, and that afterwards we would be assured a place in heaven. He would preach to us about the heaven where rich people who gave alms would go and where poor people who didn't cause too much trouble would go.

Father Romero? He went around with sheep and with wolves, and his thinking was that the sheep and the wolves should eat from the same dish, because that's what was pleasing to God.

Those were hard times. The coffee barons, the cotton barons and the García Prieto gang were eating up all the land of El Salvador and drinking our sweat in exchange for a few pennies, those ingrates! And there were so many people who weren't very aware politically, as if they were asleep, thinking that nobody could change all of that—that it was all part of our destiny written by God.

I looked at him then, Father Romero up there on the stage cradling that little lamb in his arms. But what I really thought was that if they had given him a little wolf with fangs and all, he would have received it in just the same way.

Everyone applauded and burst into tears because after 23 years he was leaving San Miguel. But as for me personally, I can't say I was too sorry to see him go.

(María Varona)

---

[2] *comadre*—A close woman friend who, through baptism, is either the mother of one's godchild or the godmother of one's child.

"Colonel Molina started his presidency on July 1, 1972."

A LITTLE INQUISITOR
Auxiliary Bishop of San Salvador (1967-1974)

I DIDN'T LIKE HIM. He was an insignificant being, a shadow that went by clinging to the walls. I don't know why, but when he arrived in San Salvador, Father Romero decided to stay in the San José de la Montaña Seminary. I was part of a Jesuit community that lived there. But he never ate any of his meals with us. He would go down to the dining room at different times so that he wouldn't run into us. It was clear he was avoiding us, and that he'd arrived at the seminary laden with prejudices.

We never saw him attend anything that resembled a pastoral activity. He didn't have a parish. And he didn't go to the clergy meetings. If he did go, he would hide in some corner and never open his mouth. He was afraid of confronting the more active priests that were being radicalized by everything that was happening in the country—and there was a lot happening! But he preferred to stay in his office buried in his papers. Or to walk down the halls dressed in his black cassock praying the breviary.

Soon after he arrived in San Salvador, we had a Pastoral Week that was a real shaker-upper! Everything went into high gear and became more radical. Plans, meetings, formation of communities[1]—a thousand things were getting underway! He stayed on the margins of all of that. Later he started to take sides, but against us. People were talking about his psy-

---

[1]communities—Christian base communities are small Bible study groups, led by lay people. Base communities flourished in the Latin American Catholic Church in the late 1960s after the Second Vatican Council (1963) which called for sweeping changes in the Church. Masses began to be held in Spanish rather than Latin, people were encouraged to read the Bible for themselves, and lay people took on new leadership roles, previously designated only to clergy.

chological problems back then. They said he took trips to Mexico to recover. It was also said that he was close to some of the Opus Dei priests here in San Salvador. He had his world, and it was not like ours. He started off on the wrong foot from the very beginning.

(Salvador Carranza)

YOU COULD HEAR HIS TYPEWRITER going full speed. Father Romero had to look at the keyboard, but he typed really fast. We would see the light on in his room until very late at night. He was a hard worker—too much so.

When he arrived in San Salvador, preparations were already underway for the Latin American bishops' meeting in Medellín—the meeting that shook the whole Church to its core.[2] And since he was the Secretary of the Bishops' Conference, he had to prepare documents, arrange them systematically, organize them so they could be discussed, mail them off and be on top of all of the ins and outs of the preparation.

His way of thinking was very different from the one that was brewing in Latin America, but as far as paperwork and documents were concerned, he put all of his effort into getting things just right. When all was said and done, it was still the work of the Church, and in those matters, he was a perfectionist.

The winds of Medellín were already beginning to blow, and many of the bishops had stopped wearing their long black cassocks. But him? Forget it. He kept wearing his. One day on the way back from one of those bishops' meetings, he told us seminarians as if he were embarrassed, "You wouldn't believe how out of place I felt. I was the only one in the whole room wearing black!"

(Miguel Ventura)

---

[2]Medellín—In 1968, Latin American bishops gathered in Medellín, Colombia. The controversial conclusions of this meeting upheld the idea of de-linking the Church from its previous alliances with powerful groups in favor of a "preferential option for the poor."

FINALLY THEY MADE HIM A BISHOP. We got the big news, and right away we started to organize a party for him. Since I was his best friend I got involved in the arrangements so that everything would turn out just right.

We had to get the word out through all of San Miguel, where he was best known. So we did. We had to rent a place, decorate it, put in a sound system and make invitations. So we did all of that, too. There was no obstacle that we didn't overcome.

"There are 40 bus loads of people coming from San Miguel!"

When we found out, we had to move quickly and find a place outside that would be bigger so that everyone would fit. We ended up at the Marists.

"Cardinal Casariego is coming!"

He was none other than the most important church official in all of Central America. The more momentum the thing gathered, the more high-level people wanted to come.

Finally the great day came. All of the Salvadoran bishops, the papal nuncio, a whole bunch of priests, nuns and Catholic school students were there, along with people from the upper crust—people with last names that meant something. A bunch of government authorities showed up too—mayors, military people . . . Then at the last minute . . .

"The President of the Republic is coming!"

With him came the police squads to guarantee the security of all these important people.

When it was all over, we realized we'd pulled off an unforgettable ceremony—just magnificent! There's a famous photo of Monseñor Oscar Romero on June 21, 1970, the Sunday that Archbishop Chávez consecrated him as his auxiliary bishop. You can see the satisfaction on his face. Next to him is Father Rutilio Grande, his friend, who Romero had asked to be the master of ceremonies that day.

(Salvador Barraza)

THEY SAY HE NEVER TOOK HIS EYES OFF THE FLOOR. The
Jesuits, who taught at the seminary and ran it, also lived there. One of
them told me that one day he found Romero practically cowering against
the wall, with the wind knocked out of him. When he saw him so upset
like that, he said,

"Monseñor, what's the matter with you?"

He was so frightened he couldn't even talk.

"Monseñor, your problem is you don't have enough faith."

This encounter took place shortly after the conclusions of the Medellín
meeting were made known. Medellín brought so much renewal to the
Church, but Romero was afraid of anything new. He didn't have the
courage to accept all those changes, and soon he began to oppose
them—to try to stop anything that looked like it was heading in that
direction. It was pure fear.

(Ana María Godoy)

***ORIENTACIÓN* WAS THE NAME** of the Church newspaper. It pub-
lished 6,000 copies weekly, and there was a plan to print and sell more.
Archbishop Chávez put Romero in charge of the paper, and in his hands
it changed completely.

At that time I was the parish priest at San Francisco, and one day several
young men came and visited me on his behalf.

"Monseñor Romero has sent us to do a report on your parish."

"All right. Tell me, what do you want to know?"

"We don't need to know anything. He just asked us to take pictures of
the church from different angles, and to take pictures of the people
coming to Mass."

"That's all?"

"Yes, that would be enough."

"Well, you tell Monseñor Romero that I would prefer that the report talk about the living communities that we're forming here in this parish, and not about the dead bricks in the church."

I was a little angry. They left. I'm sure they communicated my opinion to Monseñor Romero. But he must not have liked it, because a few days later he sent the same guys back to take the same pictures that he'd wanted all along. I let them go ahead. There didn't seem to be any point in arguing.

"All of us Romeros are obstinate," he would often say.

It's just that when he had his mind made up about something, he would be relentless—really stubborn. Like a steamroller.

(Ricardo Urioste)

HE WAS PRETTY MUCH A NOBODY to our community. What did we know about Monseñor Romero back then? That he was an ally of the rich ladies and that he went around blessing their parties and their mansions. He was always appearing in the social pages of the newspapers, today with one family of the bourgeoisie, tomorrow with another. In the photos, he always looked so happy along side those hoity toity women. It was ridiculous the number of gatherings he went to—constantly!

It was also known that he had to take trips to Guatemala for the Central American bishops' meetings. In our communities the rumors were going around that with all his travel back and forth he was making money by buying rosaries and scapulars in Guatemala in order to bless them and then sell them for a profit here. Since they were religious goods, he could get them across the border without paying taxes with a special permission given to him by his friends in the government. Who knows whether he really did that, but that was the gossip. That was what people were saying.

(Guillermina Díaz)

THE ARGUMENTS WITH HIM BEGAN. First of all, some of us "red" priests, who'd been working together since before Medellín, formed a group at the National University and wrote a public letter protesting his appointment as bishop. We denounced him openly as a conservative who was trying to put the brakes on the Church's movement toward renewal. We were pretty direct.

Earlier, when that disaster of a man named Mario Casariego in Guatemala was appointed cardinal, we'd already had a pretty big altercation with him. We wrote a document rejecting his appointment, included a list of all the corrupt activities we knew he was involved in, and published it in the newspapers. Monseñor Romero, who was Secretary of the Bishops' Conference at the time, joined the fight. He tried to undermine our authority, by condemning us in letters that he wrote and sent all over the place. It was a war of letters in which he defended Casariego tooth and nail, arguing that supporting that leper would somehow save the Church.

So Romero already knew where I was coming from and had me pretty well figured as a troublemaker when an opportunity to travel to Colombia came my way. I was supposed to get to know the work of Radio Sutatenza, an educational experience that sounded really progressive back then, but that later I realized was more conservative than tranquilizers. I was getting ready for my trip when I ran into Monseñor Romero one day at the archdiocesan offices.

"It's good to see you, Father Sánchez. Look here, here's a gift for your trip."

He gave me an envelope, and I peeked inside. It was money. I thanked him, tucked it away and ran to tell my priest friends.

"So what's he after? Does he want to buy you off?"

"When an offering is a big one, even the saint gets suspicious," quoted one, to stir things up.

"Don't exaggerate, man. I'm not a saint, and it's not that much money anyway."

I don't remember now how much he gave me, but it was enough for a pair of shoes and a suit. I was a young priest, a poor priest, in a parish where you lived off of hunger itself. I could think of ways to use that money. We all agreed I should accept it. I really didn't believe that his gift was sincere, and I didn't understand the gesture. Later I started to understand better. He was an ideological warrior, but he played fair.

(Rutilio Sánchez)

A *GRINGO*, A CERTAIN FATHER PEYTON, had dreamed up a Family Rosary Crusade and Monseñor Romero was appointed to publicize this crusade in all of the parishes of San Salvador.

When we got a letter announcing the plan at our base community in Santa Lucía, we discussed it, analyzed it and decided:

"We're not going to pay any attention to this!"

We already had too many pastoral projects with too many problems of their own to be getting ourselves into another one. Besides, we weren't convinced of the value of praying the rosary so much . . .

One Sunday, Monseñor Romero arrived in person to announce the crusade. We started telling him why we weren't going to participate.

"Look, Monseñor, we're already overwhelmed with all the other work we're doing . . ." ·

"We've already bitten off more than we can chew . . ."

"A bird in the hand is worth two in the bush . . ."

We went on like that. He just listened to us, but in his face you could see that he was taken aback by the fact that we were arguing with him—a bishop.

"We also don't like the fact that this plan came from abroad. We don't even know much about this plan . . ."

"Wouldn't it be better if you bishops set out the pastoral plans for our base communities?"

The more insistent we were, the more uncomfortable Monseñor Romero became, but we didn't stop arguing. There was one who was even more daring.

"We don't want ideas coming from outside the Salvadoran reality! This year it's Father 'Peytón,' next year it's Father 'Pleitón.'[3] Are you going bring him here too?

People snickered, and Monseñor got really mad. But he did see that we had our minds made up so he didn't try to impose anything on us. He just left. Later we heard he got back to the seminary all riled up and that he complained about us to the nuns there.

"Christian base communities, indeed! That Santa Lucía group is just a bunch of insolent children!"

(Teresa Núñez)

WE WERE ASSIGNED A TASK that brought us into contact with him. Archbishop Chávez asked Néstor Jaén and myself to lead some spiritual exercises with the clergy of San Salvador. All the priests attended, and they ran the whole gamut of the different political tendencies, even though most of the clergy in San Salvador were progressive.

One night, we were in the middle of a big heated argument on faith and politics and the role of the priest in all of it. It was a really controversial topic in those times.

Suddenly we saw a priest in black robes enter. He moved in all quiet and stealthy-like, and he just stayed there in the back, hidden, without saying anything.

"Who's that?" I whispered to Néstor.

"That's the new auxiliary bishop, Oscar Romero."

When we finished the debate, Nestor said to me: "I wonder how Romero's going to react after hearing everything we said."

---

[3]*Pleitón*—Colloquial expression, meaning someone who picks fights.

He was right to wonder. Two weeks later an article signed by Romero appeared in *Orientación* saying that two Jesuits—and it gave our names—had led spiritual exercises that didn't have anything spiritual about them, that they were pure sociology and practically Marxist sociology at that! It kept going along those lines.

I got mad and wrote him a fiery letter attacking him. I said that it was precisely those kinds of accusations that were endangering people's lives, and that Medellín had called for us to make changes in the Church. And I kept on writing along *those* lines.

"Let's see if he's fair enough to publish *that* in *Orientación*! I bet he won't!"

I was wrong. He published it. In its entirety. I grabbed the paper that day and started to read it, enjoying my own belligerence and that I'd managed to make the bishop give in. But then I saw that he'd gotten in the last word! Romero had written a closing comment: though he would allow my views to be voiced, he stood by his judgement, and he claimed that he could prove that we were Marxists. Nobody could beat him at being stubborn.

(Juan Hernández Pico)

PEOPLE SAY . . .

that a *campesino* from a faraway village came to confession at the church in Suchitoto.

"Forgive me, father, for I have sinned against love."

And since the most common sins had to do with being with women . . .

"Tell me what happened with your wife. What did you . . ."

"No father, it's not a problem with my wife. It's that I haven't joined a community organization yet. So I'm living in sin against the people around me. I don't love them."

Things were changing in El Salvador. The Church was changing too. But not everyone.

THE ELECTORAL FRAUD of 1972 was widely decried, and it marked a definitive change in the political life of our country. That year, a new coalition ran against the PCN, the eternal party of the military. The coalition was called UNO and was made up of the Christian Democrats of the PDC, the Social Democrats of the MNR and the communists of the UDN. This alliance presented the military and the economic elite with an unprecedented situation. The people understood the moment and voted massively for UNO so that things would change. But it was all in vain. The true winners of the elections, Duarte and Ungo, registered their protests with all of the relevant institutions, but as always, the military "won" in the end. It was a blatant, ugly fraud. Colonel Molina was to govern the country.[4]

On March 25, people rose up in protest in San Salvador. That was the excuse the government needed to decree a state of siege, a curfew and martial law throughout the whole country. The witch hunt began—a furious repression.

I was finishing up my theology degree and I went to celebrate Holy Week in El Carmen, a village of San Miguel. On Maundy Thursday the army arrived and took a half a dozen *campesinos* from their homes at night. Afterwards nobody could find them anywhere. On Holy Saturday, after having tortured and killed them, the army came back and threw their bodies at the entrance to the village. I felt like I would die of frustration and helplessness. On Monday I went to see Eduardo Álvarez, the Bishop of San Miguel. In addition to being a bishop, he was a colonel in the army with long-established ties to the military.

"What do you want me to do about it?" he asked when I told him about the killings.

"You should go to El Carmen and console the people there. They need it . . ."

---

[4]Napoleón Duarte and Guillermo Ungo were the 1972 presidential and vice-presidential candidates for UNO (National Opposition Union), a coalition made up of the PDC (Christian Democratic Party), the MNR (National Revolutionary Movement) and the UDN (Democratic Nationalist Union). They ran against Colonel Arturo Molina of the PCN (National Conciliation Party), a military party which had dominated the government since 1950.

"They need it?! Ha! Those people were asking for it. Now they'll just have to take what's coming to them!"

That was his only response. I felt even more powerless, and my anger was starting to choke me. Since I had known Monseñor Romero for so many years, I went to San Salvador to see him.

I told him everything. I could tell he was moved and that Bishop Álvarez's response had hit him hard.

"Are you going to go to El Carmen?" I dared to ask him.

"Well . . . no. I don't think it would be prudent."

"But Monseñor . . ."

"What you need to do is to go to the papal nuncio. Tell him about it. Tell him. It's important that he be informed . . ."

The nuncio was a close friend of the recently elected President Molina.

(Miguel Ventura)

COLONEL MOLINA STARTED HIS PRESIDENCY on July 1, 1972. On July 19, he ordered the invasion of the National University. There was a lot of violence and destruction. People were beaten with rifle butts, and about 800 were hauled off to jail. Starting then, the university was closed for a whole year. That was when things really heated up in San Salvador.

But, what do you know! The Bishops' Conference published a paid ad in the newspapers, written and signed by Monseñor Romero as Secretary, defending the occupation of the university with a rationalization taken straight from the government's statement: that the university was a hotbed of subversion, and that it was necessary to take measures against it.

We took our own measures. We decided to invite Romero to celebrate Mass with the Christian base communities in the neighborhood of

Zacamil. When he accepted—because he never said no to a Mass—we made our true intentions known.

"We'll expect you then and, just so you know, we want to reflect together in this Mass on what happened at the university . . ."

His face changed colors, but he didn't back down.

On the appointed day, about 300 people from the community were waiting for him. The meeting hall was bursting at the seams.

The Mass began. Monseñor Romero was seated in a big chair next to the altar where I was saying Mass. When it came time for the homily, I turned toward him.

"Monseñor, you already know why we've asked you here . . . We are the Church and we also have a right to speak. The first thing we want you to know is that we don't agree with what you wrote."

"Well, as a bishop, I want to tell you that I don't agree with the one-sided way in which you have been using your faith. This is a heresy that is being denounced by pastors in other countries . . ."

He had come with a briefcase full of texts from who knows what conservative bishops of South America.

"We've brought the Bible and the documents of Vatican II and Medellín!" the people from the community argued.

He read us a few paragraphs from the letter of a stridently anticommunists Chilean bishop.

"And what do you think is worth more?" a young man argued, "a letter from that man we don't even know, or the documents of all of the Latin American Bishops?"

"Didn't you sign the document? It's about justice. It lays out the Salvadoran reality exactly the way it is!" another yelled.

Monseñor Romero kept shuffling the papers in his briefcase, and the argument continued to heat up.

"And what do you think about the 100 families that the soldiers evicted from the grounds of the university when they occupied it?"

"The National Guard beat us up pretty bad, Monseñor!" yelled an old man who had been one of the evicted. He was there with his grandson.

Several others who had been beaten during the eviction were there at the Mass.

"They threw us out, and now we don't have any place to live!"

Monseñor didn't bat an eye. "We bishops have proof that there were arms being kept at the university," he told us.

He kept repeating that like a broken record. I remember that Memo Cañas, who was a professor at the university, started to cry and said to his face, "Monseñor, it's shameful that the Catholic Church should have bishops like you!"

Father Rogelio Ponseele came down even stronger. He was a big man— he weighed more than 200 pounds—and I still remember how he kept arguing, sort of half hanging onto the clothesline we had there. He was red with rage. "And you come here to tell us about an option for the poor?!" yelled Rogelio. "What do you think? Do you think we're stupid and we don't see the shameful pictures of you and the nuncio drinking champagne with the rich?"

But nobody could keep Romero from hammering away at the same point. "We have proof of what was happening at the university."

"Monseñor, how can you believe the government more than your people, more than us, your Church?" the young men insisted.

"How can you believe a government that came to power through fraud?"

"Fraud?! What kind of political judgements are these?" he said, angrily, "Now I realize that you're not doing pastoral work here at all. You're doing political work! And you haven't called me to a Mass. You've called me to a meeting of subversives!"

By then he had totally lost his cool.

"Look, Monseñor, in this environment of distrust, even though we're all part of the same Church, we don't have the conditions necessary to be able to celebrate Mass . . . So let's just call it off. The Mass is over!"

I took off my robe and stole and threw them on the altar. He looked at me, astonished.

"It's not possible to celebrate anything here! Not a thing!"

Everyone was upset and murmuring to each other. One man came up to me, trying to be diplomatic.

"Father, at least let us pray an Our Father together . . ."

"An Our Father?" I was furious, "Are we going to pray like the Pharisees? The conditions don't exist for us to be praying together here! It's over."

He left. No one went with him, or paid him any attention. The people were angry at first, then embarrassed, and then for a long time, they were just totally confused.

There has never been such a harsh confrontation with Monseñor Romero in any community in San Salvador as we had there that day in Zacamil.

(Pedro Declerc/Noemí Ortiz)

"THE SEMINARY? That place is a revolving door for women. Every night there's an orgy! And the ones who aren't running around with women, well, we know who they're running around with!"

That's what Bishop Aparicio used to say.

"The guerrillas were organized in the seminary. They make bombs there. They plan the kidnappings. Those Jesuits are all communists. It's a hot-bed of subversion!"

That's what Bishop Álvarez used to say.

Sex and violence: that's what the rumors were about, the accusations, the obsession. In early 1972 Father Amando López started to get warnings, messages and letters of that caliber. The truth was that the environment at the seminary, where we were following the teachings of Medellín, was starting to make some of the Salvadoran bishops uncomfortable and suspicious.

As the Secretary of the Bishops' Conference, Monseñor Romero used to write and send these messages, and so he turned into the spokesperson of those two slandering bishops. In their name, he started to demand the expulsion of certain seminarians . . .

"If they're not removed, we reserve the right to take other measures . . ." Trouble had already reached a boiling point a few months earlier on the day reserved to honor the pope. The seminarians had refused to participate in the festival's liturgy unless some changes were made in the traditional yearly rituals. They claimed that the nuncio was acting more as a politician than a pastor of the Church and that the Cathedral would be full of representatives of the government—and a fraudulent government at that!

It was the end of the world. Monseñor Romero went from being just a spokesperson to being a principal player. He made the problem into his personal issue. The pope and his nuncio had been attacked, and the hierarchy of the Church had been insulted. How could it be worse? He started to actively support the expulsion of the Jesuits from the seminary. We were the ones that were putting ideas into the seminarians' heads and we had to go.

There were about 100 seminarians and they all protested. They refused to continue their studies if we, their Jesuit professors, had to go.

But we had to go. With the endorsement of five out of seven Salvadoran bishops, and with Rome's approval, we were expelled from the leadership of the seminary after having held that responsibility for 50 years.

Monseñor Romero took charge of the seminary. He was satisfied. Orthodoxy had triumphed.

(Juan Hernández Pico)

HE LOOKED FOR REASONS TO BE IN CONFLICT with us. After he expelled us from the seminary, he accused us of indoctrinating the students at the *Externado San José*—our school in San Salvador—with Marxist ideology. He hurled virulent accusations at us, first in *Orientación*, the Church paper, and then in *El Diario Latino*, *La Prensa Gráfica* and *El Diario de Hoy*. Monseñor Romero said that our Marxist teachings pitted children against their parents. He said we were using "pamphlets of communist origin" in our religion classes. Outrageous accusations! He put together a whole campaign against us.

We responded in newspaper spreads, but he kept accusing us. The conflict got to the office of the President of the Republic, and finally it was no less than the Attorney General himself that had to determine whether or not we would have to leave the school. It was a national scandal, all provoked by that man.

At that time, I was the Jesuit Provincial, and I went to talk to Monseñor Romero directly.

"Look," I told him rather angrily, "You're accusing us of very serious things and I want you to tell me what you're basing these accusations on. Because the authority that I recognize—the only authority I recognize—is Archbishop Chávez, and he knows exactly what's being taught in our school. We've never taken a single step without his approval . . ." He didn't even look at me. I discovered that even though he waged heated battles, he was really a timid man.

"I want to know what you are basing these accusations on!"

He kept his eyes downcast, and responded simply: "I have reliable sources of information."

"What reliable sources could you possibly have? In the case of the school, the only sources are me, the Provincial of the Society of Jesus, and the Archbishop of San Salvador, of whom you are simply an auxiliary! What other source could you possibly have to be causing such an uproar? Tell me!"

He didn't look up.

"I have reliable sources of information." He didn't change his words or his tone.

"But I've already told you who the only reliable sources are! What are these sources of yours?"

"I have reliable sources."

That man drove me totally crazy. He didn't give me a single argument or a single reason. He didn't dialogue. He didn't ask me questions. He didn't want to know.

(Francisco Estrada)

THERE WERE SOME RICH WOMEN of the ruling class who went to a lot of trouble to get the Jesuits kicked out of the *Externado*. They were behind that whole struggle, and behind them were some older Jesuits who were egging them on. The parents of the students were divided, but there were a good number of us that supported the kind of education the progressive Jesuits were giving in the school. Father Ellacuría was supporting us.

"You should get involved too," he told us.

We divided up tasks. Beatriz Macías and I got the job of going to visit Monseñor Romero. I didn't even know what he looked like back then.

"You see, Monseñor, the Church has really been moving quickly with the Second Vatican Council and with Medellín, and we want our children to be educated in that way of thinking . . ."

"We want them to learn about the Salvadoran reality and to work to change it!"

We talked and talked. He listened to everything we had to say. He didn't contradict us or get rude with us like other bishops did. But we left with heavy hearts, and felt as if a bucket of cold water had been thrown on us because he didn't really understand anything we'd said to him. In *Orientación*, angry articles kept coming out not only against the Jesuits now, but also against us mothers and fathers that were supposedly being manipulated by them. In the end, he didn't win that battle, but he never did anything to recognize or make up for the damage he'd caused. It seemed to me that he had his head in the clouds, away from reality, up in the trees like the avocados.

(Carmen Álvarez)

HE WAS ALWAYS HIDING. In the seminary, where he lived at that time, I knew of three places where he hid away to work or just to get away from everybody. More than once I had to go around looking for him. Romero was a loner.

He had his reservations about me, because he considered me too liberal. When preparations were being made for the Bishops' Synod in Rome, we had a run-in. It happened at a meeting of the Bishops' Conference we were all participating in. That day he came to resign from three separate jobs.

"First of all, I resign from being the director of our weekly paper, *Orientación*. Secondly, I resign from the writing of the Pastoral Letter on the Family that's been assigned to me."

The third resignation had to do with me. Some time earlier Monseñor Romero had been elected by those of us in the Bishops' Conference to go to the Synod in Rome to represent the Salvadoran Church, and I'd been elected as his alternate.

"Thirdly, I can't go on that trip, but I suggest that we have another election and that Monseñor Rivera continue to be the alternate for whoever is elected."

It was clear he was doing this because he didn't want me, who he considered to be too progressive, to represent El Salvador at the Synod. He didn't trust me. Ah! But I didn't accept his proposal. I brought out all the reasons to refute it on legal grounds—and I was pretty convincing because law is my specialty.

"I have the right of succession," I insisted, "and the process by which you and I were elected was a legal process that accorded rights and responsibilities that can't be revoked unilaterally or arbitrarily."

We got caught up in a heated argument, and he didn't want to give in. "The Conference," he claimed, "has the authority to revoke that election!"

"The Conference has no such authority!"

Some bishops supported him. Others supported me. Finally my point of view prevailed. I would go to Rome.

The bishops accepted two of his resignations. He would not go on the trip, and he would not have to write the Pastoral Letter. But he would have to continue being in charge of *Orientación*. I think Monseñor Romero was going through a period of depression at the time. He looked exhausted.

That was our only argument during the four years in which he and I were the auxiliary bishops for Monseñor Chávez. In spite of all the doubts he had about me, which he didn't bother to hide, it was our first and last argument. I mention it now just to show that, at that time, he was very critical of me.

(Arturo Rivera y Damas)

"THE ALAS BROTHERS ARE ORGANIZING a coup d'état against President Molina. They're preparing a *campesino* uprising!"

My brother, Higinio, and I were both priests who worked closely with *campesinos*, and some of the landowners used this accusation against us in a legal suit. The two of us managed to go into hiding before they could arrest us. In the "absence of the accused," the judge on the case asked President Molina himself to appear and make a statement, since if there was going to be a coup, he would be the one affected.

"If you testify against the Alas brothers," Molina was counseled, "you're going to have problems with the Church. And if you don't testify against them, the problem is going to be with the military, because they're dying to get those two priests. It would be best if you didn't show up."

Molina followed the advice, and the case lost steam. So we decided to quit our hiding games and go back to the parish in Suchitoto and keep on working. Archbishop Chávez asked Monseñor Romero to make the trip back with me.

"Romero tries not to get involved in these things," Chávez told me, "but he needs to commit to something, and at least get out of his office a little."

In spite of the fact that Romero was his auxiliary bishop, Chávez would complain to me quite often that Monseñor Romero wasn't worth much in these kinds of delicate situations.

So anyway, we took the trip to Suchitoto. Everything was going fine, until we were just on the other side of San Martín. There the National Police stopped us at a checkpoint to ask us for our documents. I showed them mine, and Monseñor Romero showed them his.

"I'm the Auxiliary Bishop of San Salvador," he told them.

But it didn't make any difference. They didn't pay any attention to him.

"Get out of the car! We have orders to search this car and to take you two to Cojutepeque. We know that you are both well-known communists."

Neither he nor I was expecting anything like this. We got out of the car. Monseñor Romero was anxious. He wasn't used to these kinds of things.

"Open your briefcase!" the policeman gestured menacingly.

I was carrying some socks, some books, and underneath everything, a simple 22-caliber pistol.

"What is this?!"

"It's a pistol I use in the agricultural school we have in Suchitoto . . ."

"And might we know what you use it for?"

"What I use it for? Okay. Look, we've got cattle there. The cows are always having calves and the vultures and the dogs are always coming around to eat the afterbirth. If you're not careful, they'll even attack the newborn calf."

The guy was looking me up and down, and there I was figuring out how to tell my story . . . Since in El Salvador we call both dogs and police "chuchos," I decided to get on his case and kept weaving this big story.

"So, if a chucho comes over and decides to attack what's mine, I don't have any choice but to shoot him, and you know, sometimes, I kill the chucho! You know how those stupid chuchos are always getting in the way!"

The policeman was getting angry. Monseñor Romero hadn't heard my story. He had stood off to one side, maybe out of fear, and hadn't paid attention. But then the guy took the pistol over to Romero and put it down in front of him.

"How do you explain this pistol?"

"That's mine," he said in a sudden surge of courage, or of who knows what. "It's mine."

"I already told him we use it to kill chuchos."

Monseñor just looked at me, frightened. I was trying to swallow my laughter. He was trying to swallow his fear.

"You two are a pair of insolent subversives. And you're both going to end up in jail in Cojutepeque!"

So the policeman made us take the car to Cojutepeque. Monseñor Romero was as white as a ghost, but he was mad.

"I am the Auxiliary Bishop of San Salvador," he said to the officer as soon as we got to the barracks.

"Well, I'm the Chief of Police of Cojutepeque, and I've got an arrest warrant for the two of you."

Romero didn't take his eyes off the table.

"Let me use that telephone, will you?"

"And what do you suppose you need it for?" The guy was really rude.

"I need to make a call."

"And just who do you think you're going to call?"

"President Molina."

"Boy, you aim high, don't you?!"

Furious now, Monseñor Romero took his little phone book out of the pocket of his robe and showed it to the police chief.

"If you want to, dial it yourself. This is the direct number for the President of the Republic."

The guy looked, and his eyes got as big as a grasshopper's.

"Go ahead and dial it for me."

He looked at Romero, and then looked again at his phone book. The President's personal telephone number!

"Get out of here! Out of here, both of you! And take your pistol with you!"

On our way to Suchitoto again, Romero didn't say anything.

What impact did this first run-in with the *chuchos* have on him? Who knows? He went back to his office and kept being the pastor to his paperwork.

(Inocencio Alas)

"WHAT WE DO REGRET, more with an understanding silence of tolerance and patience than with an attitude of polemical resentment, is the explicitly worldly, violent and uncontrolled conduct of those who have tried to make use of religion to destroy the spiritual basis of religion. In the name of faith, those who have lost their faith have tried to struggle against the faith. And this is very sad, truly sad. For our part, we have preferred to adhere to that which is certain, to cling with fear and trembling to the Rock of Peter, to seek assurance in the shade of the Church's teachings, to put our ears to the lips of the pope, instead of leaping like reckless and foolhardy acrobats to the speculations of the impudent thinkers of social movements of dubious origin . . ."

(From Monseñor Romero's last editorial in Orientación, *written before stepping down from the leadership of this publication and being named Bishop of the Diocese of Santiago de María on October 15, 1974. Quoted by Jesús Delgado in* Oscar A. Romero, Biografía, *UCA Editores, 1990)*

"We lived as best we could. And there were times we almost couldn't. Our bodies and souls were destined for the harvest. Until death."

SLAPPED IN THE FACE BY REALITY
Bishop of Santiago de María (1974-1977)

THE LAND? IT WAS IMMENSELY RICH. Field upon field of good level ground. I saw with my own pair of eyes how the forests and the trees, with their beautiful spreading branches, were swept away to plant all that cotton. Cotton everywhere. Farther north it was all coffee, but to the south, there was nothing but cotton.

We are migrant workers—harvesters. We pick coffee up one row and down the other, then cotton up one row and down the other. Most of us weren't born around here. We came in from all four corners of the earth just to work—an army of people walking in from all over, going from camp to camp looking for work. The men and boys were the migrants mostly, and we women were left to fend for ourselves. And those big plantation owners that don't even live here, they wouldn't let us stay on their land. They forced everyone out and made us live along the sides of the roads.

We lived as best we could. And there were times we almost couldn't. Our bodies and souls were destined for the harvest. Until death.

(Paula Fernández)

THE FIRST THING the new bishop of Santiago de María did when he arrived at those coffee and cotton lands at the end of 1974, was to summon all of the priests in the diocese to a meeting at the plantation of a big coffee producer from there, a rich man. We all had a delicious lunch, and then the plantation owner—who looked like he might have been a good friend of Romero—left discreetly.

"I suppose you all would like to speak to your future, that is, your *new* bishop . . . so I'll leave you with him."

There were only 20 of us priests for the 500,000 souls in that diocese. The only religious order was the one that Pedro, Zacarías and I belonged to, the Passionists. We were in charge of the Jiquilisco parish and the Los Naranjos Center for the Advancement of *Campesinos*. That afternoon, Monseñor Romero asked us just one question:

"What expectations or hopes do you have for me as bishop?"

"Well, what I expect," one priest began, "is to know what kind of stipend you're going to set for baptisms, and how much we should charge for weddings . . ."

The priest got into figuring out the numbers, and Monseñor wrote something down in his notebook.

"I hope," another said, "that you won't be calling us in for so many meetings . . ."

"And if you do call us for meetings, that they won't be very long ones."

The bishop didn't say much. He just looked at them. Another one wanted permission for something or other, and another one wanted a dispensation for who knows what. Finally, it was just us Passionists that hadn't said anything. Pedro elbowed me.

"Say something!"

Romero knew perfectly well who I was and the kinds of things we were working on.

"Well, as for us, Monseñor, what we want is for you to let us make mistakes."

"What do you mean?" He looked at me, puzzled.

"Also, if we make mistakes, we hope you would try to dialogue with us and reason with us, not give us orders."

He stared at me, even more puzzled.

"We are missionaries, Monseñor, and you know that in this kind of work, you always have to be inventing new ways to do things, making commitments today and figuring out how to follow through on them tomorrow. But you have to break a few eggs to make an omelette. Don't you agree?"

He looked at me in complete silence. By the expression on his face, I figured he was not happy with what I'd said, so I didn't go on.

When we got back to Los Naranjos, I said to Pedro: "We're going to have problems, and we're going to have them soon."

(Juan Macho)

I WAS TEACHING THE MUSIC CLASS and a little of the history of El Salvador to the *campesinos*. The history classes were called "national reality" classes. Thousands of *campesinos*—peasant farmers—passed through the Los Naranjos Center, and they learned a thousand things that were new to them: first aid, cooperativism, how to lead a Celebration of the Word . . .[1] My class might have been the most politically advanced—the hottest chili pepper, so to speak. People came from Morazán, from San Francisco Gotera, from Cabañas, from Tecoluca . . . Then they'd go back to their places of origin with their eyes wide open.

I still run into people today who say:

"You! You're the guilty one!"

"What? What did I do?"

"It's your fault I'm involved in all this stuff! You convinced me when I was there!"

---

[1]Celebration of the Word—Liturgy led by lay people. Unlike a Mass led by a priest, it does not include consecration of bread and wine.

It's true. Who knows how many people were convinced, joined the movement for change and really got involved because of those little courses at Los Naranjos.

(Davíd Rodríguez)

A LITTLE OLD MAN NAMED TOMÁS was a well known Christian leader from La Cayetana. He'd lost all his teeth already, but he was a student in a course at Los Naranjos. One day, he was talking with a Nicaraguan who was telling him about the Sandinistas—how they'd taken up arms and headed for the mountains. Don Tomás decided to speak up.

"Come on! We have weapons to defend ourselves with too! Just like you folks. We already know about all that!"

That was the first time I had ever heard that there was a guerrilla movement in El Salvador. My eyes were opened.

(Antonio Cardenal)

"THERE WILL COME A TIME in El Salvador when we priests will be thrown out of the country. We will be beaten, killed, crushed like coffee grinds . . . and eventually a war will break out. And you will be the ones responsible for upholding the faith in your communities. Prepare yourselves for that time, and realize that you will also have to suffer abuses."

I heard this like a prophecy from a priest who gave us a national reality class in Los Naranjos, a long time before the big massacres began. And I felt a chill go through me.

(Alejandro Ortiz)

"NATIONAL REALITY?! That's nothing but communism, Monseñor!"

That nun made Monseñor Romero's ears burn with her talking.

She was the owner of Los Naranjos Center, so she felt she had a right. The Center was run out of a large house that had been a nuns' school and was the property of a nun in Santiago, a relative of some big coffee barons. One day the nun stood quietly in the hall listening to my class without my students or myself being aware of it. She listened to everything and then went running to find Monseñor Romero.

"They talk about rich people and poor people, and they get them to feel hatred against the rich! They get them all riled up! And they're all uneducated people! Who knows what kind of terrible ideas they'll start spreading in their own villages when they leave those courses . . ."

A few days later it was Monseñor Romero himself who stood out in the same hall to spy on me. I was in my national reality class, explaining the history of the communal lands, the problem of the big landholdings, the need for agrarian reform . . . At the end, as we always did, we read the Bible looking for words that would help shed light on our understanding of that reality. We used the famous Latin American Bible that the *campesinos* understood so well. At that point, I saw Monseñor Romero come in, all dressed up in his black cassock. I swallowed hard. He didn't say anything. He just sat in the back of the class. So I finished the lesson. He was quiet. At the end, he called all of the priests on the team at Los Naranjos to a meeting.

"Why do you teach those "national reality" classes? Explain to me what you hope to accomplish with them . . ."

"But it's not just that course, Monseñor. There's first aid. We teach them to read and write . . .The idea is that they develop themselves in a well rounded way, and that they begin to understand that the Church is not only the mother of the rich, but also their mother . . ."

He asked us other probing questions, but didn't make a single comment. He just listened.

A few days later he called in Father Juan Macho, the director of the Center.

"I don't think those classes are heresy, but I do think they're unwise, for two reasons."

"Could you tell me what they are?"

"The first is that the people in the classes are *campesinos*, and we don't know what kinds of things they're going to say when they go back to their villages, because we lose control over them . . ."

"And the second?"

"The second is that Father Davíd, the one who gives the classes, is not from my diocese. He's from San Vicente, and the bishop from there, Monseñor Aparicio, tells me that he's very concerned about this center and about these classes . . ."

Monseñor Aparicio was worried about *us*? We were the ones who should have been worried about *him*!

"Land reform is impossible in this country," Aparicio used to say, "because if we take away the highways and the lakes, there are just a few square kilometers left, and if we divided those up among all the Salvadorans, we'd only get a square meter apiece!"

He'd say things like that completely seriously; that's how ignorant he was. He put a lot of pressure on Monseñor Romero to kick me out of the center. I don't know if it was because of Aparicio's persistence or what, but at the beginning of August in 1975, Romero ordered the school to be closed.

(Davíd Rodríguez)

A BLACK CASSOCK, A PURPLE SASH and a big old cross on his chest. That's how he was dressed when he came to a meeting of the youth ministry we had organized in Santiago de María. I'd never seen a bishop that close up before. As soon as he walked in, my spirit sank. I lost all desire to talk. He sat down and started listening to us. We were discussing what young people's lives were like; different topics like drugs, unemployment and community organizing were coming up from all sides. Finally, someone asked him to say a few words, and he gave a big speech about the love of the Blessed Virgin.

"Damn! What does that have to do with what we were talking about?" I murmured to the person next to me.

"Let it go. That's the way Bishop Romero is. It's enough that he allowed us the use of this farm so we could meet."

(Guillermo Cuéllar)

El Salvador, June 21, 1975. The bodies of six people, all from one family of the name Astorga, appeared today in Tres Calles, a village in the eastern province of Usulután. According to the official government version, the dead campesinos had belonged to an underground political-military organization, and they died after opening fire on a National Guard patrol. Other versions maintain that the campesinos, all catechists trained at the Los Naranjos Center, were taken violently from their homes while the National Guard went through their village searching houses. The six bodies showed clear signs of torture.

Seven months ago a similar event took place in the hamlet of La Cayetana, in the department of San Vicente. On that occasion, seven campesinos were killed, and 13 others disappeared. The victims in that case were also catechists trained in leadership courses in Los Naranjos.

Sources linked to the popular movement say the killings are related, and suggest that they are both government responses to the growth in campesino *organizing.*

THE SUN WAS COMING UP when I saw Monseñor Romero arrive. He already knew.

"Father, let's go to Tres Calles!"

We were too late to see the bodies. By the time we got to the village, they'd already been buried, and the people could only tell us how they'd found them—mutilated, tortured almost beyond recognition. The mother was crying, the wives, the little children. We went inside their little houses. The boards still held the stench of blood. In the years to come we would become accustomed to these cruelties, but back then we were new to it.

We spent almost three hours there, but our words failed us.

"They were strong, healthy men . . . Now look what's happened to them."

Monseñor Romero didn't say anything. He just listened to everything, and watched everything. As we were about to leave the village, we saw a group of *campesinos* off in the distance. We approached them. They'd found the body of another one of the people they'd been looking for. It had been thrown in a dry ditch that ran alongside of the road. He was just a kid, at the bottom of the ditch, face up. You could see the bullet holes, the bruises left by the blows, the dried blood. His eyes were open, as if asking the reason for his death and not understanding. One of the men took off his shirt to cover him. He was practically naked. They had the wake for him there, all of them with their machetes drawn. It wasn't grief they felt right then. It was rage.

Monseñor Romero mingled with all of them and prayed a slow responsorial prayer. He didn't say anything else. When we said good-bye and walked toward the road, the *campesinos* were all standing there still, immobile with their machetes and knives ready, sharpened. I broke the silence as we walked slowly away.

"Monseñor, it seems to me that if there aren't some changes in El Salvador, violence is going to break out all over—like water bursting from a dam."

He didn't answer me. Eight well-armed National Guardsmen were coming towards us on the road toward the village. I could see that Monseñor Romero was frightened by the sight of them, but he didn't say anything. Fortunately, they didn't stop us. It wasn't until we were in the car on the way back that he finally spoke.

"Father Pedro, we have to find a way to evangelize the rich, so that they change, so that they convert!"

"Who knows, Monseñor . . . You know them. You have dealings with them. All of those rich families are friends of yours. And they're the ones that order these kinds of killings . . . Who knows if they'll change . . ."

We made the trip to Santiago in silence. The sun was setting, and I could imagine the light glinting off the blades of the machetes in Tres Calles.

(Pedro Ferradas)

HE CELEBRATED THE NINTH DAY MEMORIAL MASS for the dead at Tres Calles. That's where I met him. That Monseñor Romero made me mad. He was so wishy-washy! He talked about "the dead" instead of the people who had been "murdered" and he preached a sermon condemning violence, which practically suggested that those poor men had been killed because they were violent, that they somehow had it coming to them. I remember we had gone with a truckload of campesinos from Aguilares, all people who were participating in grassroots organizations. They went back from that Mass disillusioned.

(Rafael Moreno)

El Salvador, September 15, 1976. The President of the Republic, Colonel Arturo Armando Molina announced today to the nation that his government would begin an agrarian reform to rectify the "unjust distribution of land." The President declared that the agrarian reform would take place in spite of any opposition from the powerful landowning elite. With only 21,000 square kilometers of surface area, El Salvador is the smallest country on the American continent. At the same time, it is overpopulated with five million inhabitants. Two thousand landowners have ownership of practically the entire country and its most fertile lands.

The President's announcement raised enormous expectations all over the country. Since the massacre of 30,000 campesinos in 1932, the most important demand of the majority of Salvadorans, who are increasingly disaffected and joining opposition organizations, has been to have access to land ownership. "We will not take a single step backwards," President Molina declared firmly. The first lands to be affected will be the huge extensions of cotton land in the eastern department of Usulután.

TAKE THREE DAYS TO STUDY THE AGRARIAN REFORM: that's what Monseñor Romero asked all of the clergy, religious and lay leaders to do in the Diocese of Santiago de María, which was precisely where the agrarian reform was to begin. What could the Church contribute to that moment? That was what concerned him.

He asked me to give a few talks on the subject. I'll never forget that image: me explaining the agrarian reform to all of those priests, with Romero sitting at a student's desk in the front row, taking notes and listening to me super-attentively. The man wanted to learn.

(Rubén Zamora)

MOLINA DID NOT TAKE ONE STEP BACK. He ran backwards at full speed! The elite families raised holy hell. They took over the newspapers to attack the agrarian reform. They screamed. They threatened. They organized FARO[2]—the group that later gave birth to ARENA.[3] They blackmailed Molina. They pressured him. They put an end to his plans. And in four months the so-called agrarian reform went up in smoke. It was this victory for the landowners at the end of 1976 that opened the doors for the worst repression that El Salvador had ever seen. Eventually it pushed us to war.

"What about Monseñor Romero, who was so excited about the idea of this agrarian reform? What's he saying now?" we asked the people we knew who were organizing in the area of Usulután.

"He's been left high and dry. His hopes and dreams have fallen in on top of him, like a hat made of wax, melting in the sun."

(Antonio Cardenal)

---

[2]FARO—Agrarian Front of the Eastern Region, a landowners association of eastern El Salvador. These cotton and coffee barons funded the early death squads in the eastern part of the country.

[3]ARENA—(Republican Nationalist Alliance). Right-wing political party founded by Major Roberto D'Aubuisson in 1981. The ARENA party has held power in El Salvador since 1989.

"THE TEACHING YOU DO IS TOO PARTICIPATORY."

That's what Monseñor Romero would say most often when we would talk about the work at the Los Naranjos Center. He had finally let us open it again. Sometimes he would come at me with another kind of argument:

"I've heard it said that the government is worried about this type of teaching, too."

"The government? But who should tell me what the correct teaching is? The government or my bishop? Because if it's the government, then I have no use for you. But if it's you, then I don't care what the government says!"

You just couldn't tell about him. He couldn't just take a stand and move on it. From the very beginning, any time that I or anyone else mentioned Medellín to him, the man would get so nervous, he'd develop a tick. The corner of his lip would start trembling. It would shake and shake, and he couldn't control it. Really, hearing about Medellín and having his lip tremble were one and the same thing.

But still, he was learning. Learning from reality.

Santiago de María is a thousand meters above sea level. The harvest months are cold, and at night it's really freezing. His first year, he didn't notice. But during the second year, he started realizing that the campesinos who arrived to work the coffee harvest on the plantations were sleeping on the sidewalks, scattered around the plaza, shivering with cold.

"What can be done?" he asked one day.

"Monseñor, you can solve the problem. Look at that big old house where the school used to be. Open it up!"

He opened it. Three hundred people could fit inside. He also opened a little classroom where we used to have our clergy meetings. Another 30 could sleep in there. And that's how he started giving shelter to a lot of people.

"And serve them something hot at night—a glass of hot corn *atol* or milk." He gave that order to the people that worked in *Cáritas*.[4]

While the *campesinos* were having their drink and getting warmed up, Romero would go around and talk with them. He spent a lot of time listening.

That's how he began to understand that the problems we'd told him about so often were not stories that we'd made up.

"Father," he said to me one day, "what is this 'helper system' all about?"

"That's one big abuse, Monseñor! This is what it's like: the foremen, whether they're on coffee or cotton plantations, register x number of workers on the payroll, but they always write down fewer people than they need. What do they do then? They accept everyone else who comes, but only as helpers. And they only pay the helpers for the weight of the can of coffee or the sack of cotton they've picked, but they don't give them any food, and if they work on Sundays they don't get paid for it."

"Why do they do that . . ?"

"Because they save a big wad of money that way, and there's always a lot of cheap labor available to them. Needy *campesinos* always show up, and there's always a crop ready to be picked, so they've got the perfect setup!"

"But, how is it possible for good Christian people to do these things?"

"They do that and more! Do you know how these Christians who are such good friends of yours make up for these outrageous tricks? With little Christmas presents. On a certain plantation, where some close friends of yours live, do you know what they gave their workers who picked cotton for them, frying their backs in the hot sun like pork skins? A pair of underwear worth three *colones*! Three *colones* is what they saved every day from each one of them by not giving them any food to eat!"

---

[4]*Cáritas*—A Catholic charity organization.

"That's not possible, Father . . ."

The more I told him, the sadder he got.

"Monseñor, why don't you go to the plantation of this other friend of yours. You can see how they have no qualms about writing on the black-board that the wage per day is 1.75 *colones*, an amount completely below the legal minimum!"

"But isn't the minimum supposed to be 2.50?"

"It is."

"And what do the Ministry of Labor inspectors say about this?"

"They don't say anything. They keep quiet with the bribes that the fore-men give them."

"No, it can't be . . ."

"Don't believe me, then. Go find out for yourself."

He went to the plantation to find out.

"You were right, Father," he said to me when he came back, "but how is so much injustice possible?"

"Monseñor, this world so full of injustices is exactly what they were talk-ing about in Medellín."

"Medellín, Medellín . . ."

He listened to the word and repeated it himself. And his lip didn't tremble. After that day, I never saw that tick reappear.

(Juan Macho)

HE ARRIVED ONE SUNDAY TO CELEBRATE MASS in Tierra Blanca, there in the midst of those cotton fields, those huge landholdings.

"Monseñor," I told him, "our custom is to do the Bible readings of the day and then invite any one who wants to comment on them to do so. At the end, the priest summarizes what everyone has said and adds or corrects according to what he believes. Today your job would be to put on those finishing touches. What do you think?"

That Sunday the Gospel reading was the one about the miracle of the multiplication of the loaves and fishes. When it came time for the commentary, Juan Chicas asked to speak.

"This reading has helped me to understand that the boy who carried the five loaves and two fishes in his bag, was the one who really obliged Christ to perform the miracle."

When Monseñor heard the word "obliged," he interrupted.

"Young man, why do you think that anyone could oblige Christ to do anything? Christ was free!"

But Juan Chicas didn't allow himself to be intimidated.

"Allow me, Monseñor. One moment, and you will see. I say that he was obliged because five loaves and two fish were nothing to feed that whole crowd, but at the same time, they were all the boy had. So they were both nothing and everything at the same time. That's the thing! So what happened? When the boy offered everything he had, Jesus could do no less. He had to do everything he could, too. And he could do miracles! So he did! There, I think I've unraveled it for you. Now you understand, don't you?"

Monseñor looked straight at him and kept silent. Other people made their comments. Finally it was his turn to close the Liturgy of the Word:

"I brought with me a long homily for this occasion," he said, "but I won't give it now. After listening to all of you, I can only repeat what Jesus said, 'Thank you, Father, because you revealed the truth to the humble and kept it hidden from the learned.'"

We went back to Jiquilisco. As we were about to go our separate ways, he said to me: "You know what, Father? I had my reservations about these *campesinos*, but I see that they do better commentary than we do about the Word of God. They've really got the idea."

(Juan Macho)

HE DOUBTED UP TO THE VERY END. There was a very, very traditional priest who he completely trusted who worked in a parish next to where we were in Jiquilisco. This man would say in all of his sermons that we weren't Passionists, we were communists. That was the idea he was fixated on.

One day I was just getting up—I hadn't even bathed—when the priest arrived in a flurry as though to tell me the latest gossip: "Monseñor Romero sent me to say that the classes that Father David gives at Los Naranjos should be suspended right away, because everyone says that he has declared himself a communist!"

At that hour of the morning, and with the same old rumors!

"Well, you go and tell Monseñor Romero that I declare myself deaf, that he'd better come himself to tell me what he wants to tell me, and that he should never send another message to me through you! Big mouth! I don't want you sticking your nose into sensitive things like this!"

He left in a hurry. Doubtless he went flying straight to Monseñor to tell him about the rage I was in. I bathed, ate breakfast, and after a little while Monseñor Romero himself appeared at my house. He was a little uncomfortable about it, but I sensed that it was more a discomfort with himself than with me . . .

"The *padre* told me about your reaction, and I wanted to . . ."

"Monseñor, you know that in his sermons he publicly accuses David of being a communist, and now he's leaving him even more vulnerable. He could even be killed! How could you send that message with someone like him?! Do you think the same way he does? Because that's what that busybody would like everyone to think!"

"Forgive me, Father, I didn't realize . . ."

"Monseñor, how can I convince you that in spite of all of our defects, we are wholeheartedly committed to helping you lift up this people, this Church . . ."

"I'm sorry, Father . . ."

He kept saying that.

"It's all right. I'm not talking about the misfortune with that priest anymore. That's in the past. But I hope it helps you to understand that we want to work alongside you. We should be speaking face to face with each other. If we make a mistake, tell us to our faces. And let us tell you to your face if you're the one making a mistake . . ."

He felt so confused . . . that he got down on his knees in front of me. And when I saw him humbling himself that way, I picked him up off the ground and hugged him.

"No, Monseñor. It's not that. Just accept us . . ."

And when he saw that I was crying, he cried too. Then he broke the embrace and looked me in the eye.

"Now I understand you."

(Juan Macho)

"I'M FROM THE CENTURY BEFORE THIS ONE," he said when people would ask him his age.

We never knew how old he was. He never married. He never wore shoes either. Who knows whether that had anything to do with why his kidneys went bad.

He knew about everything . . . the secrets of all of the snakes—the coral snake, the *masacuata*. He even knew how to cut the rattle off a rattlesnake. The kids learned from him how to hunt *garrobo* lizards, and how to knock coconuts down from the trees. He taught my cousin Lito, Rafael Arce Zablah,[5] all about life.

Mariano. His job had always been carving statues of saints out of wood. Mariano, the *santero*—the saint-maker. He would carve them, paint their robes, their curls, their colored eyes, and then he'd finish them with a light layer of varnish to keep the termites and moths from ruining them when they were older.

Mariano's workshop was a little hovel made of sticks and mud, and all four of the inside walls were covered with pictures of saints. All of the saints in heaven were there, stuck on with glue or with thumbtacks. They served as models for his sculptures. Saints made of white oak, of *nogal*, of *copinol*—always fine woods. He even knew how to do Saint Bartholomew. Every house in Usulután, every chapel and all of the convents around there proudly displayed the *santos* that came from Mariano's artisan hands. He was the father of a whole brotherhood of saints.

Monseñor Romero found him on the very first visit he made to Usulután, which was also part of his diocese. And from the first time they met, they developed the kind of friendship where the two of them would just sit and talk for hours.

"Life is fine for other people. Not for me. There's no work left for me," Mariano said one night to Monseñor Romero.

"Are you going blind?"

"No, it's not that. My eyes haven't given out on me, and there's wood enough in these forests. Look how many fine trees we've got! And look at these hands! They still move like a youngster's! They don't know what it's like to feel stiff! But . . . no, it's all over . . ."

"What's the matter then, my friend?"

"Well, nowadays the saints are shipped in from abroad. They bring

---

[5]Rafael Arce Zablah—Famous student activist and early guerrilla leader. Killed in action in 1975. His nickname was Lito.

them from Spain, from Italy, from those worlds over there. They're little bitty things, made with plaster, baked and finished with enamel. They bring them by boat, so they probably turn pale from being seasick."

"You don't like those saints, then?"

"They're pretty. I'll give you that. But damn it! They're taking my work away from me! And no matter what they say, they're invaders. They're not from here!"

Mariano stopped looking at Monseñor Romero and fixed his gaze on something far away, farther than his little thatch house, farther than the tree-lined road, farther than the fence or the fields. He stared off toward some faraway unknown place.

"Those saints weren't born here. They don't have our roots, our wood, like the kind growing on these trees . . . That's what I'm not happy about."

"Then, what are you going to do, Mariano? If you stop working, you'll die right then and there!"

"What am I going to do . . ? I'll wait a little while. I have a feeling that we're going to make a saint of our own, out of Salvadoran wood, the kind that doesn't crack. And for that, I'll wait. I'm not going to die until I can see him, until I can touch him."

A breeze is blowing, and the movement of the air makes the candle's flame burn stronger.

(Rafael Romagosa)

"Tell me. Tell me, all of you. What should I do
to be a good bishop?"

BAPTISM BY THE PEOPLE
(February 22 - March 20, 1977)
The First Month as Archbishop of San Salvador

San Salvador, February 10, 1977. Media sources confirmed today that the Holy See has named Monseñor Oscar Arnulfo Romero Galdámez as the new archbishop of the Archdiocese of San Salvador. Romero has been heading the Diocese of Santiago de María for a little over two years. He takes the place of Monseñor Luís Chávez y González, who has been the Archbishop of San Salvador for the last 38 years.

WE KNEW THAT ROME HAD BEEN IN CONSULTATION with various groups since late 1976 in the search for a new archbishop, because Chávez had reached the age of retirement. The nuncio proposed Romero as a candidate and consulted with the government, the military, the business sector and the ladies of society. They asked the rich, and the rich gave their complete backing to Romero's appointment. They felt he was "one of theirs."

(Francisco Estrada)

THE UPPER CLASS HAD SUPPORTED his candidacy. That was well known in our circles. There was even talk that some people had travelled to Rome to advocate for his appointment and that one of those was Rodríguez Porth.[1] I don't know if that's true. But it is true that there was talk about it.

(Magdalena Ochoa)

---

[1] José Antonio Rodríguez Porth, a right-wing jurist, was the Minister of the President in the ARENA government, when he was killed by urban guerrilla commandos in June of 1989.

AT THE END OF THE MOLINA GOVERNMENT, after the failure of the agrarian reform, there was a time of tremendous repression against the *campesinos*. And the persecution of the Church was beginning. In February alone of that year, four priests were tortured, and four others, who were foreigners, were expelled from the country. Nuns and priests were receiving threats, and their residences and places of work were subject to being ransacked. It was an ugly atmosphere. Monseñor Chávez asked that the transition occur quickly, so that his successor would be in a position to deal with the crisis.

When he found out that Monseñor Romero would be the new archbishop, Chávez was discouraged. Romero had been his auxiliary for four years, and he was aware of his limitations.

"It's strange," he said to me, "that the Holy See didn't pay attention to my recommendation of Monseñor Rivera. He was always my candidate, and they knew it. Forty years as an archbishop and they didn't even take my opinion into account . . ."

He was hurt. Perhaps they were afraid of Rivera in Rome, because even though he wasn't a rabble rouser, he knew how to debate the law.

"That big turkey"—which is what the right wing and the military used to call Rivera—"is a communist who only knows how to cause us problems!"

Maybe in Rome they were saying: "Romero would be better. We can control him"

(César Jerez)

MY WORLD FELL APART when I found out that Romero was the new archbishop. I went to the UCA[2] crying bitterly.

"I'm not going to obey a Church with a man like that in charge! Now we'll have to go back to the days of the catacombs!"

(Carmen Álvarez)

---

[2]UCA—Central American University, the Jesuit university in San Salvador.

THE DELEGATES OF THE WORD[3] in Morazán and some other places were very upset when we found out. I remember we were evaluating the situation with the Franciscan Fathers of Gotera and we all came to the same conclusion: "This is really going to screw us up."

(Pilar Martínez)

I WORKED WITH several progressive priests in a *campesino* organization. We were in a meeting when the news arrived about Romero's appointment. Although we hadn't talked about it, we'd all been afraid it would happen. And it did. We saw it as a great triumph for the ruling class, and we prepared to confront it.

(Nidia Díaz)

I WAS IN CHILTIUPÁN in a grassroots leadership course.

"We may as well forget it! That man is going to put an end to all of this!" another priest said to me.

I hurried to San Salvador and sent a telegram to Monseñor Chávez—a farewell-and-job-well-done note. Then I sent another one to Rivera—a note of condolence. He was the one we were hoping would be archbishop. I didn't send anything to Romero. I didn't congratulate him, because it wouldn't have been sincere on my part. I was deeply displeased.

(Ricardo Urioste)

"DAMN! NOW WE'RE RUINED," we seminarians said. Monseñor Chávez had been increasing his commitment to the poor, and Rivera had supported him for 17 years. What would happen now with Romero? What could we do? It was hard for us, because if we didn't support our new bishop, we didn't stand much of a chance of becoming priests!

(Juan Bosco Palacios)

---

[3]Delegates of the Word—Lay leaders chosen from Christian base communities to receive further training, organize new base communities and learn how to do liturgies in the absence of a priest.

I DECIDED NOT TO GO to any celebration there might be for him, and I sent a telegram to Monseñor Romero: "Sorry to hear the news. Ibáñez."

(Antonio Fernández Ibáñez)

I WAS FREE OF PREJUDICES. I didn't know anything about his life. I'd never heard anyone talk about him. But when I saw him on the front page of the newspaper, dressed so elegantly in all that fancy clothing, I said, "This is just one more in a long line of sellouts."

(Regina García)

OUR CANDIDATE, like almost everybody else's, was Rivera. As the president of the Justice and Peace Commission, I had sent a letter to Rome saying that he was the one who had the consensus of the Church. I was sure they would choose him.

That day a friend brought me the *Diario de Hoy* with its big photo of Romero, and he said to me sarcastically: "There's your bishop!"

All I could do was make the sign of the cross.

(José Simán)

"WHY DIDN'T GOD deliver us from this man?"

"Don't get poor God mixed up in the entanglements of the Vatican."

"We can only hope that Romero's health is so delicate that he won't be able to withstand the pressure of being at the helm of this Church and . . . that he'll take a trip somewhere!"

(Plinio Argueta)

THOSE OF US FROM THE ZACAMIL BASE COMMUNITY received an invitation to go to his installation as archbishop. We decided we wouldn't do any such thing! And we worked to keep other communities from attending, too. We felt like sheep that didn't trust our own shepherd.

(Carmen Elena Hernández)

THE BAD NEWS had taken the wind out of our sails, but we decided to send him letters. I wrote two myself on behalf of the community council of my village, San José del Amatillo. The communities of El Terrero, Conacaste, Los Naranjos, El Jícaro, La Ceiba and El Tamarindo also wrote letters. So many of us *campesinos* had been organizing for so long, that we weren't going to just stand around and do nothing. But because of everything people said about him, we chose to write letters instead of approaching him through some other method. We asked him to declare himself on one side or the other. "What is your message, Monseñor? We would like to know if you are going to stand with the rich, or with us, the poor."

(Moisés Calles)

PEOPLE SAY . . .
that some of the older priests in Santiago de María, and other places, found out that Monseñor Romero was going to be leaving that diocese for the Archdiocese of San Salvador, and decided to give him a good talking to.

"Look, this place is not like there, and that place is not like here. In San Salvador you've got a mutinous clergy, bossy nuns that act like they're running the city and some communities that have degenerated into nothing but politics. The worst case you'll find there is in Aguilares!"

"I know a little about all that. I lived in San Salvador a few years ago, and Father Grande is a friend of mine," Romero told them.

"But in the last few years everything that was seriously wrong before, has become even more serious. And that parish in Aguilares has turned into a focal point for communist agitation. This so-called *campesino* experience has gone too far. It's a danger to the country, and you are going to have to do something about it!"

"Do you think it's really that bad?" Romero asked, frightened.

"You'd better believe it! We know when to call a spade a spade. Be careful, especially with Aguilares!"

And they say that Monseñor Romero got more worried than he already was.

ME, WHAT I USED TO DO WAS SELL FOOD. I'd carry it around on my head all over Aguilares. In the mornings I would do my route with chicken soup or pig-foot soup and in the afternoons I'd sell *atol,* a drink made out of toasted corn or pineapple. The doctor told me that I shouldn't carry hot foods on my head and that I should find some other way to make a living. So I went to work at a tobacco plant.

In Aguilares everybody knew me, not just because of the food I sold, but also because I was the primary *rezadora*. When there was a death, people would come looking for me to say the prayers. I also did the prayers to Saint Anthony, Saint Jude, Saint Eduviges, Our Lady of Mount Carmel, the Infant of Atoche, the Virgin of Guadalupe . . . There were days when I would do up to five *rezos*! Some people make money by doing prayers, but I didn't. I was doing it from my heart and didn't charge any money. My little girls learned to sing the *Ave Marías*, and the oldest would help me by leading the prayer responses. I taught all of my children about the *rezos* from the time they were very little.

If a child were dying, I was called in to sprinkle him or her with holy water; if he or she died, then I had to sing the *parabienes,* which is a farewell song that you sing at four in the morning:

I have come here to this house/ without invitation/ to sing the parabienes/ *for this enshrouded child/ The parents of this child/ cannot be happy/ because they have given up an angel/ to the heavenly home.*

When Rutilio Grande and the other Jesuit priests came to Aguilares on their evangelization missions, they asked around and found out that everyone in town knew me. In December of 1972, they visited my house for the first time. My children were home alone, and my house was full of flowers because I was getting ready for the Christmas pageant.

"Is this where the *rezadora* lives? A woman named Tina?" asked Father Rutilio.

"Yes, she lives here."

"And is this *rezadora* one of those fireworks types?"

My children didn't know how to answer that question. The priests left a message that they wanted to talk to me. I didn't understand why they would have called me such a thing, and I was a little apprehensive.

When I finally met with them, I told them all about my life and work, and they explained to me what they were planning to do. They wanted to do an evangelization campaign all over Aguilares, "so that people will be able to have a deeper understanding of Christ and the Gospel message. Do you read the Bible, Tina?"

I didn't even own a Bible! I just had a handful of *novenas* to pray to the saints. But they told me more about their plans.

"Excuse me, sir," I finally said to Father Grande, "why did you ask if I was a fireworks type?

That was what was bothering me the most.

"Fireworks Christians are the ones that only look upwards like the firework rockets we light on our feast days," said Father Tilo. "Those are the ones that just pray up to heaven, and they don't look around them or concern themselves with their neighbors."

"Well, maybe I have been a bit of a fireworks Christian."

"But that can be changed, Tina. We're counting on you. We need your help because everyone knows you."

That's how our friendship began. I felt happy, included and ready to help them. You know, a poor person like me really feels like she's been valued when she's taken into account. Up until that day, I imagined priests to be these distant and divine beings. I didn't even consider myself worthy of speaking with them. But these priests asked me to work right alongside them.

We began to work developing Christian base communities. Those famous "communities!" You know, the whole thing got started in Aguilares. That was where it was all born.

(Ernestina Rivera)

ONE DAY HE CAME RUNNING and shouting, waving his visor and gesturing with his hands like he always did.

"Oh my God! My head is THIS BIG! I can't fit anything else in it!"

He thought that his head was like a warehouse where you kept ideas, and he had learned so many new things that not even his prodigious memory was good enough to store it all.

"I need to learn how to read and write! So I can keep more in my head!"

For three years he'd been resistant to the idea of taking literacy classes from Chamba and Cuache. But once he decided, he was reading in just a few days. No one ever learned to read as fast as he did.

Polín. Apolinario Serrano. From the village of El Líbano, at the foot of Guazapa mountain. A sugar cane cutter since childhood, with fingers deformed from cutting so much cane with a machete. A swineherd who moved like smoke in and out of places all over Suchitoto with a vast network of connections that only he knew. He was one of the hundreds of Delegates of the Word who were trained as part of the parish experience in Aguilares. But let there be no doubt, he was the smartest of them all.

And not long afterwards, he was the most brilliant *campesino* leader in El Salvador. A born speaker! He could get any audience eating out of his hands. He would tell jokes, quote popular sayings or recount Bible stories. More than anything, he talked about reality.

"You can't fool us! There's no way that this Polín is a *campesino*. He must have taken ideology classes in Havana or Moscow!"

That's what the guys who aren't from FECCAS-UTC[4] say when they hear him. They don't believe that Polín could be a machete-swinging, drink-water-from-a-gourd kind of guy. They think he's a skilled politician in camouflage.

He's funny. He never talks about slums. He says "the sluburbs." And he never says proletariat. He'll say the "poor-o-tariats" instead!

But, everyone in Aguilares understands the words that come out of this catechist's mouth, because he's one of them—a regular guy. They understand him, and they organize.

(Carlos Cabarrus/Antonio Cardenal)

FOR YEARS, ALL OF AGUILARES has been organizing and growing in awareness by listening to their parish priest, Father Rutilio. This is how Father Grande talks to them:

"Some people cross themselves in the name of the father (money), and the son (coffee) and the spirit (especially if it's cane liquor!). That's not the God who is the Father of our Brother and Lord, Jesus, who gives us the good Spirit so that we can all be sisters and brothers in equality, and so that we, the faithful followers of Jesus, can work to make His Reign present here among us.

"Don't be like fireworks—all noise and hullabaloo towards the heavens way up there! We have to fix this mess here on earth. Here on earth! God isn't in the clouds lying in a hammock. He cares about the way things are going so badly for the poor down here.

"I've said many times that we have not come with the sword—or the machete. Our work is not that. Our violence is in the Word of God, the Word that forces us to change ourselves so that we can make this world

---

[4]FECCAS-UTC—The Federation of Christian *Campesinos* (FECCAS) was formed in 1964. It joined with the Federation of Rural Workers (UTC) in 1975. FECCAS was the larger of the two groups as a result of rural organizing connected to the Catholic Church, especially in Aguilares.

a better place, the Word that charges us with the enormous task of changing the world.

"Brothers and sisters, I fear that if Jesus were to return today, walking from Galilea to Judea, which for us is from Chalatenango to San Salvador . . . I dare say that with his words and actions, he'd never get as far as Apopa. They'd detain him around Guazapa, and they'd beat him up, even silence him or have him disappeared!

"The orioles have the *conacaste* tree where they can hang their nests so they can live there and sing. But the poor *campesino* is not allowed his *conacaste*, or even a little patch of land on which he can live or be buried. Those who have money and power organize themselves, and they have plenty of resources to do so. But *campesinos* don't have land, or money, or the right to organize so that their voice can be heard, so that they can defend their rights and their dignity as children of God and of this nation.

"We are children of this Church and of this country which is named after *El Salvador*—the Divine Savior of the World. We can't just say: 'It's every man for himself, as long as things go well for me!' We have to save ourselves together as a whole ear of corn, a whole cluster, a whole bagful. We have to save ourselves in community."

"THE PRIESTS OF AGUILARES came on mission to our *cantón*[5] on March 25, 1973. Before the mission, the place was a mess. The *cantón* was full of liquor and moonshine, sold illegally on every corner. People would get drunk and do stupid things. All those people—concerned only with liquor and screwing up their lives. But after the mission, all of that ended. No more drunken, disorderly behavior. People might still have a few beers, but basically they left their vices behind. The place changed in other ways too. For example, it used to be that everyone did their own thing. Now we have collective projects, and even people who aren't involved in the organization at least offer to help out in some way. The feuds that we had between the different family groups—all of that

---

[5]*Cantón*—Subsection or outlying area of a municipality, often in a remote country area without government services or Church attention.

has changed now. The people received the mission with open arms. And after it ended, we were left with a whole bunch of trained Delegates of the Word—about 30 of them, all anxious to work together. You could see the excitement in people."

(Resident of the El Tronador cantón, in El Paisnal.
Quoted by Rodolfo Cardenal in Historia de una esperanza:
Vida de Rutilio Grande, *UCA Editores, 1985)*

PEOPLE SAY . . .
that an elderly woman from one of the *cantones* near Aguilares was asked one day:

"Do you still remember Father Grande?"

"Sure, I remember him."

"And what do you remember most about him?"

"What I remember about him most of all is that one day he asked me what *I* thought . . . No one had ever asked me that in all of my 70 years."

HUGE SUGAR CANE PLANTATIONS dominated Aguilares. Sugar processing plants on thousands of acres of land. The multi-millionaires of the area—the De Sola family that owned the La Cabaña plant, the Dutch family that owned San Francisco, and the Orellana family that owned Colima—had taken over the flatlands and pushed thousands of *campesinos* to rocky areas where they were forced to rent land on eroded hillsides at higher prices year after year. When the *campesinos* started to understand that this miserable treatment was not the will of God, they organized some incredible strikes.

Before resorting to strikes, however, they had tried to do other things: community projects, agricultural cooperatives . . . But when the cooperatives started to gain strength, the paperwork was stymied in the offices in San Salvador, and it became impossible for them to get equipment, seeds or anything else. That's when the *campesinos* began to strike, began to go to demonstrations and everything. The whole thing grew like foam on the waves, and before long almost 10,000 *campesinos* from the area were on the streets of San Salvador, demanding better pay in the coffee and sugar cane harvests.

Nearby, in my parish of Guazapa, we were headed down the same road. We had started a mission there in 1976 with the same model they were using in Aguilares. We priests would spend two weeks in each *cantón* visiting the houses one by one, eating practically every meal with a different family, so that we could get to know everyone. The mission's goal was to awaken in the *campesinos* a different vision of Christianity and to motivate them to struggle for their liberation. We would apply Freire's literacy model[6] to our evangelization campaigns so that whatever change that was to come would come from the *campesinos* themselves.

"The strength of the tree lies within the seed," we would say to them. "The strength to achieve your own liberation lies within you."

We gave everyone a copy of the New Testament, even the ones that didn't know how to read. And every afternoon we would gather the community together for a general meeting. There was group work, songs and prayer, and time to reflect on some Bible passages.

It was a tremendous awakening for the *campesinos* to be able to speak and be listened to—to see that their fellow *campesinos* valued what they said and commented on it. And there was more! At the end of each mission, a Christian community was created and Delegates of the Word were elected by democratic vote. Then we would organize more in-depth courses for these leaders to take in Aguilares.

---

[6] Freire—A Brazilian, Paolo Freire (1921-1997) wrote *Pedagogy of the Oppressed.* His teaching model emphasizes that the poor already have immense knowledge that stems from their own experience. A teacher's job is to help students share and analyze experiences, and to offer some technical input, such as literacy skills, in order to help them move toward their own liberation.

After they began to read the Bible and understand it, the *campesinos* would always ask the same question:

"If God doesn't want this kind of poverty, then what should we do?"

(José Luís Ortega)

SO MANY POOR PEOPLE OPENING THEIR EYES, so many *campesinos* demanding their rights. But the only response was repression.

"The government doesn't respect me anymore."

Monseñor Chávez was very upset and complained to me about this a few days before he retired as archbishop.

"They don't even pay attention to the things I demand anymore," he said in distress. "A new archbishop needs to start governing soon."

Things were getting increasingly complicated. The presidential elections on the 20th had been another joke, a fraud. On February 22, my mother gave me the news: "You know what? I heard that Monseñor Romero is being consecrated today."

Everything was done in a hurry. Many of us priests didn't even know about it. It was a surprise ceremony.

"Well, your son is leaving the country," I said to my Mom. "I can't work with that man!"

Twenty years ago, he had been my friend, but the way things were, I wasn't going to be able to stand working with him.

Out of curiosity, I went quickly to the San José de la Montaña Seminary so I could see the ceremony. As I went in I could hear the organ music and the songs. It wasn't even in the church. I went into the chapel. Gerada, the papal nuncio, was there, and a few bishops, but there were only a handful of priests and nuns. And they had primarily come to say good-bye to Monseñor Chávez, not to receive Romero. Mostly there were diplomats, some stuck-up snobs from the upper middle class, government people and members of the most privileged classes. I looked them over. I knew so many of them. How many talks had I given them in the Christian Cursillo Movement of earlier years? And what had it all been worth? Had any of them changed?

(Inocencio Alas)

San Salvador, February 26, 1977. Today, General Carlos Humberto Romero, of the National Conciliation Party, was officially proclaimed President of the Republic of El Salvador. In the final election count, he defeated retired Colonel Eduardo Claramount, the candidate of the opposition coalition, UNO, by a margin of two to one. The results of the elections, held on the 20th, were not officially announced until today.

Meanwhile, disturbances continue in the Salvadoran capital as the opposition parties that make up the UNO coalition protest and denounce the elections as fraudulent. Irate opposition members have been occupying the Plaza Libertad continuously for the last two days, warning that they will continue their occupation until the vote count and the series of irregularities that, according to them, have characterized these elections, are reviewed. A massive protest has been planned for tomorrow, Sunday, February 27, in the same plaza.

ABOUT 60,000 PEOPLE CAME. The plaza was packed all day long. At dusk they even celebrated a Mass. A lot of people from the Christian communities were there. It was incredibly tense.

"They're going to evict us forcibly tonight . . ."

In UNO we got the information early on. The military had decided that they would be willing to commit a massacre of any scale in order to end such a concentration of people. But we weren't going to just abandon the battlefield so easily.

"What shall we do?"

We decided to look for Monseñor Romero, who had been the new arch-bishop for just five days. We wanted him to find some way to keep the killing from happening.

They gave me the job. "You know him. Go find him."

Romero was not in the archbishop's office. He wasn't in any office where I looked for him. Finally I found out he was in Santiago de María, look-ing into some problem there. I located him late in the day, by phone.

"Monseñor, it's already evening and there are about 7,000 people still here in the plaza . . ."

"Yes, I've heard."

"There are women and children. People are prepared to spend the whole night here. They're not going to leave."

"Yes, I understand."

I explained to him about the army, about the information we had, that they were going to force us out anyway they could . . .

"Yes, I understand you completely."

"So, Monseñor, we think that if you were here, maybe they wouldn't dare to act with as much violence."

Silence.

"Can you hear me, Monseñor?"

"Yes, I can hear you."

"We're begging you to come. You are our pastor . . ."

"Yes, but . . ."

"We need you here. In just a few hours they could kill a lot of people."

Silence.

"Do you hear me, Monseñor?"

"Yes, yes."

"So, you'll come? We can expect you?"

"I will lift you up to God in my prayers."

And he hung up.

(Rubén Zamora)

DID WE AGREE with UNO that we should confront the military through elections? What can we say? Anyone could tell that elections weren't going to solve anything. But we also knew that being in the plaza was a way of denouncing the regime. So the whole Zacamil Christian base community, with our priests and everybody, went to be part of the demonstration. What happened went down in history.

At night when the shooting began, the panic was so great that we were swept down the street with the crowd.

"To El Rosario! Everybody go to El Rosario!"

By the time we managed to get into the church, the first bodies were already falling at our feet. We lost our shoes in the stampede. I don't know how we managed not to lose anything else. The church was filled with people all the way to the back! We were choking from the tear gas . . .

"Chicas!! Chicas!!" We heard Odilón Novoa, one of the community leaders, shouting for us. He always used to call us the "*chicas.*"

All of this was new for the three of us *chicas*, but he had a long history of dealing with this kind of violence, and he'd brought bags of water with sodium bicarbonate and handkerchiefs for the tear gas.

There were a lot of people there that day that thought that Monseñor Romero was a relative of General Romero, the "winner" of the elections. That's how linked we felt they were in terms of power. I remember that some people even shouted in the middle of all that chaos:

"What a pair! While one Romero gives us a beating, the other one stands by and applauds!"

(Noemí Ortiz)

El Salvador. February 28, 1977. In the final hours of the day yesterday, the army of this Central American country opened fire indiscriminately against a crowd of opposition demonstrators that had been occupying the Plaza Libertad for several days. Initial reports indicate that more than 100 are dead and an as yet undetermined, but much larger, number are wounded as the result of this violent eviction.

As the shooting began, many of the demonstrators managed to take refuge in the nearby El Rosario Church, located on one side of the plaza. In the early hours of the morning, the recently-retired Archbishop of San Salvador, Monseñor Luís Chávez, and his auxiliary, Monseñor Rivera Damas, negotiated a kind of truce with the military. The agreement allowed for the evacuation of the people who had sought protection in the church when the military attacked demonstrators with bullets and tear gas. The new archbishop, Monseñor Oscar Romero, was absent from the capital during this bloody confrontation.

A STATE OF SIEGE WAS DECLARED. That day we were supposed to have a meeting of all of the clergy of San Salvador. We decided to go. There were still government trucks picking up dead bodies to dump them who knows where, and military water trucks were still hosing away the blood at Plaza Libertad.

Monseñor Romero was presiding over the clergy meeting for the first time as archbishop. He had chosen Rutilio Grande to give a talk on the rise of Protestantism in the country.

"Imagine talking about this, at a moment like this!" Rutilio had complained to us. "Romero has his head in the clouds!"

But he didn't refuse.

"Well, Rutilio," Romero said to him as he introduced him to the group, "I know your style, and I know you will have some things to say that will be very good for all of us to hear . . ."

Rutilio took over and began his talk, but every few minutes new reports were arriving . . .

"Psst. Come here. They say there are people from your community who have disappeared . . ."

One priest would leave, and another would come in. Everyone was murmuring to each other.

"OK. That's it!" Rutilio finally interrupted himself. "I don't think today is the day to talk about this. There are other, more important, things happening!"

Monseñor Romero agreed to put off talking about Protestantism to another day. That day never came. Things were moving too fast in the country. The meeting quickly turned into an exchange of information about the massacre in the plaza . . . What were we going to do?

Monseñor Romero was like a fish out of water. He was bewildered. We decided to write news bulletins to keep each other informed, and we voted to have all of the bishops publish a message denouncing the national crisis as soon as possible.

"The offices of the archdiocese will be open all day and night for any emergency," said Monseñor Romero, finally.

He felt obliged to offer something, too. But he was perplexed by the whole thing.

(Salvador Carranza/Inocencio Alas)

THINGS WERE STILL LOOKING DISMAL. On March 10 we had our first special meeting of nuns and priests. More than 150 showed up at Monseñor Romero's invitation. One especially sensitive question was raised:

"We have to talk about the situation of the foreign priests."

In those days, you could be arrested and taken to the border, or denied a residency permit for some bureaucratic reason and then be expelled. Every day there were more and more of these cases of arbitrary harassment by the government.

The situation of the priests in Aguilares was especially hard since it was a zone where there were a lot of land conflicts. The two of us there who were foreigners didn't even sleep inside the parish house anymore. We had taken to hiding.

"What do you think, then, Monseñor?" Rutilio Grande asked Romero during the plenary. "Can the ones who've been hiding, go back to their places of work?"

"Yes. I think they should. They should take the necessary precautions, but you'll see. Things are going to calm down."

He still believed in the government. We knew that Molina, the outgoing president, was his personal friend.

When the meeting ended, Romero tried to give those of us from Aguilares special consolation.

"Since you all are Jesuits, I don't think anything will happen to you. Go on back to your pastoral work on Sunday, and don't worry," he said to Rutilio Grande there in the hall. "And sometime we should talk about the whole experience in Aguilares during these last few years. You know those popular organizations. They can be radical, and sometimes even violent . . . How about if we talk about that in some of our meetings?"

"I hope we can, Monseñor. God willing . . ."

They would never see each other again. It was Romero's first meeting as archbishop. It was Rutilio's last. But neither of them knew it as they said good-bye.

(Salvador Carranza)

THREE CHILDREN COVERED WITH DIRT AND BLOOD ran through the cane fields to break the bad news in El Paisnal:

"They've killed Father Tilo!"

Several men had ambushed his jeep on the dusty road, just past the *cantón* of Los Mangos. The shower of bullets fell on Father Grande who was driving, on Manuel, an old man who was the priest's faithful companion and who tried to protect him from the bullets by covering him with his own body, and on Nelson, the epileptic boy who sometimes rang the bells in the Aguilares church.

The three children who brought the news told how they were alive because the stream of bullets had not come through to the back seat of the car where they had been.

"When the killers were shooting, we could see their faces."

"The *padre* is dead. He can't talk anymore."

People were waiting for Father Rutilio in El Paisnal, his birthplace, to celebrate the second day of the Saint Joseph novena. Now instead of the happy sounds of feast day fireworks, there is only weeping.

They run through the cane fields to see if what the children say is true. And it is. Father Tilo no longer moves. He no longer speaks. They will never again hear from him the good news of the Gospel:

"Blessed are you, the poor, because God doesn't want you to be poor anymore."

NOT HIM. RUTILIO WAS THE ONLY ONE we thought they wouldn't kill. First they would blow Chamba away. He was the Spaniard. Or me, the Panamanian. Just the day before, at lunchtime, we'd been joking because someone had carved a cross on the window of the parish car as a threat.

"First it's a cross. Next they'll plant a bomb!"

But we'd been laughing as we said it. We didn't really believe it would happen. That Saturday afternoon as I was finishing the Mass in El Tablón, a *campesino* came running up to me. "I think Father Tilo was in an accident before he got to El Paisnal. His car was seen overturned on the road . . ."

I walked the five kilometers between El Tablón and El Paisnal with him and others. When we arrived, the town was in an uproar. It was true. They had taken him from us. They had killed the most respected Salvadoran priest in the archdiocese, the spiritual father of two generations of priests from the seminary. Tilo, my brother. In the midst of the tumult, someone spoke to me from behind. But he spoke clearly so there would be no mistaking what he said:

"You got away this time, you bastard!"

When I turned around, there was no one there. Suddenly, I understood. They had planned to kill me, too. It was only at the very last minute that I'd given Don Manuel my place and decided to go to El Tablón by bus, so they wouldn't have to go out of their way to drop me off.

I headed for Aguilares. A car dropped me off at the entrance. I wanted to walk the last stretch to the parish on the empty, silent streets. It was already night. As I got closer to the plaza, I could breathe the grief. *Campesinos* were walking in from all over. I went in. Rutilio was laid out on our dinner table, blood still streaming from his back. Don Manuel was on another table. The bullets had blown one of his arms to pieces. Nelson, poor boy, had just one, perfect bullet hole in the middle of his forehead. It was true. They had been killed. And I—"the bastard" who "got away this time"—had been spared.

(Marcelino Pérez)

MORE OR LESS AT THE SAME TIME that Rutilio Grande was being killed, Monseñor Rivera was meeting with the parish team in San Salvador. Suddenly Monseñor Romero arrived and interrupted the meeting. He was anxious about something.

"What's the matter?"

All of the bishops, including him, had signed a pastoral letter, a pretty brave one, that was to be read in the churches the next day. When the word got out about the message, Romero had a flood of calls and visits from people trying to pressure him to revoke it. The calls came from friends of his from San Miguel and the people from Opus Dei who had such great trust in him.

"How is it possible, Monseñor, that you have allowed yourself to be deceived by the communists?"

"That document you signed is just going to make things worse!"

"Now that you're archbishop, why haven't you put an end to this madness?"

So Romero went to Monseñor Rivera and there, in front of everybody, showed his anxiety.

"It just seems to me that this is not the best message to be sending right now. It's one-sided. It's partial . . ."

"Of course it's partial," Rivera said, "In times like these we have to be partial. We have to be on the side of those who are suffering."

They had an argument. And Monseñor Romero went back to his office, still turning over all his doubts in his mind. After a while the telephone rang. It was the outgoing president, his friend Colonel Molina.

"Good to hear from you, Mr. President . . ."

"Monseñor, I have to give you some bad news. I've just been informed that Father Rutilio Grande has been assassinated near Aguilares."

"Rutilio . . ?"

"With my most heartfelt condolences, I want to communicate two things to you: the first is that the government has had absolutely nothing to do with this. And the second is that we will launch an exhaustive investigation to find the assassins."

Monseñor Romero didn't say anything. He hung up. Rutilio, his friend for years, murdered . . . Then, slowly, he began to arrange the pieces of paper on which the message was written—the message that he *would* read the following day.

(José Luís Ortega)

I TOOK OFF HIS SOCKS, all soaked with blood, and helped to undress Father Grande. He was dead. When I heard the news I felt as if I was being picked up in the air and thrown down on the ground. I was so shaken that I don't even know how I got to the parish house. And now I ask myself how I lived through the events of that day. I loved him. That's why, to this day, I have saved a little piece of cloth soaked with his blood.

The priests gave me permission to stay there the two nights that we held our wake for him in the parish house of Aguilares. All of us were gathered together remembering the wonderful communities that we had created with him.

It was midnight when Monseñor Romero arrived to see his body. He approached the little table where we had him, wrapped in a white sheet, and there he paused, looking at him in a way that made me see that he loved him too. I didn't know Monseñor then. That night we heard his voice for the first time, preaching.

When we heard him, it was a great surprise.

"Ay! Even his voice is just like Father Grande's." That's what we all said.

Because it seemed to us that right there, the words of Father Rutilio had been passed to Monseñor. Right there. Truly."

"Is it possible that God has worked this miracle so that we will not be left as orphans?" my *comadre* whispered to me.

(*Ernestina Rivera*)

SHORTLY AFTER HE ARRIVED, Monseñor Romero sat down next to me to talk. At about three in the morning, the people came to do the so-called autopsy on Rutilio and the murdered *campesinos*. They weren't able to remove even a single bullet, because the instruments they had were so poor. So they deduced by the way the bullets had impacted the body that the weapons used had been the same caliber as the ones the security forces use. But that's as far as the investigation went.

Romero and I were talking about this when I saw him put his hand into the pocket of his cassock and take out a few wrinkled bills and give them to me.

"Father Jerez, this is to help with all of the expenses you are going to have . . ."

"But Monseñor, really it's not . . ."

"Yes Father, these things cost money, and this way you don't have to pinch so many pennies . . ."

"But Monseñor . . ."

Finally I accepted. Romero had never trusted the Jesuits, but he had appreciated Rutilio. We continued talking about other things.

I have thought about that gesture a lot. Monseñor Romero wasn't the kind of person who carried a checkbook. He didn't have one then, or ever. It wasn't his style. He was more homebred, more familiar. That night it seemed more like when there is a death in the family and an uncle arrives and comes up to you because you're the head of the family, and he gives you a little money as if to say, "He's my loved one too. I want to do my part."

(*César Jerez*)

"PREPARE A MASS, Father Marcelino."

"Now, Monseñor?"

It was 4:00 in the morning.

"Yes, we're going to preside. You choose the songs and the readings, and we'll take the bodies to the church."

I set about getting everything ready. We couldn't count on Chamba. He'd start crying, and he wouldn't be able to stop. The patio of the parish house was filled with *campesinos* who were organized in FECCAS. We were preparing the Mass, and they were preparing a communiqué. They were burning with rage.

"Father, tell me. Are they all part of the organization? Are they all part of FECCAS?" Monseñor Romero asked me, frightened.

"Yes. They're all part of FECCAS." It was as if he were seeing devils, I thought.

"And they're going to . . ?"

But he didn't finish his sentence.

We didn't have coffins. With the help of some of the *campesinos*, we carried the three bodies, wrapped in sheets, and put them in front of the altar.

"What are the readings going to be?" Romero asked me.

"The Gospel of John: there is no greater love than to give one's life . . ."

"That's good. And the first reading?"

"That's already done."

"What do you mean, it's already done?" he asked, worried.

"The three of them are the first reading. Don't you think, Monseñor, that we don't have to say too much tonight? Didn't they already say it all?"

He didn't contradict me. Maybe he was already too shaken up by all that had happened.

(Marcelino Pérez)

" . . . TREMENDOUSLY CONCERNED by the assassination of Father Rutilio Grande and the two *campesinos* who accompanied him from his parish in Aguilares, I direct myself to you in this letter to make manifest the fact that there have been a series of commentaries about what has occurred, many of which are unfavorable to your government. I have not yet received the official report which you promised me by telephone on Saturday night, and I judge that it is of utmost importance that you order an exhaustive investigation into the events. The government, as the highest authority, has within its hands sufficient instruments with which to investigate and carry out justice in this country . . . The Church will not participate in any official act of government until the government has done everything possible to shine the light of justice upon this outrageous sacrilege that has caused consternation in the entire Church and a new wave of repudiation throughout the country against such violence . . ."[7]

(Fragments of the letter written by Monseñor Romero to President Molina on March 14, cited by James R. Brockman in La palabra queda: Vida de Mons. Oscar Romero, *UCA Editores, 1985)*

---

[7]Six weeks later, there had not even been an order to exhume the cadavers in order to do an autopsy. During his three years as archbishop, Monseñor Romero kept his word and never participated in a single official government act. Eight years later—in March of 1985—a former colonel in the Salvadoran army, Roberto Santibañez—the director of the Department of Immigration at the time of the crime—identified Rutilio Grande's assassin at a press conference in Washington, D.C. He named Juan Garay Flores, a member of a group of Salvadoran officers who had been trained in the International Police Academy in Georgetown, Washington, D.C. Roberto D'Aubuisson and Santibañez himself were also trained at the Academy.

IT WASN'T JUST RUTILIO. It was a well-organized persecution and it was only beginning. On that same day, March 12, the plan was to kill at least three other priests. At the same hour on the same afternoon when Rutilio was being machine-gunned, Father Rafael Barahona's car was also the target of a shooting in Tecoluca. Father Barahona's brother, who was driving, was killed.

The other one they wanted to kill was Tilo Sánchez, but since he was a master of disguises, he managed to escape. I don't know how he got away that day. He could have been dressed as a soldier or an opossum! I was fourth on the list. On Saturday the 12th, I was in a little hamlet and had just finished doing a wedding when the warning arrived:

"Father, the situation looks really bad. There are armed civilians driving around out there, and they're asking about you . . ."

The local dentist offered to escort me out quickly down a little-used path. Shortly after I left, those civilians—accompanied by some National Guardsmen—broke up the wedding celebration and arrested the son of the woman in whose house the community usually held its meetings.

A few days later the following headline appeared in *El Diario de Hoy*: "Arsonist Accuses Priest." I read and saw that the "arsonist" was the boy who was arrested. The story claimed that he had been apprehended while setting fire to cane fields under the orders of Father Trini Nieto— me. He had "confessed" that "all of the actions of sabotage and destruction carried out by local terrorists" had been planned at his mother's house with my participation.

Later we found out that it was all a plan put together by that devil, D'Aubuisson.[8]

I went into hiding. *(Trinidad Nieto)*

---

[8]Major Roberto D'Aubuisson—In addition to being the founder of the right-wing ARENA party, D'Aubuisson is known to be the founder of death squads. In 1993 the Truth Commission found him to be the intellectual author of the assassination of Archbishop Oscar Romero.

RUTILIO'S BURIAL was to be on the 14th. As night fell on the 13th, Monseñor Romero issued an urgent call for us to meet him at his office.

"I need you to go right now to Aguilares to make arrangements for the graves. I want the three of them to be buried together in the church in El Paisnal—Rutilio in the middle. And I want you to make it a real crypt, covering the graves on all sides with brick . . ."

"Whatever you say, Monseñor . . ."

"But you should go right now so that everything will be ready for tomorrow."

Right now? Aguilares was totally militarized at that hour of the night. Maybe he saw the fear on our faces, but he kept on asking favors of us . . .

"I also want you to speak this very night with the *comandantes*."

"With the *comandantes*?!!"

"Yes. Yes. Look for the guerrilla commanders that have links to the organizations there, and convince them not to distribute flyers or propaganda during the Mass. Tell them that I'm asking them not to turn the burial into a political event."

It was even worse than we thought! He wanted us to go around looking for "*comandantes*" at that hour of the night!

"Of course, Monseñor."

"They'll kill us for sure!" Jon Cortina and I said to each other as we left his office. And we went anyway, having decided that we were prepared to die.

We got to Aguilares at midnight. The place was green with uniforms. Right away we went to look for one of Rutilio's brothers.

"Do you know any bricklayers that can help us at this hour to open up a crypt space for the burial tomorrow?

He knew of someone. That left us with our other, more formidable, task—locating the "*comandantes*" . . .

"I know where you can find them," he told us.

We went towards El Paisnal. The National Guard stopped us at both the entrance and exit to Aguilares. That night, we ended up passing several times by the place where Rutilio had been killed.

We started digging the graves. It was hard. In the years to come, we would have to dig so many others, but this was about burying Tilo, and we weren't used to such tragedies yet.

The bricklayers worked quickly. We advanced them some money and went on to complete the other task we were dreading most.

Holy God! We walked what must have been two hours through the darkness, up and down hills, until we found some of the "boys." I don't know if they were *comandantes*, but they spoke with some authority so they must have been something. We explained to them what Monseñor Romero had asked us to convey, and we got into an argument. They had been planning to distribute flyers. Of course. He was the first priest in the country to be murdered, and besides it was Rutilio, for whom they had so much respect.

"Look, you all can pass your flyers around and then go hide, but the people stay here, and the ORDEN[9] people will come and kill them," we argued.

"But we have to express what the people are feeling!" they argued back.

The discussion was getting long. Monseñor Romero's authority didn't mean anything to them. He was an unknown quantity, or worse—the usurper of the position that many of them had hoped Monseñor Rivera

---

[9]ORDEN—National Democratic Organization—a rural paramilitary network of informers and thugs, founded in 1961 by General José Alberto Medrano of military intelligence. It was most active in the 1970s, after which it was replaced by the civil defense system.

would occupy. Finally they were convinced. There would be no political propaganda during the Mass or burial.

"But when the final blessing is said, we're free to let loose with the flyers," they said firmly.

Having negotiated the pact, we went back up and down the same hills, retracing our steps, and by dawn we were back in San Salvador.

Then I had to run around and find someone to make the marble tomb-stones that would be put over the graves. Near the cemetery there were some artisans who took care of all those things for funerals.

"What names do you want me to carve on the stones?" the first one I approached asked me.

I showed him the piece of paper with the three names . . .

"Rutilio Grande? Oh no, sir. I can't. I'm very sorry!"

At the next workshop it was the same, and at the next and the next. No one wanted to engrave those names. They were afraid—terribly afraid.

"But it's such a small thing to ask. Tell me, who's going to know?"

Nobody wanted to do it. Finally I went back to the furthest corner, way, way back, to a place that was practically hidden from sight, and I found a man with curly hair who was the only one willing.

"But please, don't tell anyone . . . I'll do it for you without a receipt."

Mission accomplished. The funeral Mass was almost beginning in the Cathedral.

(Antonio Fernández Ibáñez)

PEOPLE SAY . . .
that in San Salvador everyone was talking about Rutilio Grande's burial Mass, and especially about the single Mass that was to be said in all of El Salvador on that Sunday, March 20.

"And why do they call it the single Mass?"

"Because it will be a special Mass. Because even though it's Sunday, no priest will say Mass in any other church or chapel, or anywhere else in the archdiocese. Instead, they'll all go and participate together in one single Mass in the Cathedral. Only one Mass! So if you feel like you have to go that day to pray or light candles, that's the only one there's going to be in the whole town."

"I've never heard of a single Mass like that."

"Yeah, but a priest being killed is not an everyday thing!"

People are curious. They also want to demonstrate to the government and military that Christians are all opposed to that kind of a crime—that they are all united, like grains of corn on the same ear.

WHAT SHOULD BE DONE IN RESPONSE to Rutilio's death? After the burial came the discussions and the unending meetings with Monseñor Romero, the priests, the lay leaders and the nuns.

"What's been said and done already is sufficient," said the most conservative ones.

"We can't stop until we've broken off relations with the Vatican!" said the most radical ones.

In the heat of the debate the idea of the single Mass came up and became the center of the controversy.

"And do you really think that it would do any good?" Monseñor Romero was full of doubts.

He wanted to be convinced, to hear all of the arguments, to arrive at a truly collective decision. There were huge assemblies lasting eight or more hours, with people present from both the left and the right.

"The government is going to interpret this Mass as a provocation!"

"It *will* be a provocation. An open-air Mass with a crowd of people in the streets during this state of siege . . .We can't guarantee that there won't be shots fired and that this won't end up in a slaughter!"

"But the people in the communities are already in favor of holding a single Mass!"

Monseñor Romero was full of reservations. He finally came out with what appeared to be his biggest concern.

"And in this situation, wouldn't we be giving greater glory to God by having many masses in different places than a single Mass in a single place?"

The pros and cons were argued out again. After a while, I asked to speak.

"You know, I think that all of us here think that a Mass is an act of infinite value. So does it make any sense to be worried about saying a bunch of masses? Are we trying to add up the infinites? One is enough. I think that Monseñor Romero is absolutely right that we should be concerned about the glory of God, but if I remember right, the bishop and martyr Saint Ireneo once said, *'Gloria Dei vivens homo'*—The glory of God is that humankind should live."

I think that argument finally convinced him. In the end with the approval of the great majority of those gathered, it was decided that on Sunday, March 20, there would be only one Mass, a single Mass, in the whole Archdiocese of San Salvador.

(César Jerez)

HE WAS SMALLER THAN EVER. When the last meeting about whether or not to hold the single Mass was over, his brow was more furrowed, he was more withdrawn, more anxiety-ridden than ever. He had said yes to the idea, he had accepted it, but who knew how much criticism he would have to face.

After leaving Guadalupe Hall, four or five of us priests stayed around talking to each other. We lit our cigarettes and started exchanging our impressions.

"The man has changed."

That was what everyone was saying. Suddenly, Monseñor came straight over to where we were, and without any ado whatsoever let his question fly:

"Tell me. Tell me, all of you. What should I do to be a good bishop?"

"It's easy, Monseñor," said one mischievously. "Say you spend all seven days of the week here in San Salvador, listening to the old women who call you to meetings and invite you to tea. What you should do is change the recipe: spend six days in the countryside among the *campesinos* and just one day here. Then you'll be a good bishop!"

Then he responded with even more naiveté.

"That sounds good to me, but I don't know all of the places in the countryside yet where I should go. Why don't you make me a little schedule for those six days."

What more could we ask? When he was auxiliary bishop in San Salvador, he never even left his office. And now he was asking us to make his pastoral plan for him!

"What an incredible change," the mischievous priest said to me, still having a hard time believing it himself.

(Antonio Fernández Ibáñez)

"THREE DAYS WITHOUT CLASSES?!! These are communist whims! What is all of this foolishness coming to?"

The ruling class screamed to high heaven. Not only would there be a single Mass celebrated, but there had also been a collective decision to suspend classes in Catholic schools during the three days before the Mass so that the students could reflect together about the situation in the country. Tension was growing between Monseñor Romero and his old friends.

Overwhelmed, but convinced, Monseñor decided to go in person to the papal nuncio, Emmanuele Gerada, to communicate his irrevocable decision to hold a single Mass. He asked four of us priests to accompany him so that, among all of us, we might be able to explain it better.

The nuncio wasn't in. His secretary received us—an Italian priest who sat in front of Monseñor Romero with the expression of an inquisitor. Even though it was the archbishop there before him, he did nothing to contain his anger.

To start with, we explained to him one by one the various arguments and all the pros and cons we'd discussed in our meetings.

"*Va bene!*" he responded angrily from the very beginning, "This single Mass idea has several aspects to it. There's the pastoral aspect, the theological aspect . . . You have set out these arguments *molto bene*, but you've forgotten the most important thing!"

What could it be? Nothing occurred to me.

"The legal aspect! The aspect of canon law! The norms! There is no consideration of the law here!"

And the man began to argue that Monseñor did not have authority, according to the laws of the Church, to give anyone dispensation from Mass on Sunday or to deprive anyone of the right to attend Mass. And from there he set about scolding him—screaming at him!

I insisted that the circumstances were very special, that it was a time of repression, that it was our duty to give hope to the people and that in such a critical situation, the legal aspects were completely secondary.

"The Sabbath is for man, not man for the Sabbath," I reminded him.

But he was deaf to my arguments and continued with his scolding and his arguments about laws, and rights, and dispensations, and codes, and the various clauses of the codes . . .

Monseñor Romero was quiet. He only spoke at the end:

"I beg you to communicate to the nuncio that there will be a single Mass. This is the decision of practically all the clergy, and it is my decision as well. Tell him also that, ultimately, responsibility rests with me in this archdiocese."

No one said anything else. When we left the nunciature, Romero said to us: "These men are like the ones from Opus Dei! They just don't understand!"

(Jon Sobrino)

THE EVE OF THE MUCH-ARGUED-OVER SINGLE MASS. It was early afternoon on Saturday the 19th. We had been asked to prepare 136 signs, one for each one of the parishes of the archdiocese to carry. It was a tedious chore, and my sisters and a few seminarians were helping. In the midst of this, the nuncio, Monseñor Gerada appeared in the halls of the archdiocesan offices.

"Where is Monseñor Romero?" he asked me, irritated.

"He's not here right now. He's gone out."

He'd gone to El Paisnal to say Mass at the Festival of San José, the festival that Rutilio Grande had intended to celebrate with his people.

"Well, he should be here where he belongs!" he shouted.

"But why are you speaking so angrily about him?"

"Because tomorrow he's going to make a big mistake, and he's blind to it. He doesn't realize it! Tomorrow will be a terrible day for the Church!"

Each time he spoke, he seemed more aggressive.

"What do you mean, a terrible day? We're going to celebrate a single Mass all together, and this will be a great blessing . . ."

"Enough! Give him this for me when he returns!"

He gave me a letter, and he left. Monseñor Romero returned at about five in the afternoon. I gave him the letter and he went to his room to read it. After a little bit, he came back out, very perturbed and looking for me.

"Look at this letter. Read it!"

The nuncio was pressuring him. He was threatening him, ordering him to tell all of the clergy that the single Mass would be suspended.

"What can I do, Chencho?"

I reminded him of the oldest and most basic of all theological rules.

"You, and only you, are the bishop. And you are the one who must answer to God for the decisions you make as pastor of these people. God has given you this charge, and He has given you responsibility for the Archdiocese of San Salvador. The nuncio does not have this responsibility. Not even the pope has this responsibility. It is yours alone."

He looked at me, still searching, and I could think of nothing else to say to him. Then my thoughts went back to the past, and something occurred to me.

"Do you remember the Christian Cursillo Movement?" Fifteen years ago the two of us had been involved in that movement. "Do you remember how we said back then that when we couldn't find the answer to a problem we were facing, the best thing to do was to go and talk with Jesus? Why don't you do that? Why don't you go and talk with the Lord? Between the two of you, you can decide what needs to be done."

He went straight to the chapel of the seminary, and I went back to my place on the floor, painting letters onto signs, and fearing all the while that amidst so many pressures his confusion would overwhelm him . . .

About an hour later, I saw him coming down that long hallway. He was moving ever so slowly, while I felt my own wheels spinning faster and faster, burning up inside. It seemed like he'd never get to where I was.

When he finally stood next to me, I stayed on my knees, painting, trying to pretend I wasn't feeling that tension . . .

"Chencho . . ."

"So, did you have a chance to talk?" I stood up with a can of green paint in my hand.

"Yes, Chencho. We've talked. He's in agreement too."

(Inocencio Alas)

THE PLAZA WAS FULL TO OVERFLOWING. More than 100,000 people were there, and who knows how many more were listening on their radios. The priests dispersed into the crowd, and hundreds of people were saying their confessions on the streets. Many people who had distanced themselves from the Church for years, returned to their faith that day. Rutilio's assassination and the message given by that single Mass were alarms sounding, waking people up. Almost all of the priests of the archdiocese concelebrated that day—about 150 of us—and also priests from other dioceses who overcame all obstacles to be there.

As the Mass began, I noticed that Monseñor Romero was sweating, pale and nervous. And when he began the homily, it seemed slow to me, without his usual eloquence, as if he was reluctant to go through the door of history that God was opening up for him. But after about five minutes, I felt the Holy Spirit descend upon him.

" . . . I want to give a public thanks today, here in front of the archdiocese, for the unified support that is being expressed for the only Gospel and for these our beloved priests. Many of them are in danger, and like Father Grande, they are risking even the maximum sacrifice . . ."

Hearing the name of Rutilio, thousands exploded into applause.

"This applause confirms the profound joy that my heart feels upon taking possession of the archdiocese and feeling that my own weaknesses and my own inabilities can find their complement, their strength, and their courage in a united clergy. Whoever touches one of my priests, is touching me. And they will have to deal with me!!"

Thousands of people were applauding him, and something rose within him. It was then that he crossed the threshold. He went through the door. Because, you know, there is baptism by water, and there is baptism by blood. But there is also baptism by the people.

(Inocencio Alas)

SECTION TWO

*The vessel he was making of clay
was spoiled in the potter's hand,
and he reworked it into another,
very different one.*

—Jeremiah 18:4

"I may not have been other things, but I've always been
a communicator."

THE KIND OF BISHOP THE TIMES DEMAND

PEOPLE SAY . . .
that when Monseñor Romero had just begun as archbishop in San Salvador, the richest people in the capital wanted to give him a house and a car. He talked about it himself in the communities:

"I had no sooner arrived than those people offered me what they called 'a little house.' But it was no such thing! It was a huge house! They said I could choose one in San Benito or in Escalón. I told them 'no thank you.' Then they offered me 'a little car,' but what they really meant was a big fancy car. I told them, 'No, thank you' again. That's the way it goes with rich people. At first they try to tie you up with a little piece of string but then it turns into a big old rope and you can't escape from it.

And they say that when the hoity-toity women of San Salvador realized how Monseñor was changing, they got offended and said:

"That boy has turned out to have very bad manners!"

AFTER ABOUT A WEEK, THEY SENT HIM an immense sound system that must have cost 2,500 *colones* at that time! An expensive present, don't you think? They sent it to him with a paid-in-cash receipt from Kismet. I know, because I saw it myself.

"Be careful," I warned him. "Who knows? We could turn this thing on and find out it's full of gunpowder! It could explode on us! Or it could have a hidden microphone attached so they can listen in on all the things we do around here . . ."

"Return it," said Monseñor.

But the people at Kismet wouldn't accept the return. They said that it was paid for and that they didn't want to know anything about squabbles between clients.

(Juan Bosco Palacios)

HE DECIDED TO COME AND LIVE WITH US at the *"hospitalito"*—that's what everyone calls it. It's the Divine Providence Hospital; patients with terminal cancer are cared for here.

We sisters had a long-standing friendship with Monseñor Romero; we had known him since the time when he was a priest in San Miguel. Then, when he was the bishop in Santiago de María, he started his custom of coming to say Mass for us on the first of each month. And when he had meetings at the Bishops' Conference, he would come and have dinner with us, and sometimes he'd stay and sleep here in the sacristy. I don't know why, but he was fond of this place. Soon after he was named archbishop, he came to ask us if he could live here, and our community was very proud to be asked.

"It is a great honor for us, Monseñor," we told him.

"Well for me, it's a great opportunity to have a good place to rest," he said.

The joy of having him here came with a cost. Because we'd welcomed him in to the *hospitalito*, we were shouted at on the streets. "Reds! Communists!" they said to us; the hatred was so strong that many benefactors withdrew their contributions to the sick.

"I'm scaring off your donors," he would say, upset.

He even said that he would leave. But how could we allow him to go?

(Teresa Alas)

I WAS GIVEN AN ORDER TO GO and work in the private offices of Monseñor Romero shortly after he was named archbishop. I had already been working for several years in the archives of the archdiocese.

"There's a lot to do. We're going to need another person," Monseñor Romero said to me almost from the start.

"Perhaps another sister from my community?"

"All right."

And that's how Silvia Arriola[1] came to work in that office. Every day there was a huge amount of work, and there was never enough time. The two of us would start at 8:00 AM and stay at it past noon. In the afternoons we did pastoral work in the communities. So we were always busy, and he was always worried about us.

"You're all skin and bones!" he would say to us.

It wasn't that we had lost weight. We were just skinny people! But he kept telling us that we were too thin because we weren't taking care of ourselves.

"You two are always running around all over the place, and you don't remember to eat."

In his offices he had a small lounge and dining room. There was a little refrigerator there, but it was only used for water. One day he called us.

"Come here and look. I've made sure that this machine is full of food so you can eat. I don't want you to go hungry!"

He opened the door. There was meat, eggs, cheese, vegetables . . .

"Stay and eat your lunch here. And you can invite me once in a while!"

There was never a lack of food there, and more than once we made a little soup or fried a few eggs—any little thing like that—and he stayed and had lunch with us. But most of the time, we were too busy to eat.

(María Isabel Figueroa)

---

[1]Silvia Arriola—Member of the *Pequeña Comunidad* (Small Community) religious order. She later joined the guerrillas as a nurse and died in combat.

A GROUP OF RELIGIOUS WOMEN, especially those of us working in the Catholic schools, went and volunteered to work with him. Monseñor Romero knew how to win us over, and of course we wanted to pamper him. He was kind, but he couldn't put up with the typical attention of nuns: "Oh, Monseñor, your cassock is torn. I'll sew it for you. Oh, your trousers, your handkerchiefs . . ." Anything but that! He couldn't stand for the nuns to be bothering him about his clothes.

"This is the last time! I'll let you know when I run out, all right?" he said rather brusquely to one nun who was always giving him new socks.

(Nelly Rodríguez)

WE WENT LOOKING FOR HIM to offer our support. He didn't seem like a powerful hierarch to me, more like a brother.

"I feel more comfortable with you people who aren't Catholic than with some from my own Church," he confessed shortly after meeting us.

Monseñor added a lot of momentum to the ecumenical movement that was starting to build in El Salvador between Catholics and Protestants— Lutherans, Episcopalians and Baptists. We were all involved in the same kind of work.

(Edgar Palacios)

MY LITTLE GRANDSON WAS THE FIRST CHILD that Monseñor Romero baptized and confirmed.

"You don't know me," I said when I arrived at the church for the ceremony. "I'm the grandmother. I want to tell you that I'm with you, and if I can help you in any way, I'd like to."

He looked at me.

"What is your name?"

"Aída Parker de Muyshondt"

From that day on I started helping him with different tasks. I even packed up stacks of the newspaper, *Orientación,* in my car and distributed them at agencies and parishes. We were all willing to do anything to collaborate in some way! It wasn't all a bed of roses, though. Because of my friendship with Monseñor and the support I was giving him, my six daughters-in-laws and their families began to ostracize me. At the police station, my license plate number was on a list, and I was labelled as a communist.

(Aída Parker de Muyshondt)

I TURNED ON THE CAR RADIO. It was a Sunday and Monseñor was giving his homily. His words made such an impact on me that I never missed one of his masses in the Cathedral. One Sunday, after listening to him, I finally decided.

"Monseñor, I'm at your service." I approached him to tell him this as he was headed toward the sacristy. "I'd be happy to do any work you'd entrust me with."

"And what kind of work do you do?"

"I know accounting. I work in the audits department at a bank."

"Just what the doctor ordered! I know exactly how you can help me!" And that's how I started to help out in the reorganization of *Cáritas.* I gave him all of my free time.

(Mauricio Mendoza Merlos)

WHENEVER I WENT TO MONSEÑOR ROMERO'S OFFICE to work on the legal case concerning the assassination of Father Rutilio Grande, he would always start up another conversation when we were done.

"Tell me about *Servicio Jurídico,*" he said with great interest.

Two years earlier, a group of lawyers including myself had gotten involved in this effort. We provided legal services on land rights issues, common causes, family struggles, notary services, and all of those kinds of things that so many poor people usually couldn't afford. Monseñor fell in love with the project and dreamed about making it part of the archdiocese. Finally he was able to do that. Then the name changed to *Socorro Jurídico*—Legal Aid. In the same way, he kept bringing new projects, efforts and people under the protective umbrella of the archdiocese.

(Roberto Cuellar)

EVERYBODY AND THEIR BROTHER went to that office; many went to volunteer their services and others . . . to "convert" him.

"Look what I've brought Monseñor as a gift," said a friend of mine proudly when I ran into her one morning at the archdiocesan offices.

"What? How would you dare give him such a thing?"

It was a book entitled, *You Too Could Be Deceived By Communism,* or something like that. It was written by a certain René Ferrufino, a rabid anticommunist.

"Girl, aren't you ashamed to take a book like that to the archbishop? I don't know if you know, but Monseñor Romero is a *ve-ry ed-u-ca-ted* man!"

"He may be, but those communists can ensnare even the smartest of people, so he should also be *ve-ry* prepared!"

Her husband was involved in distributing these books to counteract the influence of the "red" priests. A few days later I received a copy, too.

(Ana María Godoy)

HE PUT A LOT OF TRUST IN US AS LAY LEADERS. He would give us work to do, and we'd feel like we had wings to fly. Sometimes he gave us surprising tasks.

"What I want you to do is to go to the various vicariates and call the parish priests together to offer them some guidelines."

What audacity! We, the lay people—most of us women—were supposed to call priests together for meetings and indoctrinate *them*!

"Oh, Monseñor," I told him the first time he suggested it, "this makes me a little nervous. I don't think some of the priests are going to like this very much."

"I want you to do it even if they don't like it at all."

"But what if they shut the doors on us?"

"Go in through the window. You have a responsibility. Go show them how it's done."

So off we would go, asking the priests what kinds of pastoral plans they used, suggesting courses, and offering to collaborate with them in their work.

"This is so we can have a better coordination among all of us, you see."

So that's how we started going through some doors and sneaking in through quite a few windows.

(Coralia Godoy)

IT WAS THE KIND OF HEAT that wasn't letting up one iota. And it was during the intense heat of that day that Monseñor Romero had to do his first rounds in our neck of the woods. He came to visit eight of the *cantones* of Aguilares. They weren't the kind of roads you could travel by car. To get there you had to walk, and he got really tired out from going here and there all day long. He even started to sniffle and cough from all of the dust that hangs in the air during the dry season. Towards the end of the day, he was irritated and dripping with sweat.

We had prepared a surprise for him so that he would feel some relief. "We fixed you some sweet corn *atol*, Monseñor. Would you like a little taste?"

"No. I just want to get out of here!"

And he left. He said he wanted to get back to San Salvador as soon as he could, and he even said it like he was mad. We were left standing with the *atol* and the other things we had fixed for him. My *comadre* and I were so disappointed that we had tears rolling down our faces.

Later we were told that when he returned to the capital he realized how poorly he'd behaved, and was embarrassed about having turned down what we had offered.

One day he returned to our area. He had thought about his mistake so much that he even asked us for forgiveness.

"Please forgive me. I had never seen such poverty. I just wasn't used to it all."

That day when we offered him a big gourd full of *atol*, he accepted.

(Rosa Alonso)

TROUBLES, COMPLICATIONS, and entanglements. Monseñor Romero knew that *Cáritas* was a mess and that someone was going to have to put it in order for it to function efficiently. When we heard about it, a group of us women offered to lend a hand, or two, or 10—whatever he needed.

"Find out what's happening in *Cáritas*," he asked us.

So we went to investigate.

"The priest in charge of *Cáritas* has put together some kind of network with his family members and they're turning *Cáritas* into their personal business. They sell what they get for twice as much as they pay for it."

"Food is getting lost, Monseñor, and they say it's because the bags are torn, but they're the ones that tear them open."

"In Chalate, they've even started a pig farm. Prize pigs are eating their fill of *Cáritas* food!"

"Are you sure these aren't just rumors?" he would ask.

But they weren't, so he encouraged us to continue.

"I'm leaving this in your hands. You need to find out what's really going on and make things right. I'll go with what you decide."

We came to suspect that someone was stealing from the *Cáritas* store-rooms in the Cathedral. Then Father Tilo Sánchez, whom Monseñor Romero had named to coordinate our work, had an idea. He hid inside an empty box in the storeroom and spent the whole blessed night waiting there. When it was almost dawn, he caught the thief with his hand in the cookie-jar. It was the sacristan!

"They say that when the river is turbulent, it's good for the fisherman. Here I guess it's been good for the sacristan," said Monseñor Romero, trying to understand.

So, little by little, we started to clean up *Cáritas* by replacing some of the old staff. We also organized the offices, the records and the accounts, and managed to whip the whole big mess into shape.

(Miriam Estupinián)

YOU NEVER KNOW what's on somebody else's mind. Take, for example, the priest in our area. His way of thinking was the exact opposite of Monseñor Romero's. He would say that Monseñor had changed and that he didn't like the change one bit. But we liked it a lot. We felt that Monseñor had taken the *campesinos'* side.

"Let's invite Monseñor to visit us," we said to our priest.

"It could cause problems," he'd say, trying to get out of it.

But in the end, we invited him ourselves, and we even went to pick him up.

Since the chapel was really small, when Monseñor arrived he asked us to take the altar table and the candles out to the park so he could say Mass there.

You wouldn't believe what happened next! Our priest gave Monseñor the cold shoulder so he wouldn't have to say Mass with him. He went off in the distance to smoke his cigarette, like he was angry.

"What an insult!"

"Oh, leave him be. Maybe after Mass he'll invite him to eat at his house and they can talk there." I told my Uncle Ambrosio to calm him down.

But our priest continued to act rudely, and didn't invite Monseñor to anything. He just went off as calmly as you please to eat by himself, leaving Monseñor there all alone.

The women of the Altar Guild were terribly embarrassed and brought him a fruit drink.

"Do you like pineapple or papaya, Monseñor?"

"I like both!"

He had realized what was going on, but he wasn't upset. Seeing him there in such a good mood, we mustered up the courage to invite him to eat with us.

"Would you like to eat some beans with us in a little diner where us poor folks go?"

He accepted right away. We fixed him up a table as fancy as we could in that little place, and as we were eating, we got a little more daring and asked him, probably a bit imprudently:

"What message do you have for the *padre* that didn't invite you to eat and acted so rudely?"

"My message to him is that he doesn't know what he's missing out on!"

And Monseñor laughed as he savored his beans and *chismol* sauce.

(Julián Gómez)

THE ARCHDIOCESAN RADIO STATION, YSAX, was a disaster. It was held together by a shoestring, and it was bankrupt financially. Bad administration—a den of thieves. And on top of all that, the government was pressuring them to remove the antenna from the piece of property where it was located.

I was travelling through El Salvador not long after Grande's assassination, exploring the possibility of setting up educational programs like the ones we had in Radio Santa Maria in the Dominican Republic. But things were tense. I didn't like the country at all, and I'd decided to leave and take my music elsewhere.

I was to return home on a Wednesday, and I'd already bought the ticket. On Tuesday afternoon, César Jerez, the Jesuit provincial, called several of us together.

"Listen up. The bishop has asked me if we can help him save the radio station."

"It's beyond repair!" I said.

All of us refused to go.

"At least come to the meeting tomorrow," César insisted to me.

"But I'm leaving the country tomorrow! I've got my ticket already!"

"Don't be so stubborn, man. You can go after the meeting."

I went solely out of a sense of obligation. I didn't know Romero from Adam. César introduced me, and told him that I had experience, that I knew a lot about radio . . .

Monseñor Romero looked at me and said exactly these words:

"I'm asking you to help me save the radio station. And if I have to, I'll get on my knees."

No one had ever gotten on their knees to ask me for anything. Much less a bishop! But the tone of his voice made me feel like he might just kneel down right there in front of me! It really threw me for a loop. It moved me.

"Bring on that radio, Monseñor!" I told him.

I didn't even remember to cancel my plane reservations.

(Rogelio Pedraz)

"YOU HAVE TO HELP ME put *Cáritas* in order, Sánchez."

I used to go every week to give Monseñor Romero a report on how things were going. That is to say, I used to go and fight with him.

We fought, especially when there were land takeovers somewhere. And there always were some. The land problem has always been at the center of the Salvadoran conflict. I would set aside some of the *Cáritas* money and food and send it to the communities that were participating in the occupation. And Monseñor didn't like it.

"Sánchez, I've found out."

"What have you found out?"

"That you're sending donations from *Cáritas* to the people who seized land in Chalatenango."

"I see you've got good sources."

"You know that I don't approve of that. It's being one-sided. You're supporting just one organization, FECCAS-UTC, and you know very well that it's an illegal group and that this could cause problems for us . . ."

"This is all true, but since they need it, I'm going to continue sending it to them. As long as we have food, they won't go without."

"But it's not like we have food to spare. You should send more to Sarah House, for example."

"I'm already sending some to them."

"Send them more!"

"No, because Sarah House will always be supported by people who like to give alms to charity. But who's going to feed the others? If we don't give to them, they're screwed. You, as bishop, should be supporting them."

"Sánchez!"

"Monseñor, those people don't have land to plant on. They're hungry, and I'm not sending them arms!"

"Sánchez, you're all passion and no reason."

"But I haven't even told you the most important reason. Giving to them is a way to educate ourselves. Because if we keep giving a glass of milk and a little bag of flour to poor people, we're teaching them to be dependent. But giving to these organized *campesinos* is the opposite! Their struggle teaches us. It can teach you, too!"

"That kind of radical thinking is what worries me about you, Sánchez."

"All right, don't take my word for it. Go and see for yourself what those people are like, see what stuff they're made of. Come on, let's go visit the place where they're camped out!"

"That's not a bad idea, but . . ."

"But what? Don't be afraid of them. Save your fear for the National Guard."

"You're always getting me involved in things!"

But we would go to the land occupations. And there the *campesinos* would talk to him and educate him—with their reason and their passion.

(Rutilio Sánchez)

IT WAS WAR. From the day of the single Mass on, the economic elite had begun an open war against him. They took out paid ads criticizing him in the newspapers. They made unfounded accusations. They made fun of him. They made offensive remarks. In the midst of all this, we decided to pay him an official visit.

"And what brings you here?" he said to us in greeting.

He was surprised that Protestants would be coming to see him. Maybe it was the first time. We were a good-sized group—the pastor and all of the deacons and their wives representing our little church, Emmanuel Baptist Church.

We explained to him how much we admired his work, and we told him that we had some good friends among the Catholic priests.

When we were about to leave, Heriberto Pérez asked if we could end our gathering with a prayer. Heriberto was the pastor who had founded Emmanuel Church. He was the eldest among us and had been brought up in that virulent anti-Catholicism that you sometimes see.

"I thank the Lord that we have met this man of God," Heriberto prayed.

He was very impressed with Monseñor, and he was expressing what we all felt.

But when other Baptists learned about this visit, they said, "You're returning to the power of darkness!"

This kind of anti-Catholic sentiment was pretty much a part of our identity, rooted as it was in the Protestant blood. But we felt calm.

A few days later, Monseñor Romero mentioned our meeting on the radio, and he talked about us, calling us the "separated brothers." That was the usual language of the Catholic Church at the time.

We continued to have more meetings, and once when we went back to visit him, Heriberto called him on the issue:

"You spoke of us in a way we don't like. We do feel like brothers, but we don't feel separated."

Monseñor was pensive for a few moments.

"Let's make a deal," he proposed. "Don't call me Monseñor anymore. Just call me brother. And I won't call you the 'separated brothers' anymore either."

"It's a deal!"

And from that day on, he called us "the brothers from Emmanuel" and we called him "Brother Romero."

(Miguel Tomás Castro)

WITH A NAME LIKE APOLINARIO one might have expected to see a big man, a titan. That's what Monseñor Romero expected, too. But then Polín appeared, a shrivelled up man with a limp—nothing much to speak of.

It was the first meeting between Monseñor and Polín, but it didn't take long for the discussion to get rolling.

"You know, Apolinario, people say that you are going around inciting the *campesinos*. They even say that you speak against the Church and against me. But they also tell me that you're a man of faith . . . How do you explain all of this?"

"Monseñor, I explain things best by asking questions."

"All right, go ahead and ask."

"Tell me then, first of all, does the archbishop know how much a *campesino* 'poor-o-tariat' gets paid for the backbreaking work he does in a day?"

"Well, I guess I don't know exactly . . ."

"Three *colones*, Monseñor! We're going around 'exciting' the *campesinos*, as you say, so that they'll pay us *two* more *colones*! Now tell me, Monseñor, what would you do if you only had three *colones* in your pocket for the whole blessed day? I mean, even if you had five! It probably costs more than that just to have your cassock washed. And we don't even earn that much slaving away from sunup to sundown in the cane fields!"

Monseñor looked Polín over from top to bottom, the scrawny guy that he was.

"But let's continue with our interview here, so the *atol* doesn't get cold! Will you permit me another question?" Polín continued, waving his hands all over the place.

"Go ahead. Throw another one at me." Monseñor was following his lead, laughing now.

"Let's see, Monseñor. Do you believe in God?"

"Of course I believe in God."

"And do you also believe in the Gospel?"

"Yes. I also believe in the Gospel."

"We're tied then! Because I also believe in God and in the Gospel. We both say the same thing, but it's different! So guess my riddle, I've got a pain in my middle! Guess, your Magnificence, what is the difference?" Polín was going strong now, having fun with his gibberish.

"I have no idea Polín. You'll have to tell me." Monseñor was laughing.

"You believe in the Gospel because it's your job. You studied it, you read it and you preach it. Your thing is being a bishop! And me . . . I can hardly read, and I haven't studied all of the 'indiology' in the Gospel, but I do believe it. You believe in it as an occupation, and I believe in it because I need to. Because God says there that He doesn't want there to be rich and poor. And I'm poor! See the difference? Do you get it? We have the same faith, but we're carrying it around in different containers."

Monseñor looked at this man Polín who was all spark. And from that day on, they became the greatest of friends.

(Rutilio Sánchez)

HE WOULD FIND YOU IN THE HALLS and—bam!—he'd pull you into his recording studio.

"Come, come help me do the program!"

So, just like that, you'd end up there. It was a crowded little room. You had to move things around to be able to open the door, and you could barely fit two people in front of the microphone.

Monseñor had come up with a weekly program. The name he gave to it was also his motto as a bishop: *Sentir con la Iglesia*—"Of One Mind and Heart with the Church." It was a general name so that any current topic could be discussed. He did his program in interview form.

"OK. You're going to interview me about family planning . . ."

"I'm going to interview *you*?!"

The "interviewer" nabbed in the hall—a seminarian, a woman who might be visiting him, a student, whoever—would be surprised. And sometimes even scared.

"No, don't worry. Look I'll show you what you have to do . . ."

But he did everything. He had all the details covered. He already had questions written out for you to ask him, word for word. He had picked out the letters he was going to answer or comment on. And the needle would already be placed on the record at the spot where the background music was supposed to begin.

"Dear listeners, this Wednesday we have with us Monseñor Romero. Today he's going to answer our questions on the topic of the family . . ." the journalist of the day would begin.

Then he would take the reins and never let go of them. Questions followed, then the answers. He always got inspired in front of the microphone. He was crazy about radio.

"And why wouldn't I be?" he'd say in his defense. "I may not have been other things, but I've always been a communicator."

That's what he called himself: a communicator. And it's true that since the time he was in San Miguel, he was always starting newspapers or newsletters or speaking on the radio. Or he'd attach loudspeakers to his old jeep so he could arrive in the *cantones* preaching. They say he brought that old contraption of a jeep to San Salvador, but being the old, beaten-down animal that it was, it finally bit the dust at the archdiocesan headquarters.

(Francisco Calles)

EL SALVADOR HAD SIX BISHOPS, and they were quite often in meetings that would last nearly six hours! They'd be locked inside the upper room of the archdiocesan offices in interminable discussions. Early on—practically right after the single Mass—we heard that Monseñor Romero had four bishops totally opposed to him. Only Monseñor Rivera supported him.

"Paco. Do me a favor," he said to me one day at the door of the meeting room. "Come and get me out of here around mid-morning, all right?"

"All right."

I arrived around 10:00 AM to get him.

"Hey," I said quietly to the secretary, "ask Monseñor Romero to come out for just a minute."

He came right out.

"And now where are we going, Monseñor?"

"It doesn't matter. We can talk right here . . . Tell me about the group of people from Zacate that came to the office yesterday."

"But you were there, too . . ."

"Yeah, but that little old lady who was all bent over. Did she say anything else afterwards?"

And we started to walk up and down those long halls, chatting about the little old lady, the little old man, the price of tea in China . . .

"And another thing, Paco. Where could I find a good cassette tape of the French trumpeter Maurice André? He's extraordinary. Have you heard him?"

Then we started talking about music—about trumpets and saxophones. After a while, he looked at his watch.

"I'm going to go back. I really appreciate this, Paco. Thanks."

He went back in. The bishops' meeting was still going on. I stood outside in the hall wondering what that had all been about.

But that wasn't the only time it happened. It became the routine every time there was a meeting of the Bishops' Conference.

"Come get me out of there. OK, Paco? Don't forget."

I came up with all sorts of reasons to call him out. One day it was that he had an urgent meeting. Another day it was a call from Patagonia. Another day, a signature that was needed immediately. I was always devising some little trick to get him out of there. I don't know how he kept justifying his departures, but he always came out. And it was always the same routine of chatting and walking up and down the hall, from east to west and west to east.

"Today, I want you to tell me about your family, Paco . . . Did you get your housing situation worked out?"

Sometimes we would spend as much as two hours talking outside. He never said a word about the bishops' meeting, nor did he ever explain to me why he wanted to get out of it.

I had to figure it out for myself. It hadn't even been six months, and already the hostility of the other bishops was suffocating him. His way of getting through it and avoiding more confrontations was to leave—to rest a while and then go back to the fray.

(Francisco Calles)

"MONSEÑOR, LOOK AT TODAY'S MAIL!!"

"That much?"

Nobody knew how to read or write in those remote villages, and still the letters poured in. From the very beginning, letters came to the archdiocese like never before. All of them were addressed to Monseñor Romero. This had never happened before. The other novelty was that many of the letters came from *campesino* communities where the letters were written collectively. Someone who knew how to write, would write in the name of the whole group. People who had never even thought about putting pen to paper took it upon themselves to direct a letter to the archbishop. But they almost never arrived through the postal system.

"That place is full of spies, and they open our mail," the ever-cautious *campesinos* would say.

So the parish priests would bring the letters in by hand.

Monseñor's radio homilies, his frequent visits to the communities and these letters provided a framework for extensive communication between the bishop and the people. And it wasn't just the people in the Archdiocese of San Salvador, the ones in his own flock, it was people all over the country. The letter-writing phenomena was happening nationally.

"Leave the letters out for me. I want to read them."

"You're not going to have time, Monseñor. Look at this pile."

He liked to be able to read them personally, but he couldn't always do that. He also liked to answer them, but he couldn't always do that, either. Often he asked one of his secretaries, Silvia, to respond in his name. Other times he would talk about issues raised in the letters during his Wednesday radio program.

"Monseñor, is it a sin to participate in grassroots organizing?"

"Is it a sin if we occupy churches to denounce the crimes that are committed against us?"

"Monseñor, what can we say to those Protestants who come to our doors telling us that God forbids us to become involved in politics?"

"Is it true, Monseñor, that St. George never existed?"

"Tell us who the Great Beast is that the Protestants keep talking about. Is he like the *Ziguanaba*[2] in our legends, or what? How can we recognize him?"

(Miguel Vázquez)

THE *CAMPESINOS* TRUSTED HIM SO MUCH that they would write him not only about community issues, or about the repression, but also about their own work in the fields.

"We don't have fertilizer for our corn fields. We want to plant when the rainy season comes, but we don't know how we're going to do it . . ."

---

[2]*Ziguanaba*—In Salvadoran legends, the *Ziguanaba* monster appears to unsuspecting men in the form of a beautiful woman and lures them to their demise.

It wasn't just one or two people who needed money for fertilizer or seed. The needs were infinite. He developed the habit of reading the letters and then writing in the corner: "Need to answer and send 'x' amount of *colones*." Sometimes he'd decide how much money to send, and sometimes he'd leave it up to us.

It became routine for Silvia and me to go with one of the seminarians to deliver his letters and the money. We would go to Opico, to Tacachico, to all of those places.

Once some very poor families in El Majagual, up there in the hills near La Libertad, asked for money for fertilizer. We went to take Monseñor's response to them. It was both spiritual and material—consolation, greetings and money. We were in one of the archdiocesan cars. We drove it as far as we could and left it. Then we had to climb up brush-covered hills to a tiny cluster of houses, crossing ravine after ravine to get there.

You should have seen the surprise and joy of those *campesinos* when we showed up. They couldn't believe that Monseñor Romero had sent them exactly what they'd asked for—enough money for the fertilizer they needed. To thank us, they loaded us down with *jocote* plums, the only thing they had.

When we got back down to the car, it was surrounded by National Guardsmen.

"What are you doing here?"

"We've come here on behalf of Monseñor Romero. We work at the archbishop's offices."

"You're guerrillas!"

The only thing that saved us that day was that one of the guardsmen recognized Joaquín, the seminarian who was with us. They were from the same village.

"I don't know about these women. They could be guerrillas, but this guy is the son of my friend."

They let the three of us go. That rainy season the cornfields of El Majagual looked more beautiful than they had in years.

(María Isabel Figueroa)

WORKING BREAKFASTS. That's what he called them. After Monseñor Romero had been archbishop for six or seven months, he began this tradition. And he kept it up until the end.

I was almost always the first one to arrive, and I would always find him in the chapel, kneeling in prayer.

"Monseñor, we're here."

And he would leave the chapel for our meeting. He would bring up national problems to see how we saw them and to hear our suggestions. He would comment on his pastoral plans and ask for advice. He didn't necessarily say much himself. Instead, he would ask us lots of questions to make sure he was well informed.

"I've often been accused," he would say, "of consulting with too many different people. But that's the nicest thing anyone could accuse me of, and I don't intend to mend my ways!"

He would usually take out a raggedy little notebook and write down some key phrases from among the things we'd said. He wasn't the kind of person who took notes from beginning to end. He only liked to put down the most essential points.

When we'd been chatting for a while, he would sometimes say:

"Let's go get some of Don Lencho's coffee."

Don Lorenzo Llach was an old friend of his, a coffee plantation owner from Santiago de María. Their friendship had suffered after Monseñor started changing, but Llach had never stopped giving him free coffee.

"If Don Lencho could see who was drinking coffee with me, he'd probably cut me off!" he would joke.

There we would drink coffee and talk about everything, and since those years were so full of happenings, there was always lots to talk about.

"History is moving too fast. Things are happening before we expect them to," someone said one day.

And Monseñor Romero said, "It's like when that French priest went to perform a wedding in a village way far away. The bride was all dressed in white and wearing her orange blossom wreath in her hair, but you could tell she was practically nine months pregnant. When the priest saw her coming down the aisle in such an 'advanced' state, he says to her, 'You should be wearing oranges instead of orange blossoms!'"

And he threw his head back and laughed.

(César Jerez)

OUR MAIN JOB IN THE SEMINARY was to chauffeur him around. That was Joaquín's and my mission. You had to be somewhat thick-skinned to put up with all of the ups and downs of Monseñor Romero's personality. Joaquín ran out of patience and surrendered the steering wheel. I took over and, little by little, started to figure out Monseñor's eccentricities.

Whenever he was really tired, he'd take a little *siesta* after lunch. One day he had to say Mass in Apopa.

"We have to leave here at one o'clock," he advised me sharply.

I arrived at the *hospitalito* at noon and ate lunch.

"Where's the man?" I asked Sister Teresa.

"Leave him alone. He's sleeping."

"But sister, it's after 12:30. We have to wake him up. If we don't, he's going to be angry with us."

"Let him sleep a little more. He's really tired. Besides, you always drive fast anyway."

It was a quarter 'til one, and he was still sleeping. One o'clock—no change. Sometime after one he woke up by himself, and when he saw the clock he started yelling at both of us. He said we'd made him late, that he didn't like to show up late and so on and so forth. By the time we got into the car it was 1:30, and he was totally furious.

"I don't know how you're going to do it," he said, "but I have to be in Apopa at two o'clock sharp!"

So I started up the car and took off in a hurry. When I stopped at the first traffic light, he jumped on my case.

"Don't stop for anything!"

When he was like that, he was a pain to drive with and it wore you out. We went on. On one of those blind curves on the way out of Ciudad Delgado, there was a bus in front of us that we couldn't get around because it was so big.

"Pass it!" he ordered me. "Pass it now!"

He was acting as my copilot. "All right, I'll pass it." I thought. But when I was pulling past the bus I saw there was a goddamn semi bearing down on us at full speed! I didn't think we could make it. It was practically on top of us. Son of a bitch! I pushed the accelerator down to the floor to try to pass the bus and get out of the way of that monster of a truck. And yes! Yes! I made it! There we were: the bus here, the semi there and me in the middle, like a piece of meat caught between two teeth!

"You son of a bitch!!!!!" the people on the bus screamed.

"Are you trying to kill us?!"

You could see the smoke from the braking tires of the three vehicles, and everyone in the bus was looking out the windows to see who the idiot was that had attempted such a maneuver . . . About that time, Monseñor Romero stuck his head out of our little Toyota.

"Holy shit! It's Monseñor!" you could hear people yell.

Some people on the bus were pissed off, and others were delighted to be able to say hello to Monseñor. I tried to apologize to the drivers of the other two vehicles, but he cut me off, unrepentant.

"Hey, we're not getting anywhere sitting here and making a spectacle of ourselves. So step on it! Let's get out of here!"

I took off at full speed. At two o'clock on the dot, we were in Apopa.

(Juan Bosco Palacios)

HE WAS EAGER FOR EVERYONE TO FEEL AT HOME. That desire was a recurring theme with him.

Once he asked a woman who worked as an upholsterer to recover some of the furniture in the living room of the archdiocesan headquarters. The day they brought him the sofa and armchairs, he took everyone that came through down to the living room to see them. It didn't matter what problems he was embroiled in.

"Come here! Come see how the furniture turned out."

He was there all morning organizing the parade of people that passed through. I remember he had the chairs done in a brown and orange striped fabric—subtle but very pretty.

"They turned out really nice, didn't they? Now it seems more like a real home."

And he exuded this same happiness with everyone who came through.

(Coralia Godoy)

I CERTAINLY DID MEET Monseñor Romero. And even if I live to be 100 years old, I'll never forget it. He visited our *cantón* for the festival of Saint Anthony. A big crowd showed up to receive him, and since there were so many of us that we didn't all fit in the church, he said we should have the Mass under a tree outside. He seemed to me to be a good-humored man, and kind of quiet, like us.

Later on in the afternoon there was a long line to see him off. I was the last to say good-bye. When he hugged me, he said, "Pray for me."

He wanted *me*, an old sinful woman, to pray for *him*! How many times does that happen? It's supposed to be the priest that prays for you and lifts you up to God, but not with him. He turned that rule upside down.

We old people live on memories and prayers. From that day on, I always prayed for him.

(Santos Martínez)

ON HIS VISITS TO THE *CANTONES*, Monseñor would sit at the door of the church after Mass and answer all of our questions. We approached him one by one to consult him.

My question was a big one. I'd been wondering about it for a long time. At that time there was a project from the United States called the "Adopt a Child" program to help Salvadoran children. If you signed up for the program, you would get 15 *colones* a month, but they would never tell you who it was that was sending you the money. I was on the list.

I told Monseñor, "It's kind of embarrassing to say so, but we receive this money every month. We accept it because we're poor and we have needs, but we're not sure if maybe later, the *gringos* who have "adopted" our kids might come and try to take them away from us. What do you think?

"I think," he said, "that you should take the money because you need it. For the people who send it, it's nothing. They're just lightening the load in their pockets by a few pennies. So take it, but be very careful about any person, plan or 'adoptive parent' that comes from that country."

(Licha Reyes)

IT WAS LIKE A MARKETPLACE with so many people coming and going. The archdiocesan office was a sea of people and even animals! Because the *campesinos* would bring him hens or roosters—even a cow on one day! Yes, that place could be chaotic!

Since I was in charge of bringing some kind of order to the files, as well as to the incoming and outgoing correspondence, some of the other workers in the offices approached me.

"You're here because you're efficient. So take advantage of that, and suggest to him that he should have a more fixed schedule for meetings and visits. If he doesn't, this place is going to be a zoo."

Every day there were more projects, more demands and more people to attend to. Priests, teachers, factory workers and *campesinos* would come in. Students, nurses and sick people would arrive . . . I put together a few suggestions and went to see him.

"Tell me, how exactly would this scheduling work?" Monseñor asked me with sincere curiosity.

"Well, it's just that some people say that often you don't follow through on meetings that have already been set—whether they're with the bishops, or priests or organizations—and that this is happening because you don't have a good schedule of appointments with specific days and hours . . ." I was embarrassed to be explaining this to him.

"Go on. Go on."

"They also say that other unforeseen visits come up, and that they break up the sense of order, and that having order is very important. So, of course, if your day was scheduled better, you could attend to everyone better . . ."

He looked pensive. And he started to slide the cross that he wore around his neck up and down on its chain . . . That was a habit of his when he'd be looking straight at you.

"Well, I don't think that kind of scheduling is going to be possible."

"No?"

"No, because I have my priorities. And with or without scheduling, I'm always going to receive any *campesino* that shows up here at any time of day, whether I'm in a meeting or not . . ."

"So . . ."

"So, the answer is no . . . Look, my fellow bishops all have cars. The parish priests can take buses, and they can afford to wait. But what about the *campesinos*? They come walking for miles, face all kinds of dangers, and sometimes they haven't even eaten . . . Just yesterday, one fellow came from La Unión. A National Guardsman had hit him so hard in the neck that he's going blind, and all because he was participating in a Christian meeting. He just came to tell me about it . . ."

What could I say? I started crumpling up the papers I'd prepared where I'd written a scheduling proposal for him.

"You know, the *campesinos* never ask me for anything. They just talk to me about the things that are going on in their lives, and that alone seems to help them. Can I schedule in the times when they're allowed to do that? I think we should just forget about this."

I went outside and threw my plans in the first wastebasket I could find.

(Coralia Godoy)

"WE'LL PUT THE SNACK BAR HERE!" he said one day.

By having a place to eat at the headquarters of the archdiocese, people would be able not only to bring their problems to the office, but also to sit down and have good long conversations over some food. That's why he did it. He fixed up the place where we used to have the photocopy machine, built on some additions to make it a little bigger here and there, and had little tables made. We opened it on his birthday.

All kinds of meetings were held in that little snack bar, and all in a more homey environment than in the offices. They served coffee, sodas, sweet bread, fruit drinks, cookies . . . things like that. After the snack bar was inaugurated, even more people started coming by the archdiocesan offices, and they stayed longer.

Monseñor Romero, who in other times had been so reclusive, had developed another style.

He would take his walks down the hall to the snack bar, and he'd sit and talk with a group of *campesinos*, or with us.

"What are you up to now, Sánchez? D'Aubuisson says you're eluding him by dressing as a woman."

D'Aubuisson had accused me of disguising myself as a woman and training guerrillas.

"Do you believe that Monseñor?"

"Well, I don't know what you'd look like as a woman—such a big burly guy, and with those hairy legs!"

He was always joking with me.

He didn't like us to be dressed improperly, and he always called us on this point. For him the sacramental vestments were really important, and that was a source of contention between him and me. I had a habit of showing up at the snack bar, or in his office, or at any place, with my boots covered in mud. Since I rode horses and was always coming in from the countryside, I could show up looking pretty filthy.

"With those boots, don't you think they're going to figure out where you are, Sánchez? You're leaving a trail behind yourself," he would say to me.

The clothes thing worried him. When he would come to our meetings of "subversive priests" we'd give him a hard time.

"Look Monseñor. None of us here are wearing cassocks. You're the only one that hasn't decided to give them up."

"Well, I don't look good in pants . . ."

Occasionally we'd get him to dress in a shirt with a clerical collar and pants, without the cassock. And he didn't dislike it.

"It's not bad. I do feel lighter."

"Well, if you want to feel younger, put on one of these shirts!"

"No, boys." That's what he called us sometimes. "I can't do that. Maybe it's the color. How could I wear a red shirt like that? I can't. And me, with boots like Sánchez? I wouldn't be able to walk. Do you even want me to change the way I walk?"

(Rutilio Sánchez)

HE SLEPT IN THE SACRISTY, right behind the back wall of the chapel. That was in the beginning, when he first came to live at the *hospitalito*. He had his bed there in a little corner.

One day he had a cold and a fever, and he decided to stay in bed and not to go to work. That was precisely the day that the nuncio, Monseñor Gerada came looking for Monseñor Romero to rake him over the coals about something.

"We'll let him know you're here," I said to the nuncio when he arrived.

"No! I don't need to be announced."

And vrroom! He walked straight into the sacristy.

"What in the world are you doing here?" he scolded Monseñor.

But it was the nuncio who was surprised because he saw how humble Monseñor's living space was. It wasn't even a room really.

Later we built him his little house. Madre Luz saw that he must have been very uncomfortable all jammed into a corner there in the sacristy, and she asked his permission to build him something of his own.

"It will be a very simple house, Monseñor."

"It better be, or I'm leaving."

One little living room, a bath and two bedrooms.

"In case you have any guests."

"No, what I want there is a hammock."

Sure enough. He was from San Miguel, and a *migueleño* is never without a hammock in his home. So one room had his bed, and the other one had the rings on the walls where he could hang his hammock.

"Don't worry about painting the walls for me. It's too much of an expense."

But we didn't listen to him on that point. On the first anniversary of his installation as archbishop, we gave him the keys. And he moved his things and started living there. We had an agreement with him about what he'd do when he arrived late at night because he'd been visiting the *cantones* or in meetings.

"Monseñor, ring the bell at the gate three times. We'll all sleep better knowing you're in safely."

That was because from early on, he had begun to receive threats.

(María del Socorro Iraheta)

MY MOTHER WAS A BAKER, and for his 60th birthday on August 15, she made him a cake. We put the cake on top of the round table that he'd given us for our youth group meetings.

It wasn't easy to light 60 candles. We burned all our fingers trying!

"All right Monseñor, let's see if you can still blow them out!"

"Of course I can! Do you think your bishop is too old to blow out his own candles?"

He took it as a challenge and sure enough, he blew out all 60 in a single breath.

Afterwards we sat down to drink some sodas and tell jokes. Monseñor told one of his own:

"Once there was a *gringo* who took a trip to Cuba. While he was there, he got thirsty. So he went up to a little stand where they sold drinks and said: 'Give me a Kennedy Dry please.' And the Cuban salesguy answered saying, 'Look here, buddy. I'm sorry, but in Cuba we don't have Kennedy Dry. We only have Orange Krushov!'"

(María Elena Galván)

EL JICARÓN IS SO FAR AWAY they say that even the devil can't find it. One day Monseñor Romero went there to celebrate Mass. To get to El Jicarón you have to leave your car at the end of the road and then walk up a hill for about an hour. The people were already up there waiting anxiously for us.

We started walking at about 10:30 in the morning. The sun was as hot as hell! And there wasn't even a cloud in the sky or a little wisp of a breeze to console us. After a half-hour or so, Monseñor couldn't go any further. He was suffocating. He'd open and shut the neck of his cassock. Finally he took it off. The fiery sun and the fields of dust we had to cross were choking him. In the distance we saw the outline of an *amate* tree, a promise of respite. When we arrived at the tree, the coolness of its shade restored his ability to speak.

"Why don't we stay and have the Mass here where it's cool?" he said, wiping the sweat from his face. "We can call the people to come here to the shade."

"All right!" I said. I started to go ahead to let people know about the change, but I'd only taken a few steps when he called out to me:

"Wait. Don't go."

"No?"

"No. I have to make it up there. The campesinos shouldn't have to adjust their plans for me. I should adjust my plans for them."

(Jon Cortina)

HE WAS SUMMONED TO APPEAR IN ROME. All of the commotion in El Salvador over Rutilio Grande's death, and the changes in him that were reflected in his first steps as archbishop, had sounded an alarm in the offices of the Vatican. I made the trip with him. We arrived in Rome at midday. Soon after we had gotten settled in our rooms, there was a knock on my door.

"Do you want to go for a little walk?"

He wanted to go to St. Peter's Basilica, so I went with him. When we arrived, he went straight to one of the altars. We knelt, and soon I could see that Monseñor Romero had entered into a deep state of prayer. It was as if he was laying all of the worries of his recent work as archbishop before the tomb of Peter, the first pope.

After kneeling for 10 minutes I had to stand up, but he stayed there in the same position, without moving, in complete concentration. He remained like that for another quarter of an hour. Afterwards we left and began to talk about what lay ahead of us.

Monseñor Romero had gathered an enormous quantity of documents to take to Rome—letters, information bulletins, minutes from meetings, internal reports. He'd brought them all along.

"So much paperwork from such a small country?! What are you thinking? Don't come back until you've done a summary," they ordered him.

That was the beginning of his dealings with the Vatican Secretary of State, and the start of the difficulties.

But he'd also travelled with his typewriter, and with it, we worked through the night.

"We have to turn these 600 pages into six before dawn!" It was a challenge both to me and himself.

The following morning we returned to the same office with dark circles
under our eyes and six pages. It seemed like they wanted to argue with
him. One *"monsignore"* especially. I heard the two of them in the hall:
"You should remember," he lectured him in Italian, "that Jesus Christ
was very prudent in all of his public life!"

"Do you really think so? Prudent?" Monseñor replied, amazed.

"Of course. He was a model of prudence!"

"If he was so prudent, then why was he killed?"

"They would have killed him much sooner if he hadn't been prudent!"

The offices we visited were full of *"monsignores"* like him. But Romero
was very encouraged by his conversation with Pope Paul VI, who died
just a year later.

"Qui, e lei che comanda! Allora, coraggio!"

"You're the one in charge. Keep your spirits up!" Pope Montini said to
him.

(Ricardo Urioste)

THEY SENT ME TO ROME, TOO, after all of the events surrounding
Rutilio Grande's death. I was to accompany Romero and Urioste on
their visits to the Vatican offices, and we would have our meals together.

The three of us had a long conversation with Cardinal Silvestrini, but
Romero went in by himself to speak with Cardinal Casaroli. He was also
alone for his appointment with Cardinal Baggio.

That evening after dinner I could tell that Monseñor Romero needed to
unburden himself. Less timid than usual, he began to tell me about his
meeting with Baggio.

"The confrontation you had with the nuncio over the single Mass was almost unforgivable!" Baggio had admonished him.

"I would like to discuss this with you at greater length, your excellency," he said in his own defense.

"Your problem is that you argue too much!"

"But it's not about arguing for argument's sake. I'd like to lay out my reasons."

"Reasons? Backtalking bishops don't belong in the Church!"

It was a difficult argument. They hadn't gotten anywhere.

The two of us were walking along slowly. Suddenly, Romero stopped short, obviously thinking about something.

"Father Jerez. Do you think they'll try to take the Archdiocese of San Salvador away from me?"

"Well, Monseñor, to get rid of a bishop they would have to have a trial and prove that you've taken money, that you're a womanizer, that you're a pervert or that you're involved in some disgusting activity that you're not involved in . . . but you're so clean you squeak! They won't be able to get anything on you!"

"So . . ?"

"So, I don't think they could demote you. But I don't think you'll advance either. Forget about that! You can be sure that you'll never get to be a cardinal in the Holy Mother Church!"

He half-smiled, then got serious again.

"But even if they wanted to, I'd rather be removed as archbishop and leave with my head held high than sell out the Church to the powers of this world."

Then it was my turn to stop short. The sentence he'd just spoken was a very revealing one, because the "powers of the world" he was talking about were not the powers of the Salvadoran government. He was speaking about the Church government, the world of Cardinal Sebastiano Baggio. It seemed that he'd decided not to be intimidated by them.

(César Jerez)

THEY SAY THAT PEOPLE WHO GO TO ROME lose their faith. Monseñor Romero didn't. He just lost his patience a little. It was a difficult trip for him. Mealtimes were the only times when we'd come up for air and relax.

One day the two of us were having lunch in the Pensionato. They served us a *lasagne a la parmesana* that was absolutely delicious, and we were enjoying it when he said to me:

"Ay, Father Jerez. If only we could be eating some tortillas with beans and a little bit of cheese and sour cream instead of this pasta."

Can you imagine? An Italian delicacy like that in front of him, and he was dreaming about beans! I was surprised by his nostalgia for Salvadoran food.

He still had half a plate of lasagna left, when I saw him bend over and go rummaging around in a bag he had under the table.

"I have something here to console us!"

And he took out a bottle of Amaretto that some nuns had given him.

"Let's have a drink to see what it tastes like!" He lifted the bottle in front of everybody.

Drinking almond liqueur with lasagna as a main course! A complete heresy! I thought to myself, "The people looking at us are going to think we're a couple of ignorant Indians who don't know when to drink Amaretto . . ." But what did he care whether it was before, during or after the meal. When I saw him so enthused about it, I decided I didn't care, either.

We had a drink, and then another. And then we had more lasagna. And, of course, we were consoled!

(César Jerez)

WE WERE WALKING ALONG the Via della Conciliazione. In the distance you could see the dome of the Vatican. It was already late in the evening. I felt like the cool night air, the darkness and the silence created a favorable ambience for exchanging confidences, so I got up my courage to try to get him to speak.

"Monseñor, you've changed. Everything about you has changed . . . What's happened?"

There I was going straight to the point, like a turkey after a grain of corn.

"Why did you change, Monseñor?"

"You know, Father Jerez, I ask myself that same question when I'm in prayer . . ." He stopped walking and was silent.

"And do you find an answer, Monseñor?"

"Some answers, yes . . . It's just that we all have our roots, you know . . . I was born into a poor family. I've suffered hunger. I know what it's like to work from the time you're a little kid . . . When I went to seminary and started my studies, and then they sent me to finish studying here in Rome, I spent years and years absorbed in my books, and I started to forget about where I came from. I started creating another world. When I went back to El Salvador, they made me the bishop's secretary in San Miguel. I was a parish priest for 23 years there, but I was still buried under paperwork. And when they sent me to San Salvador to be auxiliary bishop, I fell into the hands of Opus Dei, and there I remained . . ."

We were walking slowly. It seemed like he wanted to keep talking.

"Then they sent me to Santiago de María, and I ran into extreme poverty again. Those children that were dying just because of the water they were drinking, those *campesinos* killing themselves in the harvests . . . You know Father, when a piece of charcoal has already been lit once, you don't have to blow on it much to get it to flame up again. And everything that happened to us when I got to the archdiocese, what happened to Father Grande and all . . . it was a lot. You know how much I admired him. When I saw Rutilio dead, I thought, 'If they killed him for what he was doing, it's my job to go down that same road . . .' So yes, I changed. But I also came back home again."

We kept walking a while in silence. The light from the new moon accented the Roman sky.

(César Jerez)

"When they took me out to question me, I was always thinking, 'Now they're going to throw my body into a ravine.'"

THE SKY HAS TURNED RED

THE SITUATION WAS GETTING MORE COMPLICATED. In April of 1977, the FPL[1] kidnapped the Foreign Minister, Mauricio Borgonovo, and government security forces were put on maximum alert.

I was coming back from saying Mass in a little *cantón* near Nejapa when a National Guardsman stopped me in the street near the Reloj de Flores.

"Show me your I.D.!"

When they saw I was Panamanian, and a priest to boot, their expressions changed. They looked like dogs that had just found a bone.

"What's this SJ after your name?"

"Societatis Jesu."

"What the hell is that?"

"Society of Jesus. Jesuit."

"Oh, you're a Jesuit! Well, face it. You're in big trouble."

They took my watch off, handcuffed me, and took me in their car to the National Guard headquarters. As soon as I got there, they blindfolded

---

[1] FPL—Popular Forces of Liberation—An armed opposition group formed in 1970. It was one of five guerrilla factions to unite under the banner of the FMLN, the Farabundo Marti National Liberation Front, when the war began in earnest in 1980.

me and started the interrogation. They wanted to know about Rutilio Grande, about the *campesinos* in Aguilares, and most of all about Borgonovo. Where had we hidden him? Which one of us had written the communiqué that had come out in the newspapers? And so on.

They threw me on the floor of a basement cell, still handcuffed. "Now they're going to kill me. It's all over," I thought. After a while, a guy, whose face I couldn't see, came in and started kicking me all over.

"Son of a bitch priest! Now we'll see if you have a tongue to speak!"

He kicked me for 10 minutes, just for the hell of it. I was expecting to die, so I hardly felt the blows. He left, and I stayed there sprawled on the floor. My whole body ached.

The second night they tied me to a bedframe. Both of my hands and one foot were handcuffed to the posts. I was still blindfolded, and they hadn't given me anything to eat. Only one of the jailers brought me water when I asked for it. When they took me out to question me, I was always thinking, "Now they're going to throw my body into a ravine." Damned endless interrogations any time of day or night.

But at night there was also a different kind of suffering. I could hear the other prisoners being tortured. You could hear the blows, the screams. You could also hear the soldiers when they'd start drinking. The place reeked of liquor, and they'd go into drunken rages. I could only think "When is this going to end?"

Four days later, early Friday morning . . .

"It's all over, priest! Go and bathe!"

Bathe? Hah! I threw a little water on my face. They pushed me down the corridors, and didn't take the blindfold off until I'd gone into an office. I opened my eyes, still half-dazed.

"There you have him, Monseñor."

Behind the table was the chief of the National Guard, Colonel Nicolás Alvarenga, a well-known assassin. Sitting on the other side of the desk were "Gordo" Jerez, our provincial, and Monseñor Romero. The two of them looked at me anxiously.

"You can see, Monseñor, that we haven't hurt him. We haven't even touched him, so don't go around with your propaganda saying otherwise."

Monseñor Romero didn't even look at Alvarenga when he spoke. He turned to look at me instead.

"How have they treated you, Father?"

"Do you want me to tell you?"

"Yes, yes. Tell the bishop how we've treated you," Alvarenga cut in.

"All right. They haven't given me anything to eat for five days. They've kicked me, and they had me tied to a bed! And they've yet to tell me why I'm here and why they're doing this to me . . ."

"Well, Monseñor," said the Colonel, "you know there are always subordinates who get a little carried away."

At this point a soldier came in and served coffee to Alvarenga, to Jerez and to the bishop. I must have been looking longingly at the cups, because Monseñor got up and gave me his. Hot coffee! I drank it all at once without even thanking him.

"I want to read you the statement the priest has made," Alvarenga raised his voice.

Me, a statement? The guy began to read a piece of paper full of lies. It said I'd stated that I had been in El Salvador for 16 years organizing subversive activities, that I was a follower of the Alas brothers in Suchitoto, that I'd been detained for being an agitator during the May 1st demonstration . . . All outrageous lies!!

"In order for us to turn the *padre* over to you, Monseñor, you'll have to sign this statement."

Monseñor took the paper and, without even looking at it, asked me, "Is all this true, Father?"

"No, Monseñor. It's all a lie."

Monseñor turned to Alvarenga and looked him in the eye for the first time.

"Colonel, you'll have to decide what you're going to do. But I don't plan to sign anything."

A few hours later, I was in a plane headed for Panama, expelled from El Salvador.

(Jorge Sarsanedas)

San Salvador, May 10, 1977. The body of Foreign Minister, Mauricio Borgonovo Pohl, was found tonight on a back road leading to La Libertad. The discovery has shocked the entire nation. Borgonovo was kidnapped and held for nearly a month by the Popular Forces of Liberation (FPL), which had asked for the release of 37 political prisoners in exchange for his freedom. On April 29, President Molina stated that his government would never negotiate with the kidnappers and was holding none of the 37 political prisoners.

THE BORGONOVOS were from one of the "14 families."[2] During the days following Borgonovo's kidnapping, the family asked Monseñor Romero for help. Romero had asked the FPL publicly on several occasions to respect the foreign minister's life. At the same time he spoke up for the prisoners being held by the government, about whom it had been impossible to obtain any information. It had already become common for people to be detained and to simply "disappear." But Romero's appeals didn't work.

---

[2] It is said that at one time, a single family controlled each of El Salvador's 14 provinces and that these 14 families ran the country.

Borgonovo's funeral was held in the church of San José de la Montaña in the middle of the wealthy Escalón neighborhood. The church was full to overflowing with people from the upper class. Everyone attended. The street was bumper to bumper with Mercedes Benzes and other fancy cars, and you could already see back then the Cherokees with tinted windows full of those people's armed bodyguards.

Father Esnaola decided to go to the funeral. That Jesuit from the Basque country was an institution in El Salvador. He had been among the first to arrive in the 1930s, and had very soon after become the most famous preacher and the most sought-after confessor. People with all of the well-known last names of the Salvadoran upper crust—from the 14 families and others—had passed through his confession booth.

Esnaola wanted to concelebrate Borgonovo's funeral Mass with Monseñor Romero. He must have been about 90 years old, and he was very happy with the changes in Romero. He was also sure that his rich friends would change as well.

"These people are less stubborn than they are rich," he would say "They'll figure out what's happening. Just wait and see."

So it was with that hope that old Esnaola went to the church that day. In the homily, in front of Borgonovo's body, Monseñor spoke very firmly:

"The Church rejects violence. We have repeated this a thousand times, and none of our ministers preaches violence . . ."

Hearing that, the elite congregation that was present began to murmur and mutter. They were practically booing him. It was like they were saying, "You hypocrite. Why should we believe you?" It was a blatant show of disrespect.

When Mass ended, Esnaola went out the door to greet his lifelong rich friends. But no one would speak to him or shake his hand. No one. By snubbing him, they were accusing the Church of being responsible for the death of the foreign minister.

Esnaola went home with his heart in pieces.

"My life has been useless."

That morning, up and down the street in front of the church, the first flyers were passed out saying: BE A PATRIOT. KILL A PRIEST.

(Juan Hernández Pico)

THE DEATH SQUADS were patriotic and killed a priest the next day.

Four men arrived at Cristo Resucitado parish in the Miramonte neighborhood, and knocked on the door casually. Little Luisito Torres, the sacristan's helper, went to open the door for them. They covered his mouth and punched him in the head. Then, pressing his face down against the floor, they held a gun to his head. One of the men ran to the kitchen and held a pistol to the neck of the maid. "Where the hell is the priest?" She didn't say anything, but Father Navarro heard the noise and came through the garden. When they saw him, one of the men gave him a kick that sent him flying against the wall and broke his arm. The other two fired seven bullets into him. After putting a bullet through Luisito's head, the four escaped in two Cherokees with tinted windows that they'd left parked outside under a willow tree.

Father Navarro was 35 years old. He died from loss of blood on the way to the hospital. He managed to say, "I know who they are, and I forgive them." Luisito died a few hours later.

Many people still remember the beginning of Monseñor Romero's homily at Father Navarro's funeral:

"There's a story they tell about a caravan of people, guided by a desert Bedouin, who were desperately thirsty and searching for water amidst the mirages of the desert. Their guide would tell them, 'It's not that way. It's this way.' That happened several times until finally, that caravan of people, sick and tired of it all, took out a gun and shot their guide. But in the throes of death, he still held out his hand to say. 'It's not that way. It's this way.' And that's the way he died, pointing the way. Well, the story has become a reality today. We have a priest, riddled with bullets, who dies forgiving, who dies praying and pointing the way . . ."

ROBERTO D'AUBUISSON, that man who was my brother, was at the height of his counter-insurgency activities when Monseñor Romero became the archbishop. Roberto would come out on television disparaging all of the priests who had taken a committed stance with the poor. He would show photos of each one of them and heap insults on them. He would say:

"Look at him. This is a communist dressed as a priest."

He demoralized and confused people by doing this.

"These priests have put together something called the 'Popular Church' which is not our Church of the Vatican, the Church that the pope directs, the Church that we believe in."

Roberto was totally and absolutely responsible for the "Be a Patriot. Kill a Priest" campaign. It was him along with the people from FAN[3]—an organization that he founded that later became ARENA—who invented that savagery.

Almost all of the priests he talked about on TV were later assassinated.

(Marisa D'Aubuisson)

THE ARMY OCCUPIED AGUILARES. They "combed" the area, as they say in the military. The problem had begun the month before, right before Holy Week in 1977. There had been a land takeover on the plantation at San Francisco Dos Cerros in El Paisnal. About 500 *campesinos* who had been renting little plots of previously uncultivated land from a woman who was the landowner there, were demanding lower rent so they could afford to plant their corn.

"I'm not going to lower it even one *colón!*"

---

[3]FAN—Broad National Front—A right wing political group formed by Roberto D'Aubuisson and others in 1979. In 1981 it served as the nucleus around which the new ARENA party was created.

She wouldn't budge from her position, and the occupation of the land continued. The *campesinos* of FECCAS-UTC had organized it, and Father Marcelino was accompanying them. Monseñor Romero went to talk with the woman, but there was no change. Then the woman went to talk to the President, and he sent the National Guard and the Army to evict the *campesinos*.

The people involved in the takeover could see the soldiers approaching in the distance. There were about two thousand of them, and they even had a tank. But the FECCAS *campesinos* had a very efficient communication system, and the news spread quickly through their network.

"The *Guardia* is coming . . . !"

"The *Guardia* is coming . . . !"

"The *Guardia* is coming!"

No one was left at the site when the military arrived. They cursed and fumed, and then started "combing"—which meant they committed atrocities. They searched and looted houses, they raped women, they arrested people. About 50 *campesinos* disappeared on that day alone.

For quite some time, as a preventive measure, I had been going every night from Guazapa to Aguilares to stay the night with Marcelino and Chamba. The three of us were there that May 19 when the National Guard came to the city. It was still dark—the wee hours of the morning. Some of the *campesinos* who knew what was happening had met them on the way and opened fire. Two *guardias* and seven *campesinos* were killed. With that, the Guard let loose. They came into the city like rabid dogs.

When we could sense they were nearing the parish house, the three of us, along with Miguelito, a *campesino*, hurried up to the bell tower and began to ring the bells so that people would wake up and come out of their houses. We rang and rang but nothing happened. By that time every block in Aguilares was surrounded by armed soldiers, so no one could come out. But we had no way of knowing that, so we stayed up in the bell tower. They kicked in the door of the parish house and got into the church from there. We could hear them knocking things around, breaking glass, throwing benches . . . And since the bells kept ringing, they knew right away where we were.

"Give yourselves up, you sons of bitches!"

They started to throw tear gas grenades at us from below. Bullets sprayed over the bricks and destroyed the walls. We fell to the floor and kept taking turns ringing the bells.

"Maybe ringing these bells will save us," said Miguelito, his eyes like burning black marbles.

And he'd yank the rope, keeping the clapper clanging furiously against the bell.

"Keep it up, Miguelito! Maybe we'll get out of here alive yet!"

It went on like that for a long while. The racket of the bells so close to us kept us from hearing them when they arrived at the top of the tower.

"Give yourselves up, you priest bastards!"

There was nothing we could do but give ourselves up. When I got up, I realized that Miguelito was lying in a pool of blood, his shining eyes still looking at the bells. One of the bullets had gotten him. He was dead. A guardsman kicked him and the pool got bigger.

The three of us priests were handcuffed and taken to the National Guard post at the mayor's office. As we were being taken out, we could see how they'd destroyed the church. From the mayor's office, they threw us into three vehicles, and eventually we were deported to Guatemala. The last things I saw, as the cars started up to take us out of Aguilares, was guardsmen machine-gunning the sanctuary. Then they threw all the communion wafers on the floor and stomped on them over and over again with their boots.

(José Luís Ortega)

"MR. PRESIDENT, I CANNOT COMPREHEND how before the eyes of the nation, you can proclaim yourself a Catholic by education and conviction, and at the same time permit the outrageous abuses that are being committed by the security forces in a country which we say is civilized and Christian . . . I do not understand, Mr. President, the reasons that military authorities could possibly have for not allowing me to go in person to the Aguilares church to see for myself what was happening and to assure the integrity of the church property which belongs to the Catholic people of Aguilares. Can it be that even the person of the archbishop is seen as a danger to national security?"

(From the letter sent by Monseñor Romero to President Molina, May 23, 1977)

AGUILARES REMAINED MILITARIZED. We were already accustomed to the massacres and the repressive military operations in the *campesino* zones, but it was the first time that a whole city had been militarized for a month! No one was allowed to leave Aguilares for 30 days.

It was a month of uncertainty. What could be happening? All kinds of rumors began to spread about why the army was there.

On June 19 the army left, and it was possible to go in and out of Aguilares again. Monseñor Romero went there to celebrate a Mass, and the base communities from San Salvador decided to organize a trip to Aguilares to accompany him.

The church was totally filled, but only a few people were actually from Aguilares—a clear sign of the terror that had taken place that month. We never knew exactly what happened, but there was talk of up to 200 assassinations, of torture, of rape and of people who disappeared and were never seen again.

"It has become my job to tend to all the wounds produced by the persecution of the Church—to record the abuses and pick up the bodies. Today it is my job to tend to this church, this space that has been violated, this sanctuary that has been destroyed and, above all, these people who have been humiliated and sacrificed in such an inhuman way."

That's how Monseñor Romero began his homily. If a person were to ask a bishop what his mission is, he might say anything but that. But that day Romero said his job was to go around gathering dead bodies. Precisely. In the El Salvador of that time, the most realistic mission, the one most in line with the historical moment, was for a bishop to retrieve the daily dead, to receive them, to gather them in.

After the Mass, Romero invited us to join him in a procession through the streets, carrying the Blessed Sacrament. It was to purify the places that the National Guard had profaned.

We left the church singing. It was a terribly hot day, and Monseñor Romero was soaked in sweat under his red rain cape. He held the monstrance high. Before him there were hundreds of people. We circled the main square singing and praying. The municipal offices across from the church were full of guardsmen watching us. When we neared, several of them went to the middle of the road and pointed their rifles at us. Then more of them came. They spread their legs defiantly and with their large boots formed a wall that we could not go through. Those at the front stopped and gradually so did those further back. The procession came to a halt. There we were, face to face with the rifles. When no one was moving anymore, we turned to look at Monseñor Romero, who was at the very back. He lifted the monstrance a little higher and said in a loud voice so that all could hear:

"*Adelante*"—"Let us go forward."

Then, little by little, we moved toward the soldiers, and little by little they began to back up. We moved forward. They moved backward. Eventually they backed up toward their barracks. Finally they lowered their rifles and let us pass.

From that day on, when any important event occurred in El Salvador, whether you were with him or against him, you always had to look to Monseñor Romero.

(Jon Sobrino)

THE PERSECUTION OF THE SALVADORAN CHURCH had already become international news.

In June of 1977, the National Council of Churches of the United States and the World Council of Churches asked me to travel to El Salvador with two colleagues to see what kind of solidarity we could offer as Protestant churches.

No sooner had we arrived in the country than Monseñor Romero sent us an invitation to participate in a meeting of what he called the Emergency Committee. When I went into the meeting I didn't even know at first which one he was, because he wasn't presiding and because the introductions were being made according to the order in which the priests, nuns and lay people were seated around the table. It wasn't until it was his turn to introduce himself that I realized who Monseñor was.

At the meeting they were trying to bring us up to date on what was happening in the country. They were talking about bombs, searches, threats, torture, deportations, murdered priests and dozens of *campesino* catechists also assassinated . . . Listening to all of that, I became so outraged and so saddened that I began to sob. I tried to contain myself, but I couldn't, and everyone ended up turning around to see who was crying.

Then, Monseñor Romero stood up, walked around the table to me and put his hand on my shoulder.

"Don't feel bad, doctor. We have cried too. What we cannot do is become bitter. They're after us now, because they don't know what to do with a Church that defends the poor . . ."

I started to swallow my tears.

"And you know that in our countries, talking about poverty is like touching a high tension wire. We're not going to stop praying for those who persecute us, and we're not going to get discouraged. Remember that God may take a long time, but He doesn't fail us."

I stopped crying and started looking at things differently. When I returned to New York a few days later, I decided to use every means I could to promote ties of solidarity between the international ecumenical community and the Archdiocese of San Salvador.

(Jorge Lara-Braud)

San Salvador, July 1, 1977. With all of the usual fanfare of the occasion, General Carlos Humberto Romero was inaugurated today as President of El Salvador. General Romero has served as both the Minister of Defense and the Minister of Security for the outgoing president, Colonel Arturo Armando Molina.

The metropolitan archbishop, Oscar Arnulfo Romero, was not present at the ceremonies, thus honoring the commitment he made publicly last March to not attend any official government event until the assassination of Father Rutilio Grande was thoroughly investigated. Three other bishops were also absent. Those present at the ceremonies included Monseñor Emmanuele Gerada, the papal nuncio, Monseñor Barrera, the bishop of Santa Ana, and Bishop-Colonel Eduardo Álvarez from the diocese of San Miguel.

JUAN CHACÓN,[4] that great political leader, had a father who was a terrific man—the kind of person that God got right on the first try, you know? His name was Felipe de Jesús Chacón, but his friends called him Don Chus. I met him in one of the courses of the Christian Cursillo Movement. We worked in the same group, and even became group leaders together.

He was always struggling to improve himself. "He who loses courage, loses resolve," he would always say when he'd talk to people. And he, himself, never lost courage or resolve, no matter how much effort or risk was involved. He was born a *campesino*, but had landed a job as an accountant with the customs department at the airport. In El Salitre, where he lived, and in I don't know how many other *cantones* around

---

[4]Juan Chacón—Leader of the Revolutionary People's Bloc and one of the five Democratic Revolutionary Front (FDR) leaders to be assassinated on November 28, 1980.

there, the most respected voice there was was that of Don Chus, the catechist.

And now, there's Don Chus, thrown into this stinking dump, the dogs eating his body. I don't recognize him. They've torn the skin off his face. He's been skinned like the cattle in a slaughterhouse. His smile is gone, his hair torn out by its roots, his body cut into pieces by a machete. There's Doña Evangelina, his wife. She's come to see him and to say good-bye.

Monseñor Romero looks at him, too. He looks at him, and he can't believe it. Because he loved this man.

"Don Chus was a great Christian," he says.

Which is like saying it all, but still not saying enough.

His tears well up, and he says more: "Don Chus's life is an example."

He looks at him, and he can't believe it. There's a new government, but they keep on killing people just the same.

"How did it happen?" he asks later.

The people know how it happened. "He was getting off the bus to go to El Salitre, and some of the *guardias* and the Treasury Police got their hands on him. It's only now that his body has turned up, but he's so cut up it doesn't even look like him."

"They took another man too, Monseñor. Serafín Vázquez, a community leader. And Pablo who was staying at Serafín's that afternoon. They hacked them with machetes, and dumped their bodies by the side of the road."

"Why?" Monseñor laments.

"They're trying to instill fear in us. By making examples out of them, they're trying to stop our work."

(Inge Gabrowsky/Juan Bosco Palacios)

ONE DAY I WENT TO HIS OFFICE looking for a signature for *Cáritas*. He wasn't there, and they were anxiously awaiting him because he was late for a meeting with the other bishops. Judging by the expression on the secretary's face, it was an important meeting. Finally he arrived.

"Monseñor, the meeting can't start until you go in."

But just then, he noticed a little old woman sitting there on a bench. She looked really upset.

"And you? Have you been helped?"

"I wanted to talk with you, Monseñor," she got up slowly. "I come from a place beyond Chalatenango . . ."

Immediately he put his arm around her shoulder and walked side by side with her, listening to what she had to say.

"Monseñor, the bishops are waiting for you!" the secretary reminded him with more urgency in her voice.

"Well, tell them I'd like them to wait or come back tomorrow. But I'm not going to make this woman wait for me."

I sat down on a bench to watch him talk with the old woman. He wasn't in the least bit of a hurry. I got the sense that the woman's problem was that a family member had disappeared. Those cases had become very common by then. A half hour later, the two of them were still talking.

(Miriam Estupinián)

TILO SÁNCHEZ WAS ONE OF THE FEW PRIESTS who escaped the claws of that man who was my brother. In fact, I first met Monseñor Romero on a day when Tilo was having some problems.

The National Guard, who had been keeping tabs on him for quite some time, had stolen his car. Monseñor called in a few priests and lay people to see what could be done, and my husband and I ended up attending the meeting.

"I'm more worried about my date book than the car," Tilo explained to the group. "I have a bunch of addresses and telephone numbers of people who do pastoral work, and they might go after them."

He had left his datebook in the glove compartment, and so it had been taken too. Tilo's face showed his tremendous anxiety.

"But even more than my datebook, I'm worried about something else."

He fell silent, not sure how much to say.

"What's that?"

"In the car . . . in the glove compartment of the car . . . I also had . . . a pistol."

First there was silence, then the murmurs began, then the argument.

"Father Tilo, can you please explain your purpose in carrying a weapon?" Urioste asked him.

"Because, I might be a good person, but I'm not a fool! I may have a lot of faith, but I also have a lot of fear. And I'd rather anything happen than that they take me alive!"

More murmurs. What had he planned to do with the gun—kill someone or commit suicide?

Urioste gave him a good scolding:

"Father Tilo's attitude doesn't seem very Christian to me. Carrying a weapon doesn't fit in with the message of the Gospel. They took Christ alive, and they killed him. He didn't kill anyone, and he did *not* carry a pistol."

Tilo was on trial. Opinions flew back and forth. Monseñor Romero was the last to speak. We were all waiting to hear what he'd say.

"Brothers, we're living in very difficult times. We priests are human, and we have a right to feel fear. Sánchez," he looked straight at Tilo, "you know I don't approve of weapons. But let's not talk about this anymore. The most important thing now is to show solidarity with Father Tilo and decide how we're going to explain this blessed pistol to the government."

(Marisa D'Aubuisson/Edín de Jesús Martínez)

San Salvador, November 25, 1977. A few weeks ago, a weekly newspaper, La Opinión, emerged as a new part of the journalistic constellation of this Central American country. The newspaper is sold on the streets, and given away in the offices of large private businesses. According to some sources, copies of this paper are mailed every week from national government offices to local mayors' offices so that they can be distributed without cost in the towns and cantones. Using various genres and styles, the paper dedicates the entirety of its eight pages to critical and disparaging commentary on the sermons and actions of the archbishop of San Salvador, sarcastically referred to in the paper as Monseñor Marxnulfo Romero.

THE OFFICE OF "THE MACHETE MAN" was off-limits to most. His enormous desk was made of polished mahogany, and its surface was protected by a sheet of glass under which there were a number of photographs. As soon as you walked in, you could see the one of the naked woman. Pornography wasn't rare in our barracks, but this photo was of a female prisoner locked in the Section II cells at National Guard headquarters.

Behind the desk was Colonel Nicolás Alvarenga, the commander in chief of the National Guard. Seated in front of him were Chato Castillo, the Second Lieutenant and Section Chief, and Major Roberto D'Aubuisson. Other officers arrived soon afterward.

It was impossible to miss the framed message hanging on the wall next to the Salvadoran flag: "Nothing that is said, done or heard here, leaves this room!" On the table the sharpened blade of Alvarenga's machete glistened.

"Things are going well, but a lot of people know now. We have to be more discreet," Major D'Aubuisson warned.

He was referring to a secret operation that he had named, "One By One." The purpose of the meeting was to evaluate that operation, which had begun in March 1977 with the assassination of the Aguilares parish priest, Father Rutilio Grande.

"It's important to take out a few more priests, but we have to do it clean and fast. Once the dog is dead, we won't have to worry about rabies."

The Major took out a list of the "dogs" and read it. After each name, he stared hard at his colleagues. He was trying to incite them.

"The first one we have to blow away is Monseñor Romero. If we don't, we'll be sorry later on."

That's what D'Aubuisson was doing when I was a Captain in the National Guard.

(Francisco Mena Sandoval)

PEOPLE SAY . . .
that Father Miguel Ventura was hung from the branches of a tree in the patio of the convent in Osicala, and that they beat him mercilessly. That they kept beating him later on in the garage and that the army officer who was directing that particular operation ended up stuffing a handkerchief in the priest's mouth so that no one would hear his screams of pain.

The torture continued in a cell at the Anamorós barracks. And they say that after he was finally released, a few people went to lodge a complaint with the bishop of San Miguel, Eduardo Álvarez. He was Ventura's immediate superior. He was also a colonel in the Salvadoran Army, and he had neither said nor done anything to defend his priest. When questioned about this, the bishop-colonel responded "theologically."

"But you see, Father Miguel was tortured as a man, not as a priest."

WHEN THEY LET HIM GO, I went to Gotera to see Father Miguel because I wanted to hear directly from him what he'd been through. But no sooner had I finished talking with him in the convent when, bam!, they arrested me! Then it was my turn to suffer.

From Gotera they took me to the National Guard headquarters in San Salvador. They held me there for almost two weeks, torturing me and denying me food. There were electric shocks and other things they did that I'd like to forget. Then they sent me to the National Police where it was another dozen days of the same kind of cruelty, maybe worse.

They beat me all over my body, stabbing me with an icepick so that I'd bleed. When I was full of holes they held a mirror in front of me so that I'd be terrified at the sight of myself and start giving them the names of the "subversive" priests.

When they finally let me go, a catechist friend named Napoleon got the idea that I should go to Monseñor Romero and tell him what had happened. I didn't know him, but that was the task I was given, and I was happy to do it.

"The crime they're accusing me of," I told Monseñor, "is that of preaching the Gospel."

Then I told him that ever since I'd participated in the courses at the El Castaño Center a few years earlier, I'd come to believe what we'd been taught there: that the injustices we suffer as poor people were an offense to God, a sin that had to be done away with.

"From that idea alone, we received strength, Monseñor. And you know the saying, 'If the horse already flies, it doesn't need spurs.' What's happening now is that they're trying to rein us in by torturing us."

"People who torture their fellow human beings are agents of the devil."

Monseñor was both sad and serious as he told this to me. And from there, he started to tell me the history of the Church, chapter by chapter. He spoke to me about this path called the "option for the poor" and how choosing this path had brought us so much persecution. I remember very well a sentence he kept repeating.

"Putting ourselves on the side of the poor is going to mean a lot of bloodshed for us. All this blood is a sign of the times . . ."

"How long will this last, Monseñor . . ?"

"We don't know. We have to look up to the heavens and know how to read the signs. Right now we have this: In El Salvador the sky has turned red. We don't know how long it will last . . ."

(Fabio Argueta)

"Looking for prisoners, trying to find the disappeared, digging up
bodies to see who they were . . . That's the work
we had to do during those years."

THE BLOOD KEEPS FLOWING

San Salvador, April 12, 1978. Today it was revealed that during the traditional holidays of Holy Week, government authorities launched a sweeping military operation in the area of San Pedro Perulapán. Many campesinos in this area are affiliated with FECCAS-UTC, an illegal organization that is part of the People's Revolutionary Bloc.[1] The cantones affected by the military operation were El Rodeo, El Paraíso, La Esperanza, San Francisco, Tecoluco and La Loma. According to some sources, some campesinos organized in a paramilitary group called ORDEN joined in the army's "cleansing" activities.

"These sanctuaries have been profaned." That's how Father Luís Montesinos, who does pastoral work in the area, summarized the events. According to Father Montesinos, a large number of women, children and old people have been the victims of this military operation. "Ideas can't be killed," said the priest, criticizing the government's actions. Dozens of campesinos from the affected areas have fled to the capital, taking refuge in the buildings of the Archdiocese of San Salvador.

THEY FORCED US INTO the "garrobo" position and beat us. That kind of torture is terrible. They throw you in a stinking dungeon cell, and they stuff rags in your mouth so that no one can hear your screams. Then they make you lie face down, with your belly pressed against the

---

[1]People's Revolutionary Bloc—A coordination of several mass organizations including FECCAS, student organizations from secondary schools and universities and the ANDES teacher's union (National Association of Salvadoran Teachers). Formed in 1975 and sometimes called *el bloque*, or "the Bloc."

floor and your legs and arms bent back, the way the big *garrobo* lizards are tied up by their feet when they're sold. And then they hit you on your back with the flat side of a machete—a horrible beating.

That's as far as they went with my *comadre* and me. We were old women, after all. But with the younger girls it was worse. After having them like that, tied up like *garrobos*, they did vulgar things to them. They stood in line for their turn, as though they were possessed by the devil, and they violated them, you know, in their private parts. One man after another raped them. They even raped the little girls. Menches had a miscarriage.

(Mariana Alonso)

THE DAY THEY SEARCHED THE HOUSE was the worst. They took the men away captive, tied to each other like oxen. Their hands were tied behind their backs with *mecate* rope. Supposedly they were being taken prisoner, but they never came back, nor did anyone ever tell us where they were being taken, lined up like that, like animals.

The ones that escaped had to spend several nights outside hiding in abandoned fields and barely sleeping in order to save their lives. Some of them buried themselves in holes full of rancid garbage, and there were times they almost had to stop breathing so that the *guardias* wouldn't be able to detect them by the sound of their breath. When the *guardias* would capture somebody, they'd make him kneel in front of them, as if they were gods, and they'd make him beg for forgiveness. Then they would kill him.

Those devils also stole from us. They took everything from the change in our pockets, to our *tortilla* griddles, to the little chairs we had in our huts—everything! They killed our pigs and our chickens. Other animals wandered around adrift because they'd lost their owners. There was almost no one left here that wasn't grieving the death of a family member. And all of this happened around planting time. We were left in ruins, and we couldn't do anything.

(Tomasa Pérez)

THE COLIMA PLANTATION WAS A CHAPTER of my childhood. I learned to ride a horse there. I also learned about those mysterious events where the bull would be castrated, and where the men—and only the men—drank "bull soup" so they would be more *macho*. On Colima lands I learned the names of the trees, and I played happily during those many long summer vacations.

Colima was the property of my great-grandfather. Later it passed into the hands of the Orellana family—my uncle and aunt. When they began the construction of the Cerrón Grande Dam, much of the land being worked by the *campesinos* who lived on my uncle's land, was flooded. And so the never-ending conflicts began.

During the time of Monseñor Romero, I returned to Colima with my husband after not having visited for a long time. We went to the dam area, precisely where the conflicts were the worst.

The water level was rising but the *campesinos* and their families were still there, refusing to move and defending those lands that weren't even theirs, but on which they had planted and harvested for my uncle with so much dedication for so many years. They hadn't been relocated, and they weren't about to leave. None of their demands had been heard, and yet they went on making them.

"Ay, Chico Orellana!" they cried. "We were born on these lands, and we have worked so many years for you, and now you throw us out as if we were garbage! Ay, Chico Orellana, where are we going to go?"

There was a tragedy at every little house, and in the midst of all that confusion, I still remember a *campesina* woman who invited us to eat in her little hut, surrounded by water. The children were covered with mosquitoes, and she was fighting back her tears, but she drew what she could out of her poverty and even killed her hen and offered it to us on a table covered with an embroidered cloth.

"This water will be our grave, but we're not leaving this place."

"How ungrateful you are, Chico Orellana! Your heart is made of stone."

We went around the property. Everywhere we found the same stubbornness and the same anxiety. They broke my heart and moved me to the depths of my soul. When we returned to the archdiocesan office, we spoke with Monseñor Romero.

"The conflict over the dam, and now the military operations, are making those places unlivable," my husband told him. "Colima is going to explode."

"Monseñor, Colima's not what it used to be," I told him with nostalgia.

"Could it be that Colima was never what you thought it was?" Monseñor asked me.

I closed my eyes for an instant and returned to that beautiful farm of my childhood, to the well-groomed horses, to the parties . . . the paradise of a happy child. But now I was coming from a hell.

Monseñor brought me back to reality with another question, which was directed at me, but was really a question for my family and everything we represented:

"What do you think? Is this communism? This struggle of the *campesinos* to survive, to stay on those lands, to have a place to work . . . all of that. Does that seem like communism to you?"

I didn't know what to tell him. He repeated the question.

"Is it communism?"

(Ana Cristina Zepeda)

PEOPLE SAY . . .

that the most prominent upper class families are financing all of the printed material coming out against Archbishop Romero—paid ads in the newspapers, a special weekly paper, booklets, pamphlets . . . Today the streets of San Salvador are strewn with flyers printed with a prayer meant to be a part of one of those prayer chains. This time the prayer is "for the salvation of Monseñor Romero's soul."

"Oh Divine Savior of the World, we ask you, merciful God, to banish the evil spirit that lives within the heart of the archbishop of this city, so that he may stop sowing discord among the people, so that he will not nourish, with his seditious sermons, the destructive and criminal spirit of those who would destroy our country and bury it in an abyss of blood and violence."

The right-wing weekly paper is also reporting that there are requests being made to the pope to authorize an exorcism on Monseñor Romero, "to expel the malignant spirit from the body and mind of the archbishop."

"THE NUNCIO is receiving one-sided information, all from the same people. Why don't you go and dialogue with him and show him the other side?"

Monseñor Romero was sending us on a nearly impossible mission: to convince Monseñor Gerada, the papal nuncio, to listen to the *campesinos'* side of the story.

"Try it. Take him information. Let's see if we can get him not to criticize the archbishop so much."

The six of us, young lay people ready for this type of adventure, accepted the challenge that Monseñor put before us. In fact, it was my wife, Ana Cristina, who made the appointment with the nuncio. He accepted, but only because he knew her family. The nuncio never imagined what he was getting into.

The six of us met ahead of time to prepare for the meeting.

"It has to be something that really wakes him up. We can't just walk in all meek and humble . . ."

For better or worse we were all a bit belligerent, but then again, those were contentious times. The group chose me to read a statement, with which we hoped to open the dialogue. A direct, challenging statement? Yes, so that he would hear something he'd never heard before!

"*Avanti!* This house belongs to all of us . . ."

The nuncio received us in his office. He was alone. I began to read our statement very calmly:

"We believe that your attitude has been unchristian. You publicly support the military and this repressive government. You appear in your cassock next to them. You live in luxury . . ."

He cut me off angrily.

"Woman," he said to my wife, "you didn't tell me your husband was coming to insult me in my own house! Get out of here, all of you!"

He stood up and opened the door to throw us out.

"But, is there no room for dialogue in the Church?" said María Elena, seeing that we were failing in this mission of reconciliation that Monseñor had entrusted us with.

We managed to calm him, sit him down again and get him back to his natural color.

"I am a diplomat who represents the Holy See. And the Holy See has normal relations with this government."

That was his main argument in the "dialogue" that we managed to establish.

"But you represent the pope, not only before the government, but also before all of the people. That's why you have to talk with everyone, and you have to go to those places where the *campesinos* who are organizing are being repressed. You have to see what this military that you are blessing actually does . . ."

"The Church has no reason to be in those places!"

"Of course it does. And it's the only group that can do it! All of the other institutions have been silenced, and are in worse danger than the Church."

"The Church is in danger because of the insane behavior of this archbishop!"

"Monseñor Romero is the only one who is putting the power of the Church at the service of the poor. You should be more like him in that respect!"

It was a tremendous argument and lasted about an hour and a half. We invited him to come with us to the areas of the countryside where there were Christian communities, and where the repression was the worst, so that he could hear the testimony of the *campesinos*.

"I've already told you I have no business out there."

What he didn't have was the courage to go. You could tell how afraid he was.

"Well, if you don't want to go where the *campesinos* are, then they can come to you. We'll bring them here!"

"Unless you don't *want* to receive them . . ."

"Yes, yes. Of course. This house belongs to everyone . . . But it's also my house! So . . . *afueri!*

We left. Or rather, we were asked to leave.

"Did you hear anything . . ?" Monseñor Romero asked us hopefully when he saw us coming.

"Well, I don't know . . . You know there are none so deaf as those who won't hear."

(Armando Oliva)

HE REALLY SOCKED IT TO THEM in his homily strongly denouncing the officials of the judicial system. It was April 30, 1978.

"We can't forget," said Monseñor Romero that Sunday, "that there is a group of lawyers seeking amnesty for political prisoners. They have recently published the reasons that moved them to struggle on behalf of so many people who are perishing in the jails. These lawyers are also denouncing anomalies in the procedures used in the criminal courts where the judge is not allowing the defendants to have their lawyers present. Meanwhile the National Guard is allowed to enter and to drive fear into the hearts of the prisoners, many of whom show clear signs of torture. A judge who does not denounce signs of torture, and instead allows the prisoner's state of mind to continue to be influenced by his torturers, is not acting justly.

"I think, brothers and sisters, that these injustices can be seen all around us—in the criminal courts and in many of the other courts of our people. Not to mention in all the judges who accept bribes! What is the Supreme Court doing about all of this? Where is the transcendental democratic role of this branch of government? It should be above all the other branches, calling them to demand that those who are violating the law be brought to justice. I believe that this is key to understanding a large part of the troubles of our nation . . ."

It was like throwing a stone at a hornet's nest. A few days later the Supreme Court responded to Monseñor Romero in a full-page open letter published in the newspapers. " . . . I respectfully ask Your Excellency to provide us the names of those 'corrupt judges' to which you referred, so that we may begin a process against them and try them in court, should your accusations prove to be true."

They were challenging him. Who would win in this hand-to-hand combat? It was a very delicate situation. But he didn't allow himself to be intimidated.

"What shall we do?" he asked me, showing me the newspaper.

When I saw what the Supreme Court had said, I actually got a little scared. But he wasn't. He seemed as at home as a frog in a pond.

"Get a group of lawyers together for me," he ordered. "We're going to have to respond to this right away."

(Roberto Cuellar)

THE COURT WANTED TO STOP HIM—to put him to the test. Yes, it was a trap. A group of us lawyers got together to see what would be the best thing to do. Everyone from criminal lawyers to constitutional lawyers came that day to analyze the case backwards and forwards.

"I don't know anything about the legal consequences. I need to hear from you about this," he told us at the beginning.

He listened to us as we each attempted to untangle and clarify the issues for him.

"The crime is that you've made the accusation that there are corrupt judges—judges who accept bribes . . ."

"Because they do, don't they?"

"Of course they do, Monseñor, but the problem is that they can now accuse *you* of corruption."

"Why me? I'm not taking any bribes . . ."

"If you accuse someone of being corrupt, of selling out a case for a bribe, then you must be the one who bribed him, and that's a crime. Or you might have been a witness to the bribe, which means you participated in it. And that's a crime too!"

"But it can't be a crime to report a crime!"

"Well, technically they can accuse you of offering a bribe or of covering one up. Or worse, if you were lying, then they'd get you for defamation of character."

"But I'm not defaming anyone. You all know that everyone is afraid to talk about these things, and that's what provides them their cover . . ."

"That's true, but legally it doesn't work that way . . ."

After we'd gone over all of the pros and cons, over all the laws and jurisprudence, and after more than two hours, we all agreed on a single recommendation:

"Monseñor, you shouldn't agree to appear in Court. This is pure provocation."

"You should let the case lose steam on its own. Let it die a natural death."

"Don't hammer away at this issue. If you do, they might accuse you of contempt."

"Well, how do you like that! It's a crime if I don't talk about it, and it's a crime if I do."

Finally he agreed with us that avoiding the issue would be the wisest political and legal thing to do, given the times we were living in.

"You don't know how much I appreciate this," he said finally. "All of this has helped me a lot, and now I'm clear about all of my crimes!"

That was on a Friday afternoon. There was a lot of anticipation around the country about Monseñor Romero's homily the following Sunday. Everyone wanted to know how he was going to handle things.

A few of my lawyer friends invited me to go to the beach that Sunday. We all took our radios with us, and no one wanted to go swimming until after the homily.

"Well, it's a good thing he knows what he's supposed to say."

"This is really going to curl the hair of those Supreme Court clowns!"

Soon the homily began:

"Who would have thought that today, during this Pentecost of 1978, the Supreme Court would be like the hurricane in Jerusalem, attracting the attention of all my beloved listeners? By publicizing their words all over the country, they've certainly made this Pentecost day interesting here in the San Salvador Cathedral. I know you're all waiting to hear what the archbishop is going to say in response to the summons of the Supreme Court . . ."

Then he dropped the subject and started on the whole doctrinal part of his homily, which was always really long. When he was about to finish, and we were all in our swimsuits and ready to get in the water, he got back on track:

"I'm not the one who should be naming the people the Supreme Court could investigate. They could use, for example, the information provided by the well-known groups of mothers and family members of political prisoners, of the disappeared and the exiled. They could also use all the denunciations of corruption published in the media, not only in this country, but all over the world . . ."

The applause started, and we looked at each other with concern.

"Without any doubt, even more troubling than the cases of corruption, are these other cases that illustrate the Honorable Supreme Court's absolute disregard for the obligations ascribed to it by our Constitution, obligations that all of its members are required to fulfill . . ."

He began to list all the judicial irregularities that existed in the country: torture, disappearances, violations of the constitutional right to life, to habeus corpus, the right to strike, the right to organize . . . He hit on everything. Forget any agreement he might have made with us! Not only did he not avoid the issue, he denounced them again. And not only because there were judges who accepted bribes, but also because there was no trace of justice in the whole country! He had a heyday! And he ended with a direct challenge to the Supreme Court.

"I denounce these things because that's part of what I believe to be my role as pastor of a suffering people. The gospel requires me to do so. And if, for doing this, they take me to court or send me to jail, I'm ready for that, too—even if that only amounts to one more injustice among so many others."

The people applauded wildly.

In response to the endless ovation, he said, "Thank you so much for adding this flourish to my humble words." And then he went on with the Mass.

We stood paralyzed like pillars of salt—or of sand—in the middle of the beach.

"He didn't pay the least bit of attention to us! He came out swinging—just the opposite of what we told him to do!"

After that surprise, we felt the weight of the world fall on us. We imagined him on trial, and in our minds, we were already organizing the files for his defense, which would doubtless be followed around the world. It was nearly the end of the afternoon when we finally went swimming. Everything was calm—no Pentecost hurricane . . .

"Tomorrow the storm begins!"

We spent Monday waiting for the reaction of the Supreme Court. Nothing. Tuesday, the same thing. Not a peep out of them. Nothing on Wednesday or Thursday either. It turned out it was the Supreme Court that followed our advice to the tee. They let the case die. After that homily, they shut up. Politically, it was the wisest thing to do.

(Rubén Zamora)

"LET'S WARM UP OUR CHAT WITH A LITTLE WINE . . ."

With the people he was closest to, Monseñor had this custom: he'd try to get us to relax with a little wine.

"Let's not talk about work," he'd say. "Let's choose our 'person of the day' . . ."

That's what he liked to do over wine—propose a person and talk about him or her. It could be anybody: mutual friends, political people, or someone from inside the Church family . . . There were some people we practically *had* to talk about, but no, I won't tell you who! We'd have ourselves a good laugh.

"A little wine" was also a code phrase for when he had to call us about something urgent. One night at about 11:00, my wife woke me up. "Hey, Monseñor is on the phone for you."

"Roberto, I have some friends here," he said to me. "And we'd like to chat over a little wine."

I understood right away that something was up, and I took off in a hurry.

The man I saw sitting next to Monseñor in the archdiocesan parlor was scary looking. His beard was down to his waist. His hair was long and tangled, his eyes sunken, his skin full of cracks, and he was all stooped over.

"It's Reynaldo. He was able to escape from one of the prisons of the Treasury Police and get here," Monseñor introduced him to me.

He had come back from the dead. Reynaldo Cruz Menjívar was a member of the Christian Democratic Party who had been arrested in Chalatenango nine months ago.

"I've presented three writs of Habeus Corpus to get them to tell us where you were!!" was my greeting to him.

He could hardly speak. He was very weak. The Treasury Police had held him in a secret prison, but had never admitted it. So now finally one of the famous "disappeared" had reappeared . . .

"We have to help him," Monseñor appealed to me.

He'd already called a doctor friend to check him out. They had tortured him savagely, and then left him tied to the bars of his cell. From time to time they'd thrown him crusts of bread, and he had to fight off the rats for them. In spite of it all, he was lucky: a lot of the other "disappeared" were thrown into the ocean.

"Don't give him anything to eat. It could be dangerous," the doctor recommended.

But he did need medicines. Monseñor sent some people out to buy them, and administered the first doses himself.

"Come on, Reynaldo. This is going to be good for you . . ." said Monseñor, spoon in hand.

When I left to return home, Monseñor was still with him, trying to understand the story as Reynaldo stammered out the words.

"Don't try too hard, Reynaldo. Go slow. We have all night to talk . . ."

(Roberto Cuéllar)

OUR EYES FILLED WITH TEARS just thinking about so many people who were slowly dying. Looking for prisoners, trying to find the disappeared, digging up bodies to see who they were . . . That's the work we had to do during those years.

In September of 1976 my son, Miguel Angel, was captured and disappeared. The government had tons of political prisoners, but they never admitted to having any. In 1977, because we'd exerted so much pressure, the president himself had to speak. He said there were only two political prisoners: Miguel Angel Amaya, my son, and Róger Blandino. The two of them were moved from the secret prisons to the public prisons and given sentences of 20 years. A whole lot of other young people were left to be forgotten.

At the end of 1977, with Róger's mother and me in the lead, we founded an organization of mothers to struggle to find our children. That was the first Mothers' Committee for the Disappeared and Political Prisoners. In 1978 we introduced ourselves to Monseñor Romero, and he even let us use the seminary for our meetings, which were about sensitive issues. At the beginning, there were about 30 of us women. There was Doña Tenchita, the mother of Lil Milagros Ramírez, Doctor Madriz's mother, people from Suchitoto and from Santa Ana. We even had one father who joined the rest of us mothers. One day we decided we shouldn't have our meetings in the seminary anymore because we were endangering Monseñor Romero by doing so.

"For his security, we should meet in our own homes," we said.

But he kept supporting us in everything.

We worked like crazy. Miguel Angel and Róger supported us by going on a hunger strike with other prisoners at the Santa Tecla jail. They went around the jail trying to raise the awareness of their fellow prisoners. Because when you have ideals, you express them, whether you're at a party or in jail.

One day during the hunger strike, I went to the prison to see my son.

"He's not here. He's been transferred."

"Where?"

"We don't know."

My God, disappeared again! Róger wasn't there either. The two of us mothers went running around to all the jails to try to find them. We went to Santa Ana, Chalatenango, Cojute . . . Nothing.

"Maybe they were given the *ley de fuga*," we thought.

You know the trick: they tell the prisoners, "get out of here" and when they go, they shoot them right there, as if they'd been trying to escape. They can get rid of them easier that way. That's the *ley de fuga*, and they used it to get rid of a lot of people. With that tormenting thought on our minds, we went to talk to the criminal court judge who had the case, a certain Don Atilio.

"Why are you here? I don't know anything about those subversives!" he said, just to make us madder.

From there we went running to Monseñor Romero, all upset.

"If you could only say something in your homily . . ."

And sure enough, he talked about the case in his Mass at the Cathedral, and said that Judge Atilio would be responsible if anything should happen to our boys. In other words, he was telling the whole world about it. On Monday, the two of us mothers went back to see Atilio.

"We're here so that you will tell us once and for all where our sons are. Because now the whole world knows that you're the person responsible."

"What do you mean, the whole world?"

"Are you deaf? Don't you listen to the radio? Monseñor Romero's word is like a bee. It carries honey, but it also stings. And yesterday it stung you . . ."

"That's bullshit!" the judge said brusquely, but he knew very well what we were talking about.

Right then and there he got on the phone, maybe to the colonel in charge of the jails.

"Look. We've got Amaya Villalobos' and Róger Blandino's old ladies here, wanting to know where they are."

It seemed like the person on the other end was refusing to tell him.

"You are *going* to tell me where they are, damn it! Didn't you hear Monseñor Romero blast me in his sermon yesterday?"

He asked all kinds of questions about their whereabouts and finally hung up.

"I'm going to give you the order for them to take you to where they are."

According to the paper that he gave us, my son was in Sensuntepeque and Blandino was in Cojutepeque. The two of us mothers went rushing off, each in a different direction, still full of doubts, because who could trust a military man's word?

When I got to the jail with the order in my hand, a guardsman took me down some stairs and then more stairs to a place that was separate from and set apart from the regular jail. Finally, he led me to the furthest corner of all—a place that must have been like a secret jail. That was where they had my boy . . . Oh, how happy I was to hold him in my arms!

"Mamá, I knew you'd find us."

"We looked for you, son, but it was Monseñor Romero who found you. Without his words, you would have never appeared!"

(Alba Villalobos)

"WE WANT TO GO TO THE PLACES in the country where the Christian communities are being persecuted . . ."

A group of Dutch journalists came to El Salvador. Koos Koster, the one the army killed later on in 1985, was one of them.

"You've come at a good time," Monseñor Romero told them. "I just found out that there are problems in a place called *cantón* El Cacao, near Cinquera. If you want to go there, it would be a good time to do it."

"Is there anyone who can go with us?"

"Have you been to that *cantón*?" Monseñor turned to look at me.

"Never."

"Well, go along with them anyway, and see if you can help them get there."

That was typical. If you ever told Monseñor, "I'll help you" he really made you work! So if you weren't serious, and you really didn't want to get out there and sweat, it was better not to say anything at all.

After I asked around about how to get there, we took off. When we arrived we were astonished, because the *cantón* was deserted. There wasn't a soul to be found, and all we could hear was the sound of running water in the distance.

"I don't understand," I told them, "I can't explain why there's no one here."

When we were just about to turn back, we saw a tiny little old woman in a threadbare dress, crouched down among some rocks.

"Isn't this El Cacao, Ma'am?"

"It is."

"But where are all the people?"

"They're *monteando*."

"*Monteando*?"

"Yes, they've taken to the woods, and they're hiding in the *monte*. The only way they can save themselves is by *monteando*."

"But what are they trying to save themselves from?"

She stood up and tried to fix her dress a little.

"Every night the civil defense people have been coming here. And every night, ma'am, they kill three or four . . . Every family has lost someone. That's why they've taken to the hills; that's why they're *monteando*."

"And where are they *monteando*?"

She lifted her thin wiry arm, and pointed to a path.

"Maybe you'll find them over that way . . ."

We set off. She stayed behind and watched us go. The walk was exhausting. After quite some time we came upon a group of the people who'd been hiding.

"They call us communists so they can kill us. But we decided we're not going to take it anymore, so now what we do is *montear*."

"And what does it mean to *montear*?"

"It means we walk. We walk all day in the *monte*, and when night falls we sleep in the *monte*. So they don't find us."

"And what do you eat?"

"We eat what the *monte* gives us—roots, leaves, and fruit."

"But now that it's rainy season, what do you do when the rains come?"

"Well, we get soaked. A lot of us have fevers."

In that group there were men, women, children, and even several dogs.

"They don't bark. The animals know how to *montear,* too."

They weren't the only group. We found others scattered around the same area. The Dutch recorded interviews with them and filmed.

It was the first time I'd ever heard the word *"montear."* Later it became very common. The repression forced our *campesinos* to flee to the *monte*—to the woods, the hills. Those were the people who later took up arms. Later on some people were scandalized to learn that some of the guerrillas were practically children! Well, they were the same children who had to *montear,* either with their parents to save the whole family, or alone, because their parents had been killed.

First they took to the hills. Then they took to the mountains and became guerrillas.

(María Julia Hernández)

I WAS AFRAID OF HIM. Terrified. I won't deny it.

Monseñor Romero called a lot of ecumenical meetings, and out of fear I wouldn't go. Who among us didn't know that they were after him? I admired him because he kept taking greater risks, but those same actions made me stay away. That was my dilemma.

One day I was driving my car along one of the central streets of San Salvador, and a huge traffic jam started to build up. It was the kind of congestion that exhausts your patience. Then I noticed that right next to me, driving his little car, was Monseñor Romero.

We were there a good long while, and things weren't getting any better. Then it was as if Monseñor Romero just got fed up. He must have been in a hurry because he decided to get out of the car, leave it there, and continue on foot.

I was watching him from my car, which wasn't going anywhere. Nearby there was a pickup truck full of rich boys also stopped in traffic. When they saw Romero, they started to whistle and yell nasty things at him.

"Priests of Beelzebub! Why don't you all go to Moscow?"

"Romero, you should be the first to go!"

They goaded him, stuck their tongues out, even threw something at him—a popsicle wrapper or something like that.

Monseñor didn't even look at them. He just kept walking along. He didn't stop or quicken his pace. The whole thing made me feel terrible, as if they had done it to me.

"What if this happens to me someday?" I thought anxiously.

And, in fact, the very same thing did happen to me years later—that torture of being treated as if you were a criminal.

(Medardo Gómez)

"Every day, what he said was what gave us life. His sermons were the most eagerly anticipated event of the week."

A VOICE THAT CRIES OUT IN THE CATHEDRAL

"THE AXE IS ALREADY SET against the trunk of the tree. Christ is already threshing the harvest, tossing it up to the wind like coffee. In the basket the coffee beans are mixed in with the useless hulls and stems. They are tossed up in the air so the wind will carry away the debris, and leave the coffee beans behind. That's the way it will be on Judgement Day, like an enormous tossing in the air and a tempestuous wind. So, brothers and sisters, when the Church preaches today against injustice, against the abuse of power, against the violation of rights, it is telling you—convert, repent before it's too late, convert because God is waiting for you."

(Homily, December 5, 1977)

EVERY DAY, WHAT HE SAID was what gave us life. His sermons were the most eagerly anticipated event of the week. I was working in the communities of San Ramón, and on Sundays I would leave my house and walk to the Cathedral. I didn't have to carry a radio with me to hear his homily, because I could hear it the whole way there: there wasn't a single house that didn't have its radio on listening to him. My entire route was a homily! It was a chain of radios with a broadcast as uninterrupted as if it were a single transmission.

(Martina Guzmán)

THAT SUNDAY THERE WERE A BUNCH OF DRUNKS hanging out together on a corner. I had to pass by them, and I thought, "with my luck, these guys will want to cause trouble, they'll make me late, and I won't even get to hear any of the homily." I tried to slip by them, but then I noticed they were doing the same thing I was! They had a radio hanging from a mango tree in a yard, and they were following every word of the sermon!

"This bishop really kicks ass!" shouted the drunkest one.

And the rest applauded Monseñor whenever the people in the Cathedral did.

(Rufina García)

MORE THAN SOCCER! Even though Monseñor preached really long sermons, there were more people turning on their radios for his homilies than for soccer! And the people who listened learned about everything on heaven and earth. Those homilies weren't just catechism—they were a newspaper. I heard that people from all over the world found out about what was happening here in El Salvador just because of his sermons! You don't have to believe me if you don't want to, but I'm not lying. We had never seen anything like it before. And if for some reason you hadn't been able to hear the homily that week, you could buy the transcripts at the Cathedral and in the parishes for 10 *centavos*.

(Orestes Argueta)

THE LIGHT WAS RED so I stopped. I was listening to the homily on my car radio, when I realized there was a police patrol car next to me, also waiting for the light to change. Right away I turned off the radio. But I didn't miss anything—not even a word. I kept on listening to Monseñor, because the policemen had their radio tuned to the homily, too!

(Rogelio Pedraz)

I LOVED TO GO and hear him. He preached so beautifully that I never tired of it. From here in Antiguo, I would go to La Ceiba and from there, to the Cathedral. I was willing to walk any distance or ride any bus just to hear him.

And the Cathedral would get so full! It was packed! There were people who only heard him on the radio, and some of them doubted whether the applause they were hearing was real. There were rumors that it was prerecorded. But it was real, all right! I would say to those doubters, because there always are some:

"Don't take my word for it. If you want to know for sure, you have to go see for yourselves. Touch with your own hands, and listen with your own ears! You have to be willing to go out of your way to find the truth, so that no one can pull the wool over your eyes!"

I wouldn't be talking about this if I'd only heard it on the radio. That's why I went to the Cathedral: I wanted to be there myself, in the midst of that joyful gathering.

(Ernestina Rivera)

"WHAT DID YOU THINK ABOUT THE HOMILY?"

That was a classic Monseñor Romero question, especially on Mondays. He would ask everyone around him what they thought: me, his secretaries, Don Eduardito, the chauffeur, or the lady at the snack bar.

"So, what do you think?"

"It was a little long for my taste, Monseñor, but it was really beautiful!"

"You thought it was long? But the people there seemed happy."

"No doubt they were, but you know the Cathedral is one thing, but if I'm at home and have a lot to do, I have no choice but to turn off the radio . . ."

In our meetings with him, he was always so humble, and he never imposed anything on us. It was like he depended on us so much sometimes, you know? One Monday when he asked me about the homily, I told him what was on my mind.

"You're always so quiet when I see you, Monseñor. And then when I hear you in the Cathedral, I feel like you turn into a different person—even in the intonation of your voice. You project such strength and certainty . . . It can't all be the microphone!"

"You feel that much of a change?"

"Yes, it's like you're two people—the everyday person, and the person who gives the homilies at the Cathedral."

He stopped and thought about it for a while, scratched his head through that short haircut of his, and told me:

"You know, several other people have told me the same thing."

(Coralia Godoy)

"BROTHERS AND SISTERS, I THINK THERE'S A LOT OF SIN in society, and I think the Church has to tell Salvadoran society to convert to the true God and not worship false idols. Consider the following news:

"In the community of Aguilares a lot of bad things have been happening. I asked for reports from that parish, and it has been absolutely hair-raising to learn about how many people have been killed, captured by the security forces or disappeared since May.

"But the biggest news is about the search operation that took place on July 20. It was a combined exercise of the National Guard, the Treasury Police and the Army. They took over Valle Nuevo, Tres Ceibas, Buena Vista, Loma de Ramos, Mirandilla, and El Zapote. In Tres Ceibas they burned down the old schoolhouse, they burned the home of Luz Rivera de Calles, and they attacked Pedro Dolores Rivera, beat him and burned his feet. They beat Mariano Canales and Osmaro Contreras. They tried to burn Bernardina Carrera's house, and forced her to remove all of her belongings from the house. The only reason they didn't kill her, they said, was because she was pregnant.

"Later, on August 15 at 2:00 PM, four trucks belonging to the National Guard and the Army went into Tres Ceibas with a bulldozer and a Red Cross unit with medical personnel. They say they're not using violence, that they're building roads, giving civic education courses and handing out medicine. But, they've also prohibited meetings of any kind. After 6:00 in the evening, people can't leave their homes. The military plans to stay in the community for about three weeks.

"On the night of Friday the 17, they exploded bombs up in the hills. They've also been surveilling the wooded areas where poor campesinos have been sleeping at night for fear of being killed on their way back to their homes. It's strange. On the one hand, the military presents itself as a group of do-gooders, distributing medicine and doing educational work. On the other hand they murder and beat people."

(Homily, August 26, 1979)

TO SEE IF WHAT PEOPLE WERE SAYING WAS TRUE—that's why I went to hear his sermon. And I saw for myself that the phenomenon was real. As a communications specialist, that was what surprised me the most.

The entire population of that little country was hanging on his every word. He was becoming the only voice in El Salvador that could put forth any kind of alternative position. And the people understood that.

That Sunday, I listened as he launched into a long theological treatise that felt too conceptual and abstract to me. It was structured in a really traditional framework. But the people were following him anyway, giving him their complete attention. Then the moment came that everyone was waiting for: a kind of news report in which Monseñor Romero, with all of his authority—an authority that everyone recognized—would comment on the events of the past week.

To me, he seemed like an experienced broadcaster on a national news program. His style was exceptional—easy to understand. And when, in the midst of denouncing human rights violations, talking about bloody events and making statements, he would put forth a proposal or some kind of guideline, the crowd would burst into prolonged, sincere applause.

I had never attended—and have never attended since—a Mass that was so constantly punctuated by ovations. He had achieved complete communication with the people.

(Mario Kaplún)

HE NEVER REPORTED NEWS in his homilies that he didn't know for certain to be true. Everything was well-confirmed. He was the kind of person who wanted reliable evidence, and he would always search for precise facts before denouncing anything or coming out with any kind of statement. But Monseñor Romero measured some things with different yardsticks.

A priest, a seminarian, a nun or someone with status in the Church might approach him and say:

"Monseñor, in Aguilares five people from the same family have been captured. They've disappeared, and we think they've been taken to . . ."

"Do you know for sure this happened?" he would ask. "Did you see it? Were you there?"

And if they said, no, that so-and-so had told them . . .

"You'd better pass on all the information you have to Legal Aid, so they can go and confirm it."

But if a little old lady showed up at his place crying . . .

"Monseñor, they killed my daughter. They took her in the middle of the night, and they dumped her in the woods, all cut up with a machete. They accused her of being a communist . . ."

Immediately he would take down the name, the place and the relevant facts, and he would denounce the case. The woman's tears were enough for him, and they were more than reliable evidence. He didn't allow himself to be swayed by rumors, but when he saw people grieving, he didn't doubt them, and he would take their side.

(Juan Bosco Palacios)

"INVITE ME TO YOUR HOUSE for some beans," Monseñor Romero would say to me sometimes.

We would invite him. My mother, especially, would enjoy it when he came to eat. She had been widowed very young when the two of us were still quite small, and she'd decided to face life on her own, without begging for anything from her rich old aunts.

"I wouldn't ask them for a penny even if I was dead and needed a coffin!"

She was independent and feisty, and she was a close friend of Niña Meches, Guillermo Ungo's mother. The two of them would always argue with other women over Monseñor Romero. They would defend him tooth and nail! It was a question of honor.

One night, Monseñor Romero came to eat those beans he loved so much, and my mother told him about her adventures:

"Monseñor, you wouldn't believe it but the other day a friend came up to me, all up in arms, to tell me that the Medellín documents were evil and should be strictly prohibited because they said that the Virgin Mary had other children besides Jesus."

"And what did you tell her, Niña Mila?" Monseñor asked her with quite a bit of curiosity.

"Me? I told her that I hadn't read the Medellín documents, but that if they said that, it was fine with me. Because the Virgin Mary had a perfect right to have more children, because she was *le-gi-ti-mate-ly* married to her husband, Saint Joseph."

Monseñor roared with laughter.

"A very good answer, Niña Mila . . . That must have left her speechless."

"What about you, Monseñor, do those gossipy old ladies bother you?"

"Yes, I suppose they do bother me a little."

"Well, don't let them get to you. You can always argue with them. They're all money, but you'll see, if you scratch below the surface, they're really ignorant. They don't know about Medellín or anything else. You know, sometimes they come to me and say, 'Did you hear what the bishop said in his homily? It was sheer communism!' Do you know what I say? I say,

'Did you read what the Virgin Mary said in the Magnificat? That was even more communist!' And then they have to shut up. Those old ladies have never even read the Magnificat!"

A few Sundays later, Monseñor praised my mother's theology of the Virgin Mary in his homily. And the people applauded him.

(Ana María Godoy)

AT FIRST, MONSEÑOR'S PRESENCE was more important than his words. But little by little, his words took on more and more importance.

I had to do something at the archdiocesan office one day, I don't re-member what. He was in the middle of meeting with some priests, and some *campesinos* came in, bringing him some chickens as a gift. It made me laugh because the man had them there under the table, and they would cluck and make noise and get away from him, and he'd grab them by their feathers and put them back in the box, and they'd get out again. The whole thing was just hilarious.

After Monseñor's meeting ended, we saw each other in the hall.

"Very good, Monseñor. Your homily was very good yesterday," I greeted him.

"*Ay, padre*, what have we done now? What have we said?" he asked with fear in his voice.

"No, really, Monseñor. You were really good!"

"But what do you think will happen now?"

It was like he was afraid of what he, himself, had said. And when he was afraid, this habit of his would start: he'd hook his index finger in the collar of his cassock, and move it back and forth, this way and that way. He was a coward, and he knew it. He was a prophet, and he didn't know it."

(Carlos Cabarrús)

"I WOULD NOT BE A FAITHFUL PREACHER of the Word of God if I did not mention that this particular Sunday in April of 1978 is framed in a reality so tragic that we need the beautiful image of the Good Shepherd to stand out above these shadows of blood and pain, of depression and desolation.

"We could not comprehend all of Christ's tenderness during this time in El Salvador if we didn't take into account the nature of these times. And what are these times in El Salvador? It seems impossible . . . our history is so full, brothers and sisters, so packed with events, from Sunday to Sunday.

"When a Sunday ends, I think to myself, 'What can I possibly say next Sunday? I've already said it all!' But then another Sunday comes and brings with it so much more history, so many things happening at once . . . Truly we are living in a country during a time when we are protagonists of very decisive events."

(Homily, April 16, 1978)

I STARTED THINKING ABOUT BECOMING A PRIEST. The idea kind of wormed its way into my head. It was because of those homilies of Monseñor Romero. They were so inspiring! You would listen to them and just feel like you were on fire.

"This priest thing is too much for you! You're too worldly," Chepito would say to me. "You weren't born for such things. You'll never get past the front door!"

So he'd make me doubt myself. Then I'd hear another homily, where he'd be denouncing things and giving them hell, and I'd go back to the idea of studying to be a priest. I wanted to be able to tell off the rich and let loose against all the injustices and abuses in the country. I wanted to change all of El Salvador and turn it into a place where there wouldn't be any poor people!

With every homily I heard Monseñor give, I became even more convinced. To become a priest like that—a brave man, an iron man, like him . . . That was the best thing I could imagine in the whole world.

"I'm going!" I said.

"You're going?"

I went. I packed up my bags. I said good-bye forever to the military-led agricultural school where I had a scholarship, and I enrolled in seminary.

"Let me try, at least," I begged the priests who were the directors there.

They accepted me based on my enthusiasm alone, and I began to learn about seminary life.

In the mornings we had to sweep and clean the whole building. They had these enormous brooms and these immense mops, and we had to make those halls, that were as long as railroad tracks, shine. One day I was going along with that monster of a mop—*whoosh!* here, *whoosh!* there—shining up the hall in front of the chapel on the top floor. As I went by, I saw that at that early hour of the morning, there was a priest praying in one of the front pews. He was all alone, kneeling.

I kept going down the hall—*swish!* here, *swish!* there. After a while I had practically polished the whole floor, and he was still in there praying. The fool didn't even move! I went down another hall and got it all shiny, and then went back and peeked into the chapel. There he was, still kneeling! "What's he doing there, praying so much?" I thought. Another 15 minutes went by and he was still there. "Why so much prayer? With so much happening in this country, all he can think of to do is pray? He should learn a few things from Monseñor Romero, a man with fire in his heart and in his words, a man who doesn't waste his time! Hadn't he even heard that song, 'Praying Is Not Enough?' He ought to listen to some of those homilies!"

I was angry with the praying man, whoever he was. "If he doesn't come out, I'm going in to mop the chapel!" I needed to clean it, but I also wanted to see whether maybe he was just sleeping.

Finally I went in—*whoosh!* here, *swish!* there—making it shine with the mop. I wanted to get a good look at the man so I could tell the rest of the guys at breakfast.

I went up and down with the mop, getting closer and closer to that motionless lump of a man, and I looked at him from head to toe . . . It was Monseñor Romero.

He didn't even move. When I left the chapel, he was still there, kneeling and praying. I left with my bubble burst and the mop over my shoulder like an empty musket.

(Juan José Ramírez)

NIÑA REFUGITO AND I were moving towards ecumenism. It was a new thing, something we'd never seen in El Salvador. Monseñor Romero started holding these meetings frequently, calling them "ecumenical," a word we weren't acquainted with.

One time we Catholics went to the Protestants' worship service, and Monseñor preached a sermon there. Then the Protestant minister preached another one. You should have heard how the people applauded for both. Listening to both of them, we could see how similar their messages were.

"People have twisted religion around," I commented to Niña Refugito, "and now look, their homilies are like two drops from the same cup of coffee!"

The next time, the Protestants joined us in the Cathedral with the big crowds of people there. We felt so happy.

"God willing, the churches will get together. We're already taking steps!"

The next time, there were even more people. We couldn't even fit into any of the Protestant chapels! I don't know why, but the Protestant houses of prayer are tiny little places—not like the Cathedral where truckloads of people could fit.

One week we'd be at their churches and the next week they'd be at ours. One week they'd be with us, and the next week we'd be with them. And each time more people took part in that ecumenical spirit! It was another world where we dreamed about the unity of all people.

I used to talk about ecumenism a lot with a woman who came around to my house selling fish. She was a Jehovah's Witness. When my husband saw the two of us talking so friendly over religious matters, he asked me:

"What's this with you and her? Aren't you trying to mix oil and water?"

"But, can't you see? Now we are all part of the same stew! We're all waking up to the words of Monseñor Romero."

(Ernestina Rivera)

WITH JUST TEN KILOWATTS OF POWER, YSAX Radio broadcasts could be heard in almost every part of the country, and Monseñor Romero's homilies were reaching every ear that wanted to hear. Soon the homily had the largest listening audience of any program in the country. Monseñor was always alert to what was being broadcast. If we let a Monday go by without playing his Sunday sermon again, he'd be at our doorstep right away to complain.

"You don't let anything get by you, do you?"

"Nope. I'm always checking up on you."

And he was. Our station's—well, *his* station's—most faithful listener was himself!

He always put so much work into preparing his homilies that it occurred to me that the best birthday present I could give him would be the homilies themselves! I recorded all of the ones from his first year and a half as archbishop, I put them in order on new cassette tapes, and I arranged them in a nice little wooden case that a carpenter made for me without charge when he found out it was a gift for Monseñor.

"Here you go, Monseñor. Now you can listen to them when you get old."

He liked it a lot and congratulated me on the idea. I even saw him put the little case in a place of honor in his office. But then, much to my surprise, I began to realize that from the very beginning he started re-cording over those tapes with other programs, like his famous Wednesday interviews or some other such thing. When he got his hands on them, he messed them all up, and he erased them! He was erasing himself.

I didn't rerecord the collection for him. And he didn't ask me to, either.

(Rogelio Pedraz)

PEOPLE SAY . . .
that a Democratic congressman from the United States, Tom Harkin, who was passing through El Salvador, went to Mass one Sunday at the Cathedral. The church was full to overflowing.

He was moved by the piety of all the poor people and by the archbishop's homily. But what really made an impression on that *gringo's* heart was the lousy shape the Cathedral was in.

It needed paint. It was only half-finished. It was full of scaffolding and patches. Birds were flying around inside the sanctuary, coming in through broken windows and out through the open door frames with non-existent doors.

"This church doesn't give good impression," Harkin lamented in broken Spanish, "Doesn't Monseñor Romero take care of his most important church?"

"Monseñor Romero spends his energy taking care of others."

They told him that when Monseñor had become archbishop, he'd begun a plan to rebuild the Cathedral, but that soon he'd changed his mind.

"This is not the most important thing," he said, convinced.

For Monseñor, people came first. And that's why he said the Cathedral would remain that way: halfway done, as a monument to the people who don't have a roof over their heads or land to plant on, people who have neither bread nor peace.

EVERY WEEK MORE PEOPLE CAME to the 8:00 AM Mass at the Cathedral. Even the plaza outside filled up with people, so they put loudspeakers there, too. And they weren't the only people who heard the homily! Practically all of El Salvador was listening to it on the radio!

"The hardest thing is after the Mass," Monseñor told me once. "I'm exhausted when I finish."

It was because he had the habit of greeting everyone at the door of the Cathedral. And there were so many people! Everyone wanted to touch him, hug him, give him flowers or money or some little gift, or shake his hand, give him their babies to hold for a moment, or kiss his ring. It would get to be midday, and there would still be crowds of people pressing in on him in the hot sun.

Sometimes a few of us priests who had concelebrated the Mass with him would go to the door with him to help receive the little gifts that the people brought. One day I stayed with him. After a while, I saw a little old woman, who must have been more than 80 years old, making her way through the crowd. She came up to me.

"*Padre*, with all of these people here, I don't think I'm going to be able to get to Monseñor."

I remembered the Gospel stories of people who didn't get to see Jesus because they were squeezed into crowds like these.

"And what did you want, Ma'am?"

"I've brought him a gift."

"If you'd like, I could give it to Monseñor for you."

"Well, all right."

The little woman reached into an old paper bag that she had in her apron pocket, and she pulled out . . . an egg.

"Sure. I'll be glad to give it to him."

"Wait. I have more."

She pulled from the bag . . . another egg. "God help me if this woman keeps taking eggs out of her bag," I thought.

"No problem. I'll pass these along to him."

"Wait. Wait."

She put her hand in the raggedy little bag one more time and pulled out . . . a wrinkled one-colón bill. It was worth about 40 cents on the dollar at the time.

"This is also for Monseñor."

"Thank you very much, Ma'am. I'll make sure he gets this."

"Oh I hope so, God willing."

I looked at her more closely. She seemed so poor, so old . . . I stepped aside to chat with her a little more. It was a way to thank her, since it was going to be impossible to get her to where Monseñor was with so many people . . .

"Tell me, what is your name?"

"Remedios."

"And where are you from?"

"From Nuevo Edén de San Juan."

From there? Blessed Virgin! It was way out on the border with Honduras! You'd have to go down to Ciudad Barrios and get on the San Miguel highway before you could get into San Salvador . . . I figured it was more than 100 kilometers.

"But Niña Remedios, the bus ride must have cost you more than what you are bringing for Monseñor . . ."

"No, because I came to San Salvador on my own two feet."

"You walked?"

"Yes, I walked."

We exchanged a few more words, and she went away happy. I'm sure she returned home on foot as well, with all her 80 years weighing on her.

That Sunday, with a crowd that showed no sign of waning, I couldn't give Monseñor either the *colón* or the two eggs. In fact, I never did give them to him. I'm not even sure what I did with them. They were such insignificant things. But one day I did tell him about the little old woman. And at the very next Mass that he celebrated, he thanked her by name. Way out there by the Torola River, in Nuevo Edén de San Juan, I'm sure that Doña Remedios heard him, and I'm sure both her heart and her feet were happy. Maybe she felt like Simeon, that old man in the Bible who was ready to rest because he'd seen his dreams come true.

(Antonio Fernández Ibáñez)

"IT PAINS THE CHURCH that there are people who idolize money and turn their backs on God. Those people are on the road to ruin. They will be condemned. They might say: 'That's a long way off. Life must be enjoyed here on earth.' They are like children when you ask them whether the moon or the mountain is bigger. Children say the mountain is bigger. Since the moon is so far away, they can't see that it is many, many times larger. That's what happens with the myopia of the rich."

(Homily, September 18, 1977)

THE RICH DETESTED HIM. They were outrageous in their disdain for him. It got to the point where you couldn't go to an afternoon tea, canasta game or a dinner if you admired Monseñor Romero, because you would only hear insults and contemptuous remarks about him. They were the kind of people who could write 100 books about one nasty rumor but couldn't write a page about 100 truths. So, it was painful. Besides, why be a sounding board for them? It was better not to go.

I had a family friend who was very well off—a businesswoman, but one who liked Monseñor Romero. The poor thing had one foot in both worlds, and she had to listen to all of the venomous things people said.

When she was fed up with hearing so many insults, she asked him, "Monseñor, wouldn't it be better if you weren't so direct in what you say? Maybe if you were just a little more careful . . ."

"But I never mention a single family by name, and I'm not hurting anyone personally. I only say what's in the Gospel, and there's no way you can go wrong there . . ."

So the poor thing had to continue with her schizophrenic life. One day I asked Monseñor:

"Have you tried to go and talk to those hardheaded rich people?"

"Well, yes. I've gone several times to the parishes they attend. I've tried to approach them, because I don't have anything against them personally."

"And what happens?"

"They laugh at me. They make fun of what I say. They don't like me. So I say, let them keep on laughing. Let's hope that somewhere along the way, they can deal with their own baggage. I can't do anything else."

One time I was at a gathering where there were people from all layers of society. One woman went right for the jugular.

"Look," she lit into me, "I can accept the fact that you love your Monseñor Romero so much, but don't ask me to. Because I don't know if that man's a communist or what, but he's always attacking wealth. And I'm rich! So he's attacking me all the time! It's as clear as a bell! So keep him to yourself!"

(Coralia Godoy)

"WHENEVER THE TRUTH IS PREACHED against injustices, oppression, and the abuse of power, that truth is going to cause pain. I know I've already mentioned this simple comparison that a *campesino* made one day. He said to me, 'Monseñor, if you put your hand into a pot of salty water and your hand is healthy, nothing happens. But if you have a scratch or sore of some kind, ouch it hurts! The Church is the salt of the world, and naturally, where there are wounds, the salt is going to burn . . .'"

His homilies were full of truths. That's why so many people wanted to listen to them. When I made breakfast, I would get everything ready ahead of time so I could sit down and listen.

"I don't like to listen while I'm doing chores. I want to be sitting down so I can understand everything from beginning to end," I told my *comadre*.

My husband Pablo liked to listen sitting down, too. He'd get up extra early on Sunday mornings to haul the firewood so he'd have time to sit down and listen to the homily when it came time. Sometimes Chita, Marta and Señor Toño would come and listen with us, because they didn't have radios at home. Others would come, too, whenever their batteries ran out.

When you're poor, you feel like you've been forgotten. But with these homilies, that changed. For us, Monseñor was like a father who was always looking out for us. After listening to him so much, I had the desire to meet him personally.

"I wonder what he looks like," several of us would say, because we only knew him by his voice.

When it came time for the Festival of St. John the Baptist, the news started to circulate around all of the *cantones*: "Monseñor Romero is coming to celebrate Mass for the patron saint of Chalate!"

Everyone went to town to meet him. They came in from all over! There were people from Minas, El Jícaro, La Ceiba, La Cuesta, Ojos de Agua, Los Ranchos, Potonico, Las Mercedes, Azacualpa, Upatoro, Guarjila . . . and so many other places, I couldn't list them all. I put on my best dress—a blue one with polka dots. Everyone else did the same, all dressed up in their Sunday best. The church has never been as full since. We sang, firecrackers went off outside . . . It was a lively Mass. His face? You know, it didn't seem that old to me. His features were distinct, as if they'd been carved from a *copinol* seed.

But the most joyful moment was when we went back to our *cantón*. A woman named Doña Brígida had an idea: "What do you think? Wouldn't it be great if Monseñor Romero came all the way out here to visit us?

"Yeah, that would be great!" we all said.

"Hell, yeah!" said Fabián. He was always vulgar with his speech.

We started to make the necessary preparations for him to come to our little valley of 40 homes. And meanwhile, we kept listening to his homilies.

(María Otilia Núñez)

"MONSEÑOR, YOU HAVE TO PUBLISH YOUR HOMILIES!"

"Don't say it, and don't even think about it." He spoke as if I'd just suggested something sinful.

"Monseñor, words are carried away by the wind. We have to have them in writing."

"Well, talking is cheaper. Publishing is expensive, so forget it!"

He was so curt with me that I left in a hurry. I didn't forget about it, but I didn't want to bring up the subject again. One time Isabel and Silvia, his secretaries, both had the flu at the same time, and Monseñor was getting anxious about all the mail that was piling up. He distributed the correspondence among several of us, and I got a big pile of letters. They contained greetings for Monseñor and news from the communities. And, much to my delight, they all made the same request:

"We would like to have your homilies in writing so we can read and reflect on them together . . ."

I went to his office right away with my stack of letters.

"The people have spoken!" I said, and put them on his desk. He looked at me perplexed.

"I'm not the only one. The people agree. Read them!"

He looked at some of the ones on top, but he didn't say anything.

"It's going to cost a heap of money."

"Not so much. You'll see . . . Let's do it. We can figure out how much it costs later!"

At the end of 1978, Monseñor finally decided.

"Let's send out our Christmas greetings this year with the homily from the first Sunday in Advent. We'll publish the first one that way. What do you think?"

"I think there's never a first without a second!"

He sent it to his friends and to the communities as a gift, and dedicated it with the following words: "I'm the first to recognize the deficiencies in this Ministry of the Word that I try to carry out in the Cathedral every Sunday. I also realize that there might be less interest in the written version than the oral teaching, which is given in an historic moment within the living framework of a Cathedral that pulsates with life and prayer . . ."

But later it became the custom to transcribe all of his sermons the day after he gave them. We began to publish them in our weekly paper, *Orientación*. Now we have several volumes of them.

(María Julia Hernández)

IT WAS A COLLECTIVE EFFORT, with participation every step of the way. Monseñor Romero always planned out his homilies with a group of people, in community. The applause from the listening community was the affirmation that completed the circuit.

Every week he met for several hours with a team of priests and lay people to reflect on the situation in the country, and afterwards he would put all of that reflection into his homilies. That was one of the keys to his sermons.

The other key was prayer. The meeting would end, he'd say good-bye to the group, and then he'd sit down to organize his ideas and prepare himself. I'm a witness, having seen him on more than one occasion in his room, on his knees, from 10:00 on Saturday night to 4:00 in the morning on Sunday, preparing his homily. He would sleep a little while and then be at the Cathedral by 8:00.

He never wrote down his homilies. Never. It seemed like he did, but he didn't. The most he ever took to the Cathedral was an outline, a letter-sized sheet of paper with two or three ideas written down.

It makes me laugh when someone who never knew Monseñor Romero says that other people used to write his sermons. If anyone wrote them, it was the Holy Spirit!

(Rafael Urrutia)

WE WOULD GO ON OUTINGS to one of the beaches at least once a week. The two of us would be there, lost to the world!

Monseñor Romero loved the ocean. He liked to look at the sea when it was calm. He liked to swim too, though he wasn't such a great athlete.

He would take along his breviary to pray with. And above all he'd take a huge stack of books—practically a library. And his hammock. He'd look for some trees, install his hammock and crash there. Then he set about preparing his Sunday sermon.

"Hey, how would it sound to you if I said this . . . ?"

Sometimes he would tell me something about what he was planning to say in the homily—like a little kid cooking up some mischief. Of course, he couldn't tell me everything he planned to say, because he would talk about so many different things when he preached. He went on forever! The good thing was that he never repeated himself. You know, one day he had to celebrate five Masses and say five homilies. I heard them all, and I can tell you he didn't so much as repeat a comma in any of them. He was definitely not a parrot! Another good thing was his ability as a speaker. Even though his homilies were long, nobody went to sleep, not even the children.

One time we were at the beach. I was basking in the sun like a *garrobo* lizard, and Monseñor was in his swimsuit with a book half-open in his hands. The sun was beginning its descent.

"Aren't you going in today?" I asked him.

"We ate so much, I'm afraid to . . . I'm likely to go in, get a cramp and never come out!"

"Yeah, it's dangerous. We really stuffed ourselves didn't we? But I really feel like going in. The ocean is so beautiful today . . ."

Monseñor Romero stayed silent for a while with his eyes on that distant border, that little blue line that defines the horizon . . .

"Hey," he said to me, "are you afraid of dying?"

"Me? No, not at all!"

"Well I am. I really am . . ."

"You're just afraid because you won't be able to preach up there in heaven. You won't be able to find anyone who needs to hear your sermons!"

"Be serious, man! Do you know what I'm going to miss most up in heaven? Beans and avocados. Going without them will be awful."

(Salvador Barraza)

"He never fell into the trap of being a 'political bishop.' It wasn't hard for him. He didn't look like one because he wasn't."

STUMBLING BLOCKS

EVERYONE WAS ON EDGE—nervous.

"What could be the matter? Why isn't he here yet?"

"I don't know. Monseñor is usually so punctual."

He was already a half hour late for his appointment. The big, burly security men at the United States embassy were getting impatient.

The appointment was with Mr. Terence Todman, who had recently been named Undersecretary of State for Inter-American Affairs.

It was early 1978, and the subject of El Salvador was already controversial in the United States Congress. There had been several very critical reports issued about human rights violations being committed by the Salvadoran government. Those were the Carter years, you know, and Monseñor Romero's homilies were having some impact internationally. So the US government was also interested in having contact with him.

When he finally arrived, Monseñor Romero didn't apologize.

"How are you, sir?" he said, extending his hand to Todman. "I've just returned from visiting my communities."

He wanted to make it clear that the communities took priority over diplomacy. And just like that, he walked into the meeting room as calmly as you please. Todman went straight to the point.

"We don't think it's a good idea for there to be such strong discord between you and the Salvadoran government."

Monseñor listened. Todman went around and around on the same point, driving it home.

"We think it would be more constructive for there to be a good relationship between the Church and the State, just as there always has been in the past . . ."

Monseñor kept listening, his eyes downcast, his hands on his knees.

"For the good of the people, the Church and State should work together . . ."

Finally, like a water jug that breaks after too many trips to the spring, he got tired of hearing the same thing. Monseñor raised his head and looked Todman in the eye, stopping him in his tracks.

"It seems to me that you don't understand what the problem is."

"Why do you say that?"

"Because the problem is not between the Church and the government. It's between the government and the people. The government-people relationship is the key issue. It's not the Church, much less the archbishop!"

It was Todman's turn to listen.

"If the government improves its relationship with the people, we will improve our relationship with the government," Monseñor told him firmly. "We will always measure our actions according to how things are going for the people."

(Roberto Cuellar/José Simán)

San Salvador, February 14, 1978. On the first anniversary of his installation as Archbishop of San Salvador, Oscar Arnulfo Romero was given a Doctorate Honoris Causa in Humane Letters by Georgetown University in Washington, D.C.

The degree was presented in an exceptional way—not, as would have been customary, in Washington on the grounds of the university, but rather in the Cathedral in San Salvador.

Church sources disclosed that various Vatican representatives had pressured the Georgetown Jesuits up until the last minute; they didn't want such a high honor to be bestowed on the controversial Archbishop Romero.

THAT AWARD THEY GAVE HIM was even better than the big one in the lottery! When they gave it to Monseñor Romero, I said to my *comadre*:

"I wonder what this *honoris* thing looks like . . ."

I went to the Cathedral so I could be there at such a special Mass. He preached so beautifully that day! And when he said that he didn't deserve such a great honor, and that instead he would dedicate it to the Salvadoran people—that he was donating it to his people because he was unworthy . . . Girl, you should have seen us cry! Tears of joy. And the applause poured out of us, straight from the heart.

(Esperanza Castellón)

"THE SALVADORAN BISHOPS' CONFERENCE called an urgent meeting. My first instinct was not to attend . . . I arrived at the meeting and saw that everything had been set up. Monseñor Rivera was in Guatemala and had sent a telegram asking that the meeting not be held without him, as the matter at hand required the attention of the full plenary. His request was ignored in spite of the fact that I had supported it.

Four bishops—Monseñor Aparicio, the President of the Conference; Monseñor Barrera, Bishop of Santa Ana; Monseñor Álvarez, Bishop of San Miguel; and Monseñor Revelo, Auxiliary Bishop of San Salvador—all voted against me, naturally. It was four against one: the meeting would be held . . .

I was the object of many false accusations by the bishops. I was told that my preaching was subversive and violent, that my priests were stirring up an environment of violence among the campesinos, and that we had no cause to complain about the way the authorities were abusing us. The archdiocese is being accused of interfering in other dioceses, causing division among the priests and pastoral discontent. They also accused the archdiocese of sowing confusion in the seminary . . . I chose not to answer their charges."

(Based on Monseñor Romero's Diary, April 3, 1978)

"WHO IS THIS MONSEÑOR ROMERO?" my friends in Parliament said when I came to them with the idea.

In 1978 we decided to nominate Romero for the Nobel Peace Prize through the CIIR[1] in London. A few years earlier I had learned how the Nobel machinery works. That experience was useful for this occasion.

Time Magazine had just published an article on the situation in El Salvador and had praised Romero. That was just what I needed. Armed with our own letter of recommendation and with copies of the article, I went to party conferences to collect signatures of support from among the British parliamentarians.

"I've never heard of this Romero," they would say.

"He's a Catholic archbishop who's defending the poor and struggling for human rights, and his life is being threatened . . ." I said as I gave them the letter and the *Time* article.

And when they finished reading, they would come to the same conclusion: "Well, yes, then. We should do it."

And they would sign. That's how I gathered 118 signatures from parliamentarians of all of the various parties. Between the House of Com-

---

[1]CIIR—Catholic Institute for International Relations—An independent charity, based in London, that works for socially just development.

mons and the House of Lords there are a total of 600 Members of Parliament, so 118 was a significant number. I really hadn't expected so many.

We stirred up quite a bit of publicity in London and sent the nomination letter to Oslo. In Venezuela and in other countries, there was also a significant amount of organizing around his candidacy. We understood that whether or not he won, just nominating him was a way of providing some protection for him.[2]

In El Salvador there was complete silence on the part of the government. The media decided not to say anything either until finally, *La Prensa Gráfica* was forced to. They published the news in about two inches of text on some forgotten corner of page 30-something. But the people in the archdiocese enlarged the tiny article and turned it into a poster. "Monseñor Romero nominated for the Nobel Peace Prize," it said. Posters were distributed in all of the parishes, and immediately they went up on the walls and doors of churches and chapels around the country. Every one ended up hearing about it, and almost everyone was happy. A small group of people, the same ones as always, were angry.

(Julian Filochowski)

"HABEMUS PAPAM!" We had a new pope. During the days in which Karol Wojtyla was elected pope, Monseñor Romero came to a celebration in Opico. After Mass, the priests in the area had lunch with him, and the new Polish pope kept coming up in all of our conversations.

We didn't know much about Wojtyla—John Paul II. We were full of questions. Monseñor Romero was eating and listening to us talk . . . He looked very pensive.

"I'm concerned about this new pope," he said abruptly, after having kept silent for so long.

---

[2] In 1978, Mother Theresa of Calcutta won the Nobel Peace Prize.

"Why, Monseñor?"

"I'm afraid that he doesn't understand the reality of the people of Latin America. He's from Poland. He's had a different kind of experience . . . Who knows? He might back the United States government, in order to fight communism, you know, believing he can defend the faith that way— that it's the best thing for the Church . . ."

"Do you really think so?"

"I don't know, but that's what I'm afraid of."

(Trinidad Nieto)

A VERY ROMAN, VERY CATHOLIC, very apostolic, very conservative Lithuanian *gringo* was in charge of the information agency at the US Embassy in San Salvador.

Since I directed the archdiocesan radio station, and since he dealt with media issues, we had what could be called a "friendship." One day we got together to chat, and he said something very strange to me.

"I've heard that Monseñor Romero wrote a letter to the pope making some pretty strong criticisms of one of the Salvadoran bishops and of the nuncio. What can you tell me about that . . . ?"

"I don't believe it," I told him.

I was feigning ignorance. That such a letter existed could be true, but how would this man know about it? Who could have told him? I decided to investigate. I found out that Monseñor had indeed written a report to the pope in which he told of his latest run-ins with the nuncio and about a really ugly experience with Bishop Revelo. Revelo, with the manipulation and support of the government, had changed the statutes of *Cáritas* in order to remove Romero as its director and install himself.

I told Romero what the *gringo* had said.

"I would like you to find out for me," he said, "if the letter the embassy man has seen is signed or not."

The signature was the key.

"If it doesn't have a signature," Monseñor explained, "it's a copy that someone stole from my files. But if it has a signature, it's a copy that someone from Rome sent to the *gringo* embassy. I'll be concerned whether it's a thief in my office or a spy in Rome, but I'll be a lot more concerned if it's a spy . . ."

So I continued my investigation. I went back to visit the Lithuanian, and since I was the one playing dirty this time, I brought up the subject myself.

"You know, I don't think there's any way that Monseñor Romero would have written anything like that . . ."

"I have the document to prove it."

"I won't believe it until I see it."

I wanted him to show it to me, so I could find out.

"I'll show it to you right now!"

He brought it over to me, eager to prove the content of the letter. But I only wanted to see if it had a signature or not. It did. That meant that from the pope's offices in Rome, they'd sent a copy of Monseñor Romero's letter—a very private letter, of course—to the US Embassy in San Salvador, "for your information."

I followed the lead a little more and discovered that there was a Lithuanian *"monsignore"* in the Vatican, and that whenever he came across something that was against, might be against, or that he hoped would be against Monseñor Romero, he would make a copy of it and send it to the US Embassy, convinced that by doing this service to the empire, he was also serving the Holy Mother Church.

I told Romero.

"But then, whose side is Rome on . . ?" he asked me with pain in his voice.

(Rogelio Pedraz)

HE CAME LIKE A TRUE INQUISITOR with his entire bag of tricks. At the end of 1978, the Holy See sent him to San Salvador with the title of "Apostolic Visitor" so that he could investigate what Monseñor Romero was doing. He was Antonio Quarracino, an Argentinian bishop who later became a cardinal.

"He's already talked with everyone in the right wing of the Church," Monseñor Romero told me. "I'd like you to spend some time with him and give him your point of view."

I agreed. Monseñor had already taken him a big pile of written homilies, newspaper clippings, letters and minutes from the meetings of the Bishops' Conference. In other words, Quarracino had plenty of information at his disposal.

I talked with him for about two and a half hours at the nuncio's office. The "visitor" had his head full of every prejudice you could imagine and then some. And he was not at all favorably disposed to people in the grassroots organizations. He just couldn't let go of it.

"They're violent, and they're Marxists!" he kept insisting.

"They say that hunger justifies the means," I said, smiling, but he didn't understand where I was coming from.

"And the worst thing is that they've infiltrated the Church because Monseñor Romero has allowed them to!"

"Why don't you look at it another way? They're in the Church because they're the sheep of his flock, and Monseñor Romero knows them by name . . ."

He didn't go for that, either. It was hard for him to understand. He wanted a simple explanation of the Salvadoran reality. And he didn't understand where I was coming from because I was neither poor, nor a member of a grassroots organization, nor an atheist. Rather, I was from a working-class Catholic family that had managed to earn a lot of money.

"They've brainwashed you, too!"

His visit ended after three or four days. I didn't think he had come to understand much of anything by the time he left. Monseñor Romero came to one conclusion:

"If they don't want me here, they can fire me as archbishop and send me back to being a parish priest. But I'm not going to change what I say simply to keep that from happening. I'm going to speak according to my conscience," he told us.

Quarracino came to a conclusion of his own. As he was leaving to go to the airport and was going down the stairs at the seminary, suitcase in hand, he said:

"I can't say anything negative about Monseñor Romero. If I say anything against him, and they find out here, these Salvadorans will have my hide!"

Well, maybe he'd learned something after all.

(José Simán/Rogelio Pedraz)

THE CLERGY COUNCIL: very few people know what this institution is in a diocese. It's a group of priests who, by right, appointment or election, advise the bishop and help him make decisions. It's not a very well-known entity, but it's very important in making a bishop's governance more democratic and pluralistic. Naturally, this can only happen if the council functions. Most bishops—even the most orthodox ones—have a council but don't use it. They tend to govern alone, like monarchs.

I was part of the clergy council of the Archdiocese of San Salvador. Monseñor Romero had appointed me, in spite of the big argument we'd had in 1973 over the *Externado* High School. And he never, ever reminded me of that previous episode.

I can testify to the fact that Monseñor Romero never excluded or imposed a veto on any priest because he thought differently than he did, or because he didn't subscribe to the same pastoral methodology. There were people of all different stripes in Monseñor's council, including those who attacked him openly.

Because of this pluralism, we had some very tense moments and even some crises in the council. One day, a priest started to upbraid him:

"You're going down the wrong path, and you're dividing the Church because of it!"

"I would really like to know," Monseñor Romero said to him, "if this is your personal opinion, if it's the opinion of a particular group, or if it's a more general feeling, because I don't want to cause any harm to the Church . . ."

"You might not want to, but you are! Your intentions don't matter. Results do! The road to hell is paved with good intentions!"

"Then it occurs to me that we should do an opinion survey to evaluate my actions as archbishop. It needs to be very well done. We should enlist the help of people who are professionals in the area."

Everyone liked the idea, even the priest who was arguing with him.

The archdiocese asked some technical experts from the Central American University (UCA) to formulate and carry out a survey and to give us the results so that we could evaluate them objectively. It surprised me, really. I mean, when do bishops ever do something like this? The results were encouraging. The majority of the clergy of San Salvador supported his way of thinking.

(Francisco Estrada)

TEN YEARS AFTER MEDELLÍN, it was again time for a meeting of the Latin American bishops, this time in Puebla, Mexico. The Salvadoran Bishops' Conference didn't elect Monseñor Romero as a delegate to Puebla, but he had a right to attend as a nonvoting participant because of a nominal post he held on a Vatican committee.

He got to Mexico City a few days before the meeting began.

"Be Romero's chauffeur today for some errands he has to run, OK?" asked Rafael Moreno, who had travelled with him from San Salvador.

I took the Volkswagen and went to pick him up. The Mexican newspapers those days were full of reports about the bishops' meeting and about the new Polish pope who would be making his first trip overseas and would be coming to Mexico to officially open the meeting. What more could they ask for? That was all they talked about. I was going to bring up the topic with Romero, you know, just to get him talking.

"You know what, Monseñor?" I said as I started up the car. "There's a Puebla newspaper that has published a list of the 'red bishops' that are coming to the meeting."

"Oh really? Tell me, who's on the list?" he asked me with a certain timidity, although he was clearly curious to know.

I told him the names I'd seen. Now after so many years, I can only remember that one of the ones on the list was Miguel Obando, the Archbishop of Managua. When I finished running off the names . . .

"But, tell me," Romero's voice was even more timid, "isn't my name on such a prestigious list?"

"No, Monseñor, you're not on it."

I'll never forget the look on his face when he heard he wasn't on that list. It was profound disillusionment and disappointment. He didn't say anything else about it after that. Instead we talked about enchiladas and Mexican fried foods.

(Gonzalo de Villa)

THERE IN PUEBLA he finally met one of the first and most famous "red bishops" in Latin America, Sergio Méndez Arceo, the Bishop of Cuernavaca.

I stood next to him during a conversation between the two of them. That was typical of Romero. When he didn't feel very secure about a private conversation, he would always ask someone else to accompany him, and he'd feel more at ease that way. That's what happened with Don Sergio. Romero was always intimidated by the political or ideological positions of some of the most progressive people in the Latin American Church.

Don Sergio was extremely supportive of him, and he was very grateful for that. So a personal friendship began, but it was not an ideological meeting of the minds.

In Puebla the person with whom Romero did find that kind of resonance was Monseñor Leonidas Proaño, the Bishop of Riobamba in Ecuador. Yes, they were twin souls. They had been on very similar paths, working and evolving along the same lines. The two of them really connected.

(Rafael Moreno)

AT LAST, MONSEÑOR ROMERO . . . How many times had he come to Cuernavaca while I was a priest or an auxiliary bishop? And he'd never wanted to see me. He always refused. In those days he came to Cuernavaca just to rest.

I heard that the priest of the parish where he was staying had asked him, "Why don't you go visit the bishop?"

"I don't think I should. Monseñor Méndez is pretty burned politically," Romero said about me.

So, we never saw each other. Later when he came through Mexico City, he was a bit burned himself—or I should say he'd already gone from the frying pan into the fire. I was the one who sought him out. I made several efforts and finally was able to talk to him. I started the conversation, and we chatted.

"Well, you just never know what turns life will take! The two of us are in very similar situations now. We're both facing heavy opposition to what we're saying from the pulpit, and we've both had to suffer through having former friends turn their backs on us. But you and I both have something important we can depend on, too: the majority of our priests support us . . ."

He listened to me, but he didn't say much. His face was a bit serious, but I think he was happy to have met me. I was *very* happy to have met him. It seemed to me that Don Oscar Arnulfo, the bishop I met that day when he was already a well-known figure, was a deeply shy man and not at all ideological.

(Sergio Méndez Arceo)

I WENT TO PUEBLA AS A JOURNALIST. I had a good relationship with the team of liberation theologians that had been denied entry to the meeting by the Latin American Bishops' Conference (CELAM). They were working "outside the walls" in connection with many of the bishops who were inside. I made it my job to be a bridge between the two groups.

Monseñor Romero arrived in Puebla as a celebrity of sorts, and even though he wasn't the kind to make a lot of noise, he was one of the bishops that the journalists and the curious onlookers were most eager to talk with.

Monseñor Aparicio, on the other hand, did make a lot of noise. He was the one the Salvadoran bishops had sent as their representative. I went with a friend of mine to interview him and see what kind of position he was taking. That man said the most outrageous things! Among other things, he blamed Romero for everything that was happening in El Salvador: for planting bombs, for kidnapping people, for training children as guerrillas. He even said that the disappeared were just people who were hiding so they could make the government look bad . . .

When Aparicio's comments got around, everyone was anxiously waiting to hear how Romero would respond. A press conference was organized, and soon he came looking for me.

"Which journalists are going to be there? Tell me what kinds of things I should say . . ."

"Well, Monseñor, there will be journalists from all over the world. I think most of them sympathize with you, but not all of them. Don't get to thinking you're in San Salvador where things you say don't leave the house. What you say here could be published in any country. So, if they ask you something you don't want to answer, don't answer. Don't fall into traps. Just respond to the things you're really sure about, because whatever you say is on record forever."

Basic advice. He seemed really nervous to me, but when he was in front of the sea of journalists, it was like it was with his homilies. He became another man!

When they asked him about the divisions among the bishops of El Salvador, he answered:

"Unfortunately, there is division. But I think there's a verse in the Gospel that speaks of such things. It's when Christ says that he has not come to bring peace, but a sword. When he goes on to explain this, he talks about divisions in the family. That's because true unity is not romanticism. It's not appearances. The kind of unity that Christ calls for is unity in truth. And that truth is hard sometimes. It means giving up things we like. True unity means that kind of sacrifice. So it's not hard to understand that even within the Church there might be division."

He never fell into the trap of being a "political bishop." It wasn't hard for him. He didn't look like one because he wasn't.

(Julian Filochowski)

"I THOUGHT IT WAS JUST A SPECK of something but it's an ulcer. I'm going to have to go to the hospital over the weekend for treatment."

He was a little anxious about an eye problem that had come up in Puebla. Romero was a bit of a worry wart about his health, although they say that he was never in better health than he was after he went through his big change.

That eye problem was the reason we got to know each other. I was in the same hospital where he ended up. I was feeling a little delicate because I was still convalescing after an operation, and the incision hadn't completely healed yet. So even though I was representing the Nicaraguan clergy at the Puebla meeting, I had to eat and sleep in the hospital.

One day, when I came in for lunch, Monseñor Romero was there with his eye bandaged up.

"Now the journalists are going to start saying that the bishops have resorted to fistfights in the meeting!" he said to me.

We laughed, but his bandaged eye worried me, and not so much because of the eye itself.

"Monseñor," I began, " you should write a note to the executive committee explaining that you won't be able to attend for a few days . . ."

"Do you really think it's necessary . . ?"

I did think so. Monseñor Romero was a stone in the shoes of Monseñor Alfonso López Trujillo, the Secretary of CELAM, and the other conference leaders. That bunch was trying to manipulate the meeting so it would take an anti-Medellín direction, and they were trying to find ways to cut out the progressive bishops. I had already heard them make several comments against Romero.

"Monseñor," I told him, "be careful so they don't use your bandaged eye as an excuse to tape up your mouth as well. You don't have a vote, only a voice, and there are people who will say you shouldn't be allowed to participate at all because you were absent without notifying anyone . . . It hasn't turned into a fistfight yet, but you know they're not that far away from it!"

He wrote the note, and I took it.

"Here," I said to Diego Restrepo, one of the priests who assisted López Trujillo, "I've brought you this note from Bishop Romero to the executive committee . . ."

Diego opened it, read it and yelled at me, "What difference does this little piece of paper make? I don't care if he's got one bad eye or two. He's still not doing this conference any good!"

I got back to the hospital late that night, still pretty angry about how rude he'd been. I met Monseñor Romero at the door to the chapel.

"How's that eye?" I greeted him. "How'd your day go?"

"Well, now that I'm not in there doing things for myself, I'm depending on God. I spent my time in the chapel, praying for things to go well at the meeting. And you? Tell me, tell me . . . How did things go today?"

I told him other things, but I didn't tell him about Restrepo's rudeness so as not to upset him. The next day, I went to the eye doctor who was taking care of him and asked him to write me the note. This time I took it to López Trujillo himself. I found him in a hallway, surrounded by his followers and putting on airs. I interrupted him and began to explain that Monseñor Romero had sent me, but he cut me off.

"Another piece of paper from that man! If he's so sick, he should stop bothering us!"

He didn't even want to touch the note.

"Listen," I said angrily, "I'm not your mailman, and you don't have a choice. Take it!"

He had to take the note from me. And I think that little piece of paper did some good. When Romero got back from his treatment, López and company continued to bad-mouth him, but they couldn't stop him from speaking. They had to keep contending with him.

(José Ernesto Bravo)

WHEN PUEBLA ENDED, Monseñor Romero returned to El Salvador carrying the documents that were officially approved and signed by all the Latin American bishops who participated in the meeting. The documents were said to be very important. That's why all the Salvadoran bishops decided to take them to San Miguel to lay them at the feet of El Salvador's patron saint, the Virgin of Peace, so she could give them her blessing.

A lot of us from the Christian communities travelled from San Salvador for that festive occasion, because the documents were so important. And because it's always fun to go to San Miguel. Besides that, since Rivera was the only one backing Monseñor Romero in the Bishops' Conference, and since everyone else gave him such a hard time, we wanted to go as a show of support for Monseñor.

Eighty priests, a lot of nuns and a whole bunch of us Christians went. You could see during the Mass how the other bishops were edging out Monseñor Romero, not giving him his proper place. But when the Mass ended we got back at them for snubbing him. Right there in the church we cheered for him. "*Viva* Monseñor Romero!" we cried. "Long live Monseñor Romero!"

We made such a scene that when the ceremony was over, the other bishops went straight out the back door and left Monseñor alone. "*Viva* Monseñor Romero! *Viva*!!*" As we kept on shouting our "*vivas*" for him, Bishop Barrera turned to the group of women that was shouting the loudest and yelled at us: "You should say '*Viva*' to the Virgin instead!" I think they were all green with envy at how many people supported Monseñor. They didn't even have a dog on their side!

Monseñor Romero left and walked all through those streets of San Miguel that he knew so well. Who knows what he was thinking about, maybe about all of his years there, about his San Miguel friends—you know, his rich friends from before, so many of whom had turned against him . . .

While he was remembering, our crowd scattered all over the place, still shouting our "*Viva*, Monseñor Romero!"

Beneath the bright glare of the midday sun, a woman in a wheelchair made her way to him on the street. She wasn't all withered yet, but some kind of disease had left her twisted and almost unable to move.

"Monseñor," she said, "lay your hands on me, and I know I will be healed."

He stopped, looked at her for a long while and gave her his blessing.

(María del Carmen Pérez)

"When the demands these organizations make are just, they must be heard . . . Joining an organization is not a sin.
For a Christian, sin is losing sight of God."

THE "OLD MAN" AND THE ORGANIZATIONS

POLÍN AND MONSEÑOR ROMERO were sitting next to each other in an auditorium at the UCA, taking part in a panel discussion on the grassroots organizations. Apolinario Serrano—Polín—was already the secretary general of FECCAS-UTC, which had thousands of *campesino* members and was part of an umbrella group, the Revolutionary People's Bloc.

There wasn't room for everyone. The auditorium was bursting at the seams and there were even people who climbed trees to be able to hear. Someone from the audience asked Polín a question:

"Is it true that priests have awakened your political consciousness?"

"What awakened us was reality. When we get home after working ourselves to death under the hot sun like beasts of burden, and we haven't even earned enough money to buy medicine for our sick child, what do you think is waking us up?"

That earned him an ovation. And Monseñor Romero applauded enthusiastically, too.

> *(Cited by Plácido Erdozain in* Monseñor Romero: mártir de la Iglesia popular. *CELADAC. Lima, 1981.)*

THE MORE PEOPLE JOINED organizations, the more repression there was. That was their rule, and the blood flowed. And the more blood there was, the more people joined the organizations. That was the *campesinos'* rule.

In Aguilares, the National Guard used the slightest excuse to go in and wipe out a complete family. Girls were raped, houses were burned, and young men were disappeared.

One day the *campesinos* who were part of the movement—the ones who were organized and angry—took over the parish house to see if they could raise the profile of their protest against so much injustice.

"If a baby doesn't cry, he doesn't get nursed, and if he cries in church, he'll definitely get fed!!!" said Andresito, who was always coming up with some wise crack.

So they took over the sanctuary. There were about 100 of them. The National Guard was watching them warily, but inside the church they were strong with their banners, their graffiti and their denunciations. I went rushing off to San Salvador to find Monseñor Romero.

"Is there danger of a massacre?" he asked me worriedly.

"When isn't there? What do you think we priests and nuns should do?"

"What the *campesinos* are doing is only just, and you should always be at their side. What the National Guard is likely to do is unjust. If they attack, you should be there next to the *campesinos*. Accompany them. Take the same risks they do."

He didn't hesitate. We, who had been the hesitant ones, went back to join the protest.

(Jon Cortina)

"NO ONE CAN TAKE AWAY the right to free association. The repression that seeks to tear apart organized groups is doing great harm, because the right to organize is a human right that no one can violate. When the demands these organizations make are just, they must be heard. Organizing is a right, and in times like these, it is also a duty. Because social and political demands cannot be made by individuals, they must be made by the strength of a people who together clamor for their just rights. Joining an organization is not a sin. For a Christian, sin is losing sight of God."

(Homily, September 16, 1979)

OCCUPYING CHURCHES: that form of struggle became commonplace for the people's organizations. Every week churches were occupied in San Salvador. The Cathedral was the preferred site.

Monseñor would get frustrated. "What do they want? I've already told them this isn't the way to go about reaching their goals!"

What he didn't like was the fact that if a church was occupied, you couldn't go in to pray or to celebrate Mass. So he wasn't in total agreement with the strategy, and he'd get angry.

The ones who organized the occupation would go visit him afterwards and explain their reasons for doing it. He'd receive them and even write down their demands, but he would always be insistent with them:

"Think of some other way to do this. It's not right to keep taking over churches."

He would always be scolding them. But he acted the same with people on the other side too. I remember when some group took over the El Calvario Church. The Somascan Fathers were the parish priests there, and they decided to cut off the water supply in order to force the protesters to abandon the church. When Monseñor Romero found out, he admonished the friars:

"Think of some other way to do it. It's not right to leave them without water."

That's the way it was. He was concerned about the security and about the food and water supplies of those who were involved in the take-overs, but he still scolded them in private and in public. And he would chew them out something fierce!

(Francisco Calles)

"YOU'RE RIGHT. Since the Church is the house of God it belongs to everyone, and everyone can use it. But it's not here so that some people, like you, can create chaos and destroy it! You should have seen how you left that church! A bunch of benches broken, graffiti on the walls! You even left one of the saints naked so that someone could wrap himself up with the cloth at night! How can people who call themselves Christians behave like this? You can make denunciations from the church, but you can't show disrespect. I do not accept it, and I'm not going to tolerate it!"

*(Monseñor Romero to Odilón Novoa,
leader of the People's League of February 28 (LP-28)[1])*

"COMPAÑEROS, we are going to occupy the church. But if you damage anything, even so much as one of the damn candles, we're going to penalize you. Monseñor Romero has already scolded us up and down because we've left his churches all filthy and disorderly. So please, everyone take along a bucket of some kind, any kind, to relieve yourself in. We are going to show that we are respectful, clean, orderly people of revolutionary stock!"

(Odilón Novoa to the members of the LP-28)

"IN ORDINARY TIMES no one would occupy a church. In ordinary times, when there are ordinary channels of expression, the churches would be only for the expression of religious sentiment. But we are not living in ordinary times. We are living in times of emergency. If we had the misfortune to be hit by an earthquake, the churches would open up to care for the victims and the wounded, and no one would say that it was 'profaning' the church. Well, we are also in times of emergency today, and we must understand that in times of emergency, it is not easy to condemn acts that could be condemned during ordinary times."

(Homily, September 2, 1979)

---

[1]People's League of February 28 (LP-28)—Another mass organization, this one was linked to the Revolutionary Army of the Poor (ERP), one of the five factions later to unite into the FMLN guerrilla movement in 1980.

WHAT WAS AN OCCUPATION of the Cathedral like? I was lucky enough to be able to participate in several.

First of all, we would discuss at the grassroots level what we were trying to accomplish. It was always the same kind of thing: to denounce the repression of the government and to demand something of them. The leaders would tell us what time we should get there, and we campesinos would come in from the countryside in groups. Then we'd go into the church when Mass was being celebrated, and when it was over we would just stay inside.

The leaders of the occupation would explain to the administrators of the Cathedral—if we were in the Cathedral—that we were going to occupy the church and why. They would also explain everything to the people who were in the church praying so that they'd support us too. We didn't want any misunderstandings.

"We're counting on all your support, because unity brings strength, and we're going to need strength to put the brakes on all of the injustices and thankless treatment of campesinos. We're going to put an end to it once and for all!"

Most people supported us. The people of San Salvador—workers, market women, the Christian base communities, people who lived in slums and others—came and joined us. They came during the day or night to keep us company in the church or to bring us food or water or medicine. During the afternoons, we had educational activities so that everyone would understand why we were involved in the struggle.

We always had two groups at any occupation: those inside the Cathedral who coordinated everything and talked with the church authorities, and the support people who slept outside on the sidewalk.

Wow, a church occupation was a fun activity, really. It was a festive occasion. Because you would be there sharing with other people—a whole bunch of other people—and we campesinos would be there right along with the city people. We learned a lot by spending time with so many different kinds of people. And since everyone helped each other, that brought us closer together. When I went to one occupation with

Sonia, my two year-old daughter, the women from the ANDES teacher's union brought milk and diapers to all of us *campesina* women who were there with small children.

"Today we help you. Tomorrow you'll help us," they said.

It was festive, but it was also dangerous. Some very conservative Church people would go there to try to find out who the leaders of the occupation were so they could accuse them by name and denounce them. Sometimes government spies would come inside the Cathedral to see who we were so they could capture us when we left. But we always had our lookout people lined up on the street around the church, and anyone that came in had to identify themselves.

How long did an occupation last? Three to five days or more, depending on how the negotiations were going. Once we had as many as 1,500 people inside the Cathedral.

And Monseñor Romero? He had his points of disagreement with us, and he'd get after us. He'd say we were messing up his Sunday Masses. But he never criticized *campesinos* in a disrespectful way. He took our intentions into consideration.

(Gabina Dubón)

THE WORKERS FROM THE LEON FABRICS FACTORY were on strike, and a delegation of strikers came to talk with Monseñor Romero.

"Paco, meet with them on my behalf and tell me about it later," he asked me.

That day he was very busy. Actually, he was busy every day. There wasn't enough time to attend to everyone who came looking for him. This type of delegation usually came to tell him about a complaint the workers had, and to ask Monseñor to say something about their struggle in his homily.

News was so restricted by then that you could only find out about what was happening in the country by listening to YSAX and Monseñor's homilies. The rest of the media was either being censored, was censoring itself or had just decided to be unhelpful and talk about meaningless things.

I listened to the workers, and before they left I went to tell Monseñor what they were proposing.

"Tell them we'll help them, but get some good information for me. We have to have the story exactly right."

He was leaving his office when he called me over with a mysterious look on his face.

"Hey, Paco." He lowered his voice. "Do you think they need money?"

"I'm sure they do. When they're on strike, they always take up collections to help each other out."

"Then tell Manuel"—Father Manuel Barrera was the treasurer—"to give you 300 or 400 *colones*, and give it to the workers for me."

Wow, that was a surprise! In the atmosphere we lived in, if anyone had found out, they could have accused him of financing strikes. Not because it was so much money, but just because he had given any money at all.

"Monseñor has asked me to give you this on his behalf," I told the workers as I gave them the money.

They were just as surprised as I was.

"Would you look at the 'old man'!" That's what they called Monseñor in their organizations—the "old man." "He's coming along a little more every day!"

(Francisco Calles)

ON HOLIDAYS THEY GAVE US seminarians some time off.

"Today is a holiday. You're free to do what you please. There's a game at the stadium. There are some good movies showing. You can walk over to the pools at *Los Chorros*, or climb up the volcano to the *Boque-rón . . .*"

But there were about six of us older students who were fired up about the popular movement and everything that was going on in the organizations. So that May 1[2] we decided to go to the union march. We weren't from FECCAS; we weren't from MERS;[3] we weren't workers; we weren't anything—just spectators who felt like we were with the people. There we were, watching the workers and all of the crowds of people from different organizations go by with their banners, shouting their slogans.

The priests of our formation team at the seminary were already suspicious of us. And it turned out that some other people from the seminary went to the march, too. Only they went to see who was there and to report on what we were doing. That evening the directors of the seminary called us in.

"You want to be involved in politics? Well then, you'll have to leave the seminary. Our decision is final."

The team informed Monseñor Romero, and the next day he called us in to talk with him.

"I wonder where he is in all of this . . ."

We weren't sure when we got to his office. He asked us to have a seat and began to tell us about the report he'd received about us. He had it there in his hands.

"It says here that you're helping out the radical priests who are the most involved in politics. It says you do everything *they* say, but that you don't obey the authorities at the seminary . . ."

---

[2]May 1—International Workers' Day
[3]MERS—Revolutionary Student Movement of El Salvador, an organization of secondary school students.

He looked so serious that we started to get worried.

"It says you're attending political meetings, that you hang out with people who participate in organizations, that you take part in demonstrations, and that they've found you reading the books that the people in the organizations distribute . . ."

The list of accusations was long, and Monseñor looked like he was enjoying himself. Finally it ended.

"And what do you have to say about all this? Are they making a mountain out of a molehill, or is there something to this?"

How could we begin to answer him? We started where we could.

"Well, we do go to the demonstrations because that's where the people in our neighborhood go, our families, our friends . . ."

"On May 1 we saw a lot of them there. The people who are in the organizations are our people."

"You can learn a lot by reading about politics. It's nothing to criticize us for . . ."

"Politics aren't bad, Monseñor. You get accused of the same things just because you talk about what's really happening . . ."

We laid out our arguments. When we were through, he still looked serious.

"So, Monseñor . . . Are they going to expel us from the seminary?" we dared to ask him.

"Look," he said to us solemnly, "you're in seminary to learn, and you have to learn to obey, to sacrifice and to respect authority . . ."

He paused, and we knew the six of us would be kicked out on the streets.

"But, you also have to learn about the realities of the people, because you come from the people, and you came here to learn how to serve the people. So . . . don't worry. You're staying. If they throw you out, they'd have to throw me out, too!"

When we left his office, some other seminarians were in the hall waiting to see what the bishop would say . . .

"We won!" we shouted with joy.

And they were happy too. But the religious formation team, led by Father Goyita Rosa, was fuming.

(Miguel Vázquez)

"DOWN WITH THE POLICE! Long live the revolution!" "The people will not be silenced by tanks and machine guns!" "We shall overcome!" And the other one that appeared one day, "COME, LORD. SOCIALISM IS NOT ENOUGH!"

Every day we would see the new writing on the walls of San Salvador, graffiti spreading like vines on the streets. Monseñor Romero didn't like the painting of slogans, and would always criticize it.

It was Polín who made him change his mind.

"Explain to me, Apolinario," Monseñor asked him, "what you think about all of this unruliness, and see if you can help me understand . . ."

"Look, Monseñor, we don't have a newspaper . . . And on what building or corner are they going to let us put up a sign? Do you know how much they charge for an ad on the radio? And even if we had the money, do you think they'd run our spot? So how do we deal with the problem? We set a couple of our guys on watch on the side of the road armed with sticks and scythes, while another couple of guys go and write a message on a wall. Of course, if the soldiers see us, we have to take off running! Graffiti is communication. It helps us communicate with our people! Walls are the newspapers of the poor! Now do you get it . . ?"

He started to get it. Things like that and other things. He had so many good and challenging conversations with Polín that sometimes he'd say to him:

"You know, Apolinario, instead of prayer today, I'm going to have a chat with you."

And he'd spend his prayer hour talking with Polín. The whole hour.

(Rutilio Sánchez)

I HAD TO GO INTO HIDING. I was already well-known in San Vicente because of the land takeovers and the *campesino* organizing struggles. They were watching my every move, and they were hungry for me. At that time, my bishop, Monseñor Aparicio, had already excommunicated me, suspended me *a divinis*, and punished me in who knows how many other ways. He would talk about me in public during his 9:00 AM Mass, and my poor mother would suffer when she'd hear him heaping insults on me.

"Don't pay any attention to him, Mom, and go to another Mass." I tried to calm her down when I got a chance to pay her a clandestine visit.

"Well, how else am I going to find out about where you are?"

For her, Aparicio's sermons served as news bulletins about my life . . .

I found a place in San Salvador, where I wasn't being watched so much. Since I was already participating in the movement, my work with some communities was only semi-public. I'd celebrate Mass in people's homes, and occasionally I'd go to the countryside to do a wedding . . . We used to call it the "catacomb ministry."

It was in this capacity as a clandestine priest that I made contact again with Monseñor Romero, that contradictory bishop of Santiago de María for whom my "national reality" classes at the Los Naranjos Center had caused so many headaches.

Mother Teresita was always providing us a space in some corner of the *hospitalito* for those "catacomb" meetings. She would even bring us refreshments. But Monseñor Romero didn't know about them. One day she kind of half gave me some advice:

"Look, Davíd, if there's nothing wrong with what you're doing, why are you doing it behind Monseñor Romero's back?"

She was right. I decided to go say hello to him and tell him all about it, but I was a little uncertain. Who knew what he would say? Could he have really changed so much? I told him everything so I wouldn't have to run around with secrets . . .

And he took it as though it were nothing. He was a totally different man.

"You have my support, son. I know you. I know all of you, so don't worry. But tell me, where are you living?"

"I live where I can. I have to keep moving around. I don't have a fixed place to lay my head. I go to Zacamil, to Mejicanos, to Marichi's house . . ."

"Well come over here too. You've always got a place here."

So on many a night I went to sleep in the guest room in his house at the *hospitalito*. He liked me to visit so I could talk to him about what I was doing. I never told him I had joined the movement, although I'm sure he figured it out from the fugitive life I was living, but he never asked. I would tell him mostly about the work I was doing in the *campesino* communities.

"I've even had to celebrate Mass with coffee and *semita* bread instead of bread and wine!"

"Hey, but those Masses don't count!" he said, somewhat alarmed.

"They're being celebrated by communities of people who are all ready to give their lives for each other. Does that count or doesn't it?"

He was very interested in that whole experience, and he'd make me talk about it. For me it was a form of protection to be there. I would wait for my contacts there or prepare a course I was going to give in the communities, depending on the plan that my friends in the movement would make for me. One day, I dared to ask him something else.

"You know what it's like for us there in San Vicente with Monseñor Aparicio. He's excommunicated several of us. The priests there need to have some safe territory, far away from that man, to have their meetings . . ."

"That territory is here!" he told me, laughing.

So we were also able to have several meetings of the San Vicente group there in the *hospitalito*.

(David Rodríguez)

MONSEÑOR ROMERO WROTE four pastoral letters. Without a doubt, the third one was the most important. It was about the grassroots organizations.

I remember there were about six working breakfasts with priests and lay people where we looked at the topics that would be analyzed in the letter. The relationship between the Church and the grassroots organizations was one topic—especially the *campesino* organizations, and even more especially FECCAS-UTC which had more than 80,000 members, the majority of whom had come from the Christian base community movement. We also looked at a Christian's right to join organizations, the issue of violence and so on . . .

We formed commissions to come out with the first drafts. At the third breakfast, Father Fabián Amaya came up with an idea:

"There are a lot of people in the Christian communities that are participating in organizations, and they have their own opinions and experiences on all of these subjects. Why don't we pass around a few questionnaires so that they can participate too?"

Monseñor Romero didn't think twice.

"What a great idea! God willing, and with all of their contributions, this letter will be from the whole Church, from the whole archdiocese, not just from Oscar Romero."

The communities were consulted through the parish priests with questionnaires that we prepared based on biblical reflections. Hundreds of completed forms were sent in to the archdiocese. Monseñor Romero read all of them, and there are traces of each one of them in his pastoral letter.

(Juan Hernández Pico)

"NETO LIVES WITH ONE FOOT IN THE STIRRUP."

That's what people said about him because he was impatient. But being a priest in the world of labor organizing is never easy. When we got together with our priest friends doing pastoral work in these conflictive arenas, Neto always came in with the workers' perspective. It was always interesting to listen to him.

"I've invited Monseñor Romero to participate in a gathering with workers this weekend over in Ayagualo," Neto told us one Monday.

"And is the 'old man' going to go?"

"The 'old man' is going, but you know, the workers don't mince words, and I'm a little afraid that Monseñor Romero might not like the way they put things. He's kind of sensitive, and those guys are downright brazen. Anti-clericalism among the workers is pretty damn strong."

"Leave them alone, Neto. Don't get worked up about it. Let them say what they want, and let the 'old man' respond. They'll get to know each other that way."

After the meeting, Neto went to eat lunch with one of us at Juan Chon's restaurant, across the street from the old penitentiary. He wanted to keep talking about things.

"Listen, how do you manage," Neto asked "to keep the people in the movement from losing their Christian identity? With the *campesinos*, it's easier. Faith and politics are all integrated for them. But not with the workers . . . It's hard!"

The next day, there was a military raid on a house where Neto was staying with three friends who had also taken up arms: Valentín, Isidoro and Rafael. They were all killed. Some of us didn't know that Neto had joined the guerrillas. We couldn't tell you when, exactly, he'd joined up. Ernesto (Neto) Barrera was 30 years old—the same age Christ was when he began to speak out.

(Based on Orientación, December 10, 1978)

"PACO, FIND A FORENSIC EXPERT and go with a camera right now. Take photos of him. I'll be there as soon as I can!" Monseñor Romero asked me with urgency.

I went to the funeral home. As a boy I'd worked with Father Neto in the Soyapango parish, and later on also in the ministry to workers along with Pedro Cortés.

It was getting late in the evening. The shooting had been that morning, and the army was already spreading the propaganda that Neto had died in combat, in an armed confrontation.

I went in. He was naked, lying on top of an aluminum table riddled with bullets. Some of the bulletholes were on his arm, as if he had tried to protect himself when they began to shoot. His skull was shot to pieces, and touching him was like touching a bag of ice. And there were little burn marks all over him, like the marks of cigarettes being extinguished on his body. His eyes were half open. I wanted him to look at me again with that old sparkle in his eyes, but his eyes stayed open, looking only at death.

The pathologist examined him, and made note of everything. It was my job to take photos.

When I got back to the archdiocesan office with all of the information, the first priests were already arriving to weep and gnash their teeth.

"If he took up arms, he didn't die as a Christian. He died as violent man," pronounced one.

"If he joined the guerrilla movement, he wasn't a priest anymore. He wasn't even a Christian," another condemned.

They came and went, looking for Monseñor Romero.

"If he died in combat, he can't be buried in a church," advised one.

"And you, Monseñor, shouldn't show your face at the funeral. He was a guerrilla!" another warned.

"It would be better to do it discreetly—a burial that no one knows about." Everyone agreed on that point.

A few hours later pamphlet bombs went off in the streets of San Salvador. The papers carried a clear message: Neto Barrera's name in the movement was "Felipe," and Felipe was a member of the Popular Forces of Liberation, the FPL.

"He died the way he lived, Monseñor. You should be very careful," the Pharisees continued to say.

(Francisco Calles)

HE CONSULTED WITH PRACTICALLY EVERYBODY. He always did, but Neto's case was special. It was a tremendous challenge for him and for many of us as well.

"Don't go, Monseñor. They'll just use it against you."

"It should be a quiet burial."

"Just go and give your condolences to the family. Don't do anything else."

At night, he called us together to advise him—eight sad and frightened priests called because we had been so close to Neto. We were birds of a feather, priests with the same ideas.

We felt like there was a noose around our necks. Now the government had the proof it was looking for: guerrilla priests. We had never felt that our safety was guaranteed, but now they would finish us off for sure, we thought fearfully. And on top of it all, there was our sadness for Neto, so beloved and so dead. You can imagine, we arrived at that dinner as pale as ghosts. We had no idea what to say to him.

The meal was served. We sat down, and Monseñor Romero started to eat. We couldn't even swallow.

"The situation is very delicate . . ." I said.

"In moments like these we have to reflect . . ." said another.

"It was just so unexpected, you know? None of us expected this . . ." said a third.

Everything we said was so meaningless. Each one of us was more prudent and restrained than the next. And the beans were getting cold. No one was eating, just Monseñor Romero who was listening patiently to the brilliant advice of the radical communist advisers he had sought out in the eleventh hour. When he realized that we were playing cat and mouse and trying not to reveal too much, and that we were just going to spout foolishness, he decided to speak.

"In order to make the decision I need to make, I'm just asking myself one question right now, just one."

We, who had arrived trembling, were even more frightened now. What would he ask us? If Neto had or hadn't joined the guerrillas? If he carried a weapon or not? If we . . .

"What I'm asking myself is this. What must Doña Mariíta, Neto's mother, be thinking now? Would it matter to her if Neto was carrying a weapon or not? If he was a guerrilla or not? Would she care? Neto was her son, and she was his mother, and so Doña Mariíta is there by his side now.

The Church is also Neto's mother, and as a bishop I am his father. I should be by his side as well."

We looked at him. He looked at each of us one by one.

"You have to be at his side too. We're going to say good-bye to him with a Mass, like the priest that he is, and we're going to bury him in a church in the parish of Mejicanos. Come! Let's go get things ready . . ."

He got up. We got up. Eight full plates remained on the table. Only Monseñor's plate was empty.

(Astor Ruíz)

"I thought I knew the Gospel, but I'm learning to read it in another way."

ALL ROADS LEAD TO THE COMMUNITIES

"I WAS HERE YEARS AGO in this community and in this very place, with many of you who are now gathered. Do you remember?"

Of course we remembered. That argument we'd had with Monseñor Romero in Zacamil in 1972 had left its mark on our community.

Six years later, Monseñor was there with us again in the same place. But this time it was a welcome party we'd invited him to. We had cake, songs, streamers, music . . . It was a real party!

No one was going to mention the problem we'd had with him years ago. No one but him, that is. He brought it up as soon as he got there.

"We couldn't even celebrate the Eucharist that afternoon because of the run-in we had between me and all of you . . . We were insulting each other . . . Do you remember?"

We swallowed, unable to say a thing. The guy who was running the record player decided to turn it off, and the person opening soda bottles dropped one on the floor and it broke.

"I remember it well, and today, as your pastor, I want to say that I now understand what happened on that day, and here before you I recognize my error . . ."

Adelita wanted to say something, but the words didn't come.

"I was wrong, and you were right. That day you taught me about faith and about the Church. Please forgive me for everything that happened then."

Well, all of us, young and old, started crying. Excitement and joy were all wrapped up together. We broke into applause, and our applause melted into the music of the party, just like our tears dissolved into the drinking of the *atol*. "Quincho Barrilete," the song that Monseñor liked so much, was playing. All was forgiven.

(Noemí Ortiz)

"YOU DON'T SEE ME AS A PASTOR, only as a politician."

"But Monseñor, how can I see you as a pastor if I've never been a sheep in your flock? I don't know any more about religion than the dogs of San Roque."

That was the argument he had with me whenever I went by YSAX to see how things were going in our work with the radio station. In spite of his scoldings, I never felt like he wanted to "convert" me—that bad habit that priests sometimes have.

Back in those days I was trying to get involved in the movement, and I wasn't sure how to go about it. I went with a friend of mine from the FPL one day to see what they called a Christian base community in a *cantón* of La Libertad. I wasn't going because of the religious aspect, but rather to see how people were organized and how it all worked.

We went to La Libertad by bus, and people were waiting for us there. It was two more hours on horseback. The riding partner assigned to me was an eight year old boy, Emilio—he rode in front and I behind.

"Giddyup, horse!"

When the horse started moving, I started to smell a nauseating odor of something rotting. Where was the stench coming from? I noticed the boy's foot. It was one big open wound full of worms.

"Hey, what happened to you there?"

"I cut myself with a machete."

We continued on. The smell was awful. We arrived at the community, way up on rocky slopes only fit for planting sorghum. I could only see old people, women and children. They must have been people who had opted for the armed struggle, because there weren't any men.

Talking with them, I discovered they had deep religious convictions. That was what led them to be involved in the movement, not political ideas. And just like this community, there were a whole lot of other communities, groups and people all over the country—people who were led to the struggle by their faith.

When it was late in the afternoon and we were ready to leave, I spoke with Emilio's mother.

"Let me take him to be treated. If I don't, I'm afraid the boy is going to lose his leg."

She gave me permission, and I took him to San Salvador with me. Emilio had never been out of his *cantón*. When he first saw the cars he asked, "Are we in San Salvador now?"

"This is it. Do you like it?"

"I would like it more if you would do me a favor, ma'am. There's something I'd really like."

"Ask me for anything you want, Emilio. Tell me what you want most in life, and I'll get it for you."

Would he want a bicycle? Or maybe a trip to the ocean?

"What is it? Tell me."

"I want to meet Monseñor Romero."

That was what he wanted most in his eight-year-old life.

He had to be in San Salvador for two months for his leg to heal, and in that time he got to know other things: streets, cars, streetlights, escalators, elevators, stores, amusement parks . . .

"Ma'am, do you remember? You owe me a favor," he would remind me from time to time.

One day in the hospital where the nuns were treating him for me, I saw Monseñor arrive. Emilio saw him too, and he was fascinated to see him there in person.

"Monseñor," I told him, "I'm here with one of your admirers, and what this little guy wants most in life is to meet you."

"Well, let's go get acquainted . . ."

He put his hand on the boy's head, and started to walk with him.

"So, what's your name?"

"Emilio Valencia. I'm from El Almendral."

He sat down and put Emilio on his lap.

"Tell me about your *cantón*. I've never been there."

I can't describe the look of joy on the face of that child. He was happier than if Santa Claus had appeared on Christmas Day. They spent a good long while talking with each other.

Afterwards, he didn't even want to take a bath because Monseñor had touched him. And from that day on, his main concern was to not forget anything so that when he got back home, he could tell everybody what the two of them had talked about.

Emilio had the pleasure of going back home cured, and telling all of his stories. But there were only a few pleasures left to him in life. He lived for only two more years. A few days before Monseñor Romero was killed, the National Guard attacked and burned down his entire *cantón*, killing him and the rest of his family.

(Margarita Herrera)

I WAS MAKING SOME VISITS in one of the *cantones* of Aguilares with four *campesinos*. One of them was the famous Polín.

"We're going to meet for a while to study the Bible," one said.

"Will the honorable priest join us?" asked Polín.

"All right. I've got the afternoon free. Let's go!" I told them.

And we started walking until we got to the shade of an *amate* tree. The houses were off in the distance now, and we were surrounded only by the scenery of the countryside.

"Shall we get it out?"

"Yeah, get it out!"

They had the Bible hidden, buried under the ground in a plastic container. In those times, the Bible was one of the most subversive books you could have, and it wasn't infrequent that the army would kill someone for carrying a Bible.

They unpacked it. They'd been meeting for some time now to read and reflect on the Gospel of John.

"You just sit right there," they told me, "and if you hear us saying something that's totally wrong . . . well, you just straighten us out!"

They read. They made their comments. They had some quiet prayer-like time. They chatted. I was all eyes and ears listening to them. They'd been at it for more than an hour, when way, way off in the distance we saw a little dot of something moving towards us.

"Don't worry. It's an animal!"

They kept reading, but they also kept looking out of the corners of their eyes.

"It is not! It's a person!"

They got alarmed and hid the Bible under some leaves.

"It's a woman. She's wearing a skirt."

"That's not a skirt! It's a cassock!"

"It's a priest!"

Then when he was closer . . . "Hey, it's Monseñor Romero!"

He was walking by himself way out there.

"Monseñor, what are you doing here?"

"That's what I say. What are *you* all doing?"

"We're reading the Bible—the Gospel of John."

"Would you allow a pastor to sit down with you?" he asked them.

"Pull up a chair, Monseñor!" Polín said.

He sat down on a patch of grass. And the men went on for another hour with their reflections—reading calmly and speaking calmly, like the *campesinos* do, thinking things out so that words aren't wasted.

Monseñor Romero didn't open his mouth. When they were through, I turned around and saw that his eyes were brimming with tears.

"What's the matter, Monseñor?"

"I thought I knew the Gospel, but I'm learning to read it in another way."

And there was Polín, with his mischievous smile.

(Antonio Fernández Ibáñez)

THE COMMUNITY OF SAN ROQUE WAS SO FAR away that you couldn't get there by car. It was alongside a path—well, not really a path, more like a ravine. And to tell the truth, it wasn't really a community, it was more of a slum where the buses won't go even today.

And someone like Monseñor Romero was going to come there! When the news was confirmed, we couldn't even believe it. But it was true. He came to celebrate some First Communions.

He left his little car on the street and walked and walked and walked. The most amazing thing was that everyone who went out to greet him ended up joining him. Soon there was a big line of people walking as if in a procession, but it wasn't a mourning procession, it was a happy one!

I met him there on the road to the church, and I joined in the walk too, going up and down the gullies. It was there that I spoke with him for the first time.

"Monseñor," I said to him, "you're holding up well in spite of all the walking!"

"Well, I like to be where the people are, and you know what they say: no pain, no gain!"

He loved it. Some people called to him from their houses.

"Monseñor, would you like to come in?"

He never snubbed anybody or turned up his nose at an invitation, and once inside the house, he'd stay a while to greet the family.

"Now, this little one I'm taking with me!"

He picked up a little girl and held her in his arms, and then all of the other kids wanted to be picked up too. They were running after him, hanging on to his cassock.

When he finally got to the church of San Roque to celebrate Mass, there was a crowd of people surrounding him. It looked like a hive swarming with bees.

After the Mass and the party they had there, he made his rounds on the other side of the neighborhood, coming back by a different path.

"This way I get to meet everybody, and nobody goes without a greeting."

And no one went without a greeting.

"Damn! Only he could be capable of sacrificing so much to celebrate a Mass in such a remote place!"

That's what Don Tito, the shoemaker, said when that great day ended.

(Hilda Orantes)

THEY WERE TRIPS WE TOOK JUST FOR FUN, not for work. We went on a lot of little outings, I don't know how many.

I gave him my time so that he would rest and relax some. And with all of our wanderings I got a little rest, too. Years before we had come to a friendly agreement:

"You don't tell me about your problems, and I won't tell you about mine," he would say.

That was our secret. That's why we enjoyed our time together so much. How many times did I go to Guatemala with him? I remember he was always looking for a new cassette of marimba music. He loved those melodies. But not just that. He also loved classical music, which is the most refined.

He would make me go to the theater to music concerts that were kind of boring and deadly slow, and I'd fall asleep on him. He'd elbow me to wake me up.

"When are you going to learn that this stuff is beautiful?!" he'd say.

He was selective in his tastes. On one trip we took to Mexico, he said to me one night:

"What do you say? Let's put frugality aside today, and treat ourselves for once."

"To what?"

He had bought box seats to see the Folkloric Ballet, and *that* was truly a thing of beauty that no one could sleep through.

But his greatest pleasure was the circus. That was something he'd brought with him from childhood. There was never a circus in or outside of El Salvador that he knew about that he didn't go see.

"But aren't you too busy?" I'd say. "Are you going to be able to take the time?"

"You get the tickets, and let's go!"

So we'd go to the circus. When the tightrope walker or the trapeze artist would do their jumps and turns way up in the air, he would get so nervous his hands would sweat. But it was nervousness he enjoyed. He loved it. And the clowns! The ones with names like "Firuliche" and "Chocolate." One of them would do a few silly tricks, and he would just roar with laughter. I never saw him laugh so hard as he did with the clowns.

(Salvador Barraza)

LA JOYITA, AGUA CALIENTE, EL PEPETO, Plan Piloto, El Vaticano, San José del Pino, La Periquera, Sesunapán, El Naranjo, La Presita. They were all projects of the Basic Housing Program, which had built almost 5,000 houses in 10 years and was about to build another 8,000. Entire subdivisions were being built with nice houses that were our very own, built with our own hands and the sweat of our brow.

"Them? They build little houses, and then they build barricades with the cement blocks they have leftover . . . They're using this house-building stuff as a front to organize subversive activity."

That's what the army officers would say. They were watching us closely. So then the repression came. In La Periquera didn't they kill our entire community council in a single day? And didn't the community elect new leaders right there in front of the dead bodies of their friends? And didn't the army do away with the second leaders in a flash? And what about San José del Pino? There was so much harassment from soldiers trying to terrorize them that they decided to sleep with strings tied from house to house. Everyone tied the string to their thumb before going to bed. And thumb to thumb everyone was connected with strings so they could sleep and still be alerted. If one person moved, everybody felt it and they were all on their feet! Others spent nights up in trees, keeping a look out for the National Guard, so they could give a warning.

For the tenth anniversary of the Basic Housing Program, there was a party in the El Pepeto neighborhood of Soyapango. Inviting Monseñor Romero was only going to make us seem more subversive, but we didn't want to miss out on the joy of having him with us just because of that.

"On the night before the party, only the pig dies," said one old woman to calm our fears.

He came. After the Mass we organized a meal where we were going to all sit down and eat together. But of course, since we were so happy to have him with us, each family still prepared a little something extra to offer just to him. At lunchtime, he didn't stay at the special table they'd prepared for him and for the community leaders. Instead, he got up and made the rounds.

"I'd like to see your houses. What you've built with so much effort deserves to be seen."

With that disposition he went into each one of our houses: 530 families. They offered him something at every house. And he was so polite, he accepted a bite at every one of them: a pupusa, a glass of fruit drink, beans, sour cream, a chicken leg, some guacamole . . . 530 bitefuls. One by one. He didn't snub anybody!

When he got back to the special table, he was happy.

"Aren't you going to eat anything, Monseñor?"

"Well, I don't have to eat now. I've already eaten!"

And he laughed with satisfaction.

(Antonia Ferrer)

"I'VE BEEN TOLD THAT D'AUBUISSON has his eye on me and that he thinks I'm a priest. I've also heard that at the National Guard they call me the "*padre* with the beard . . ."

"And how is it that you're still alive and in one piece?" Monseñor Romero asked me with a laugh.

"Because they also know that I hang out with the Salesians. And since the Salesians hang out with rich people, that's my defense against the death squads!"

I'd gone to talk with Monseñor Romero about my pastoral work at the Center for Celebration and Prayer of Don Bosco. I had grown up in that kind of work—that kind of spirit—and now I was still educating hundreds of kids as a catechist and a soccer coach. Monseñor had gotten to know us a short while ago, and he was enthusiastic about our experience.

"What screws us up," I told him, "is that the Salesians 'convert' people, but they do it backwards. Their preferential option is for people with money. They put more priority on their school for rich kids than they do on the prayer center for the poor. It's the opposite of what Don Bosco himself would have done!"

Monseñor listened to me. I think he shared my concern, but with more wisdom.

"That kind of falling away from ideals happens with other religious orders too . . . I guess that's why they say that every soup gets cold eventually and that every brush loses its bristles. It's the law of life. But everything can also be renewed. Don't you lose that Salesian spirit or your patience. You're very impatient!"

At the end of our long conversation, Monseñor came up with an idea that he posed to me:

"Do you think we could organize prayer centers like that in all the parishes?"

"Sure, we could . . ."

"Parish prayer centers for the formation of young people, using catechism and sports, music and theater . . . What do you think?"

I got excited about the idea. We started in Colonia Luz in Mejicanos. There was a basketball court there so we started with that. Soon it was a community of 100 young people.

"When are we going to start one up in another parish?" Now Monseñor was the impatient one.

"We've already spread the Salesian spirit around. Now it's just a question of time," I encouraged him.

But we weren't able to go any further. There wasn't time. The repression clipped our wings.

(Francisco Román)

LA BERNAL IS LIKE A PIT OF MISERY in the middle of several middle class neighborhoods. It's sunk down in a hole, with nice housing developments all around it.

We arrived at La Bernal to work as catechists. The church was just a big space with a roof and no walls, but there was already a very lively community there. That year we prepared about 30 kids to receive their First Communion on the afternoon of December 24.

"Why don't we invite Monseñor Romero?"

The kids had the idea—an idea that was coming up quite often in all of the communities. Inviting him was practically a guarantee that he would come, because he rarely refused. He would always find a little time to go to the communities' celebrations, and he'd even show up at birthdays and *piñata* parties.

Well, he came to La Bernal. Some didn't believe he'd come until they saw him appear and heard the sound of the jeep. That's because the place was so poor. But afterwards the people crowded into the church like ants on an anthill to receive him. And there was lots of pushing and shoving to be able to greet him in person.

I still remember what he said when he began his homily:

"Today we have moved the pulpit from the Cathedral to the neighborhood of La Bernal so that from this small, poor community we can announce the good news of Christmas to the entire community of El Salvador . . ."

After the Mass and the First Communions, we fixed up two tables really nice. They were kind of long tables with white tablecloths that hung down to the floor. The children who had received their first communion sat at one table, with Monseñor at the head. The rest of the community sat at the other table. Tamales had been made.

"Two apiece!" said the women who were handing them out.

There was one regular tamal and one sweet one for everyone. Suddenly a little boy appeared out of nowhere. He was a tiny little kid, about four years old. Light haired and covered with dirt. Barefoot, and with a nose full of snot. He came up to Monseñor Romero from behind and pulled on his cassock with his grubby fingers.

"You want some?" Monseñor asked him.

The little boy nodded his head a few times. Yes. This kid was filthy with dirt and stains. Monseñor picked him up, put him on his lap and started feeding him from his tamal. He'd eat one bite and give the next bite to the boy. One for him, one for the boy, one here, one there . . . And so just like that, the two of them ate tamales together that Christmas eve.

(Guillermo Cuéllar)

WHEN I STARTED SEEING A YOUNG MAN who had been a seminarian and who was working with the communities, I didn't say anything at home. Not because he'd been a seminarian, but because my parents were against everything—against my having a boyfriend, against my getting married, against my living with anyone . . . So I was silent. I was afraid of the scene it would cause.

When I got pregnant, the guy behaved badly and left me. I was afraid of an even bigger scene so I kept even quieter.

But him. I did have to tell him. And his was the scolding I was most afraid of.

I'd been working for him for about 10 years as his secretary, and practically his housekeeper, since the time he'd come to San Salvador as the auxiliary bishop, then later in Santiago de María and now as archbishop. I wrote letters for him, I cleaned up his desk, his files and his recording room everyday, I made his bed . . . I took care of his scheduling. And I always brought him the boldo tea he liked to drink mid-morning when he needed to calm his nerves. And the honey for his throat which would get irritated from so much preaching. By now, Monseñor Romero was like my father, and the anger I most feared for being pregnant and without a husband was his.

But I had to tell him. Some people already suspected, and they were going to go to him with the gossip anyway. Or he'd figure it out himself since he saw me every day in the office. But, but how? How could I work up the courage tell him, and what could I say? What if I started shaking and I got a frog in my throat? How could I begin? I couldn't just deal with the problem by myself either, because he was my father and also my confessor. But how could I survive a scolding from him? He wouldn't just scold me, he'd fire me, and I'd be left without work, and then what would I do? How would I earn enough . . . It would be me and the baby on the streets without money, without a soul we could count on. Dear God, what are we going to do in the streets . . ?

But I had to tell him. I went over it again and again in my mind for I don't know how many days, and finally one day I tiptoed into his office with that glass of orange juice that he liked to drink at 10:00 in the morning. I was sick with worry and fear.

"Monseñor, your orange juice . . ."

"Oh good. It's so hot today . . . Sit down, Angelita. I wanted to say a few things to you . . ."

"I have something to say to you too, Monseñor. It's just one thing . . ."

"Well then, ladies first!"

My whole body was shaking from head to toe when I started to tell him. And I told him everything from the beginning—from the time I'd started seeing the seminarian to the time of my swelling belly which was now beginning to show . . .

"And he's going to be born in five months . . ." I was sobbing.

He looked at me and smiled. And he stayed like that for just a minute or so, but it seemed like an hour to me.

"It's all right, Angelita. The first time is forgiven."

"What did you say, Monseñor . . ?" I was so flustered that I didn't even understand him.

"Don't worry, *hija*. The first time is forgiven. Right now you have to do what you can for that baby that's going to be born."

He kept smiling, and it was *me* that felt like *I* was being born again!

From that day on, he helped me out with everything like a worried father. He told Silvia Arriola to help me, and so the two of us went out to talk several times. He asked his sister Zaida to take care of me until the baby was born. He even spoke with my parents to tell them what was happening, and if they ended up forgiving me, it was only because of his intercession.

During the last month of my pregnancy, he said:

"You have to go and rest, Angelita. I'm not running you off, mind you. When you feel better, you've always got your job here and I'll be waiting for you. Better yet, I'll be waiting for the both of you—you and the little guy!"

It was a little girl. Claudia Guadalupe. I named her Guadalupe after Monseñor's mother, so that her memory would be alive in my daughter.

(Angela Morales)

JANUARY 19, 1979. OCTAVIO SPENDS ALL MORNING with pen in hand at the offices of the archdiocese, writing out the conclusions of the "Week of Reflection on the Meaning of Priesthood," in which more than 70 priests of the archdiocese have participated. Every day the priests are clearer that the primary purpose of their vocation is to identify with the people.

After eating lunch, Octavio goes to another meeting. Monseñor Romero is presiding. It's about urgent affairs at the seminary. Octavio is in charge of the spiritual orientation of the youngest aspirants to the priesthood. This year, 27 young men who have recently finished high school have asked for admittance into the seminary. Every day it's more dangerous to be a priest in El Salvador, and every day there are more candidates.

From there Octavio runs to the parish of San Antonio Abad to celebrate the Eucharist. It's already night when he shows up in El Despertar, the retreat house in the neighborhood. From 5:00 PM on, those who are going to participate in the "Introduction to Christianity" retreat that Octavio is leading have been arriving. It's Friday. Twenty-eight young men are to be here until Sunday.

Octavio gives the first talk that evening before they go to sleep. The subject is Jesus' sermon in the synagogue in Nazareth. "I have come to free the oppressed . . ." Afterwards Madre Chepita and Ana María prepare the questions for the next day's discussion groups. They go to bed pretty late, and at midnight, tired from all the excited energy that's always generated at these gatherings, everyone is asleep and dreaming.

January 20. At 6:00 in the morning, they all wake up. The house is shaking with sound. It's not a landslide like Ana María first thought. It's a tank and a military jeep breaking down the gates to the central garden. Bullets are flying. The noise is frightening.

"Crush him! Kill him!" men are shouting.

The military operation is over in just five minutes. When the soldiers take the half-dressed boys out to put them in the patrol cars surrounding the house, Madre Chepita realizes what has happened. Octavio's body is lying in the patio, with his face smashed in, in a puddle of blood. Close by, another four bodies are riddled with bullets from the machine gun fire. She didn't know who they were until later: Angel, a 22 year-old carpenter, David and Roberto, 15 year-old students, and Jorge, a 22 year-old electrician and student.

Octavio Ortiz Luna was 34 years old. Monseñor Romero had known him since he was a kid in seminary there in San Miguel. Octavio was the first priest Monseñor Romero ordained after becoming a bishop.

(The Community of San Antonio Abad)

THE ISIDRO MENÉNDEZ MORGUE WAS FAMOUS. That's where the bodies went after they were found on the streets, in the ditches, or in the garbage dumps of San Salvador. There were times when there were six, seven, eight of them every day. The garbage truck would pick them up and take them there until someone came to identify them. Sometimes no one came. They were afraid of reprisals.

That's where they took Father Octavio and the four boys after the National Guard killed them in El Despertar. The news spread quickly through the neighborhood. I went with my father, Beto, who had been a friend of Father Octavio since I was a little girl. We went to the morgue looking for our dead.

The entrance was totally militarized. Monseñor Romero arrived the same time we did, and he went in right away, wracked with sorrow.

"Where are they? Where are they?!"

No one stopped him or anything. The guardsmen just looked at him from the door, curious to see the archbishop going into such a place of ghosts. We went in behind him.

The floor was one big puddle of blood. The five of them were there, thrown on the floor. Streams of blood were still coming out of them. Around them were some of the people in the community that had arrived before us.

"Where is Octavio?"

"Here, Monseñor. This is him." They pointed to him.

You couldn't tell it was him. His body was completely flattened, his face destroyed to the point that it looked like he didn't even have one. I had seen Father Octavio in my house eating with my father so many times . . . and I couldn't even recognize him.

Monseñor Romero knelt on the ground and held his shattered head.

"It can't be. This isn't him. It's not him . . ."

Tears streamed from Monseñor's face as he held him close with all of his affection.

"They ran over him with a tank and smashed his head, Monseñor."

"I can't believe they could be so savage," he said.

The guardsmen looked in through the door. Monseñor's cassock was covered with blood and he was crying, cradling Father Octavio in his arms.

"Octavio, my son, you have completed your mission. You were faithful . . ."

Marichi came in, completely distraught.

"You don't have a camera, do you?" Monseñor asked her.

"Not here. It's at home."

"Go get it. Take pictures of Father Octavio for me, with his face like this, the way they left him."

She left quickly.

"Afterwards try to see if they can fix his face up at the funeral parlor," he asked us. "Take care of these boys too . . ."

And he stayed on the floor without moving, just holding Octavio and looking at him.

"Octavio, my son."

(Carmen Elena Hernández)

OCTAVIO WAS THE SECOND of my 12 children. He wove hammocks and planted corn with us until one day, when he was 13 years old, he left the nest to fly on his own. He decided to go to seminary in San Miguel where Father Romero was in charge of the boys that wanted to be priests.

When he reached that goal, and I saw my son lying prostrate on the floor in front of the bishop, face down, like they do in the ordination ceremonies for priests, I told Exaltación, my wife:

"He's going to be a priest, but he looks like he's dead."

When they killed him, I saw him lying prostrate again, and I said to myself:

"I saw him like this before, and now I'm seeing him again in the same way."

These are the mysteries that life holds.

After he became a priest, he stayed in San Salvador working with the Christian base communities. That's what he wanted to do most.

On January 20, on the same day and at the same time that they killed him, I was getting on a bus in Cacaopera to come and visit him in San Salvador.

My wife said to me, "Tell Octavio to set aside a day to go to Esquipulas and see *El Cristo.*"[1]

That was the message I was taking him from his mother, but when I got to Ilopango, I realized I would never be able to give it to him. The news was already coming out on the radio that he'd been assassinated. It was saying that they were all guerrillas, that they'd caught them firing pistols from the rooftops of the place where they met their end. They were repeating those lies. But the only weapons Octavio and the boys had on that retreat were a guitar and a Bible. The people who tried to defame them—they were the ones that were armed to the teeth!

When I got to the Cathedral, it was already night, and the five bodies were there.

"Don Alejandro," Monseñor said to me after giving me a hug of condolence," we're going to have a meeting to see what kind of arrangements to make."

He was exhausted and upset, but he still wanted to help decide on what kind of burial we were going to give him. Monseñor Modesto López was at the meeting, too. It was the two of them on behalf of the Church, and there were five of us there from the family—me and my daughters who lived in Ilopango. There were also a whole bunch of people from the community of Mejicanos where Octavio had been working. I don't know how many.

Monseñor Romero began. "We would like to have Octavio buried here in the Cathedral as a martyr."

---

[1] *Cristo* at Esquipulas—Many Central Americans make pilgrimages to Esquipulas, Guatemala to take their prayers to the image of the *Cristo Negro*, or Black Christ.

It didn't seem like a bad idea to me.

"But what do you think?" Monseñor asked me. "Shall we keep him here, or do you want to take him to your village to the cemetery there?"

Octavio was the only priest to have come out of Cacaopera. I think he was the only one from the whole department of Morazán. It didn't seem like a bad idea to bury him there in the land where he was born, in the land where his umbilical cord was buried.[2]

"I don't know, Monseñor. I don't want to decide without talking to his mother. We need to think about it."

At that point, the people from the base communities indicated their unhappiness with the two options. It was if they had already thought it out and decided.

"Octavio was with us in life, and he should stay here with us now!"

They said it with all the weight of their great conviction.

"Octavio is not dead. *Octavio vive!* He is living with us still!"

That's what they were saying—the kinds of things that lift our spirits when we hear them. They consoled me a lot in the midst of my grief.

"Octavio must stay with us!" they were all saying with strong voices.

"Well," Monseñor Romero said to me, "you can see that there are two of us, five of you and a whole lot more of them! We could be here all night, and we would never convince them. I think they've got us beat, Alejandro. What do you say? Maybe we should let Octavio stay with them."

"All right, then."

---

[2]An indigenous tradition is to bury the umbilical cord of a child near the home where he or she is born.

There were a lot of them, and they were already well organized apparently, because as soon as Monseñor Romero made his desires known, three brick masons, who the communities had already hired, left to go open up a space for a crypt inside the church in San Francisco Mejicanos.

At midnight, Monseñor said the first Mass for Octavio and the boys. The mothers and fathers of all four of the boys were there. That night I heard the father of Jorge Gómez, one the boys who was killed, say something that stayed in my mind:

"I am proud that my son gave his life alongside a prophet."

Octavio, my son, a prophet . . . Life holds such mysteries, and God has us walk along such unforseeable paths! He was the first of my sons to be killed. They killed all of them later. Angel in 1980, Santos Angel and Jesus in 1985 and Ignacio in 1990. So in the struggle for our people, I lost all of my sons. The ones I have left are my daughters and my grandchildren. We've named one of the little ones Octavio, thinking that maybe this little Tavito will grow up to be a priest someday.

(Alejandro Ortiz)

"WHILE IN MEXICO, OUR PRESIDENT said that there is no persecution of the Church here. Instead, he said, there's a 'crisis in the Church because of priests with a third world bias.' He denounces my words as 'political preaching,' and says I don't have 'the spirituality of other priests, who do, in fact, continue to preach.' He says I'm taking advantage of my preaching to promote my candidacy for the Nobel Peace Prize. How vain does he think I am! When asked if there are '14 families' in El Salvador who own everything, the President responded with denial. He said no such thing exists. In the same way, he has also denied the existence of political prisoners and the disappeared.

"But here in the Cathedral, we see the proof that he is a liar! A priest murdered by the National Guard, and four young men killed with him . . . Lord, today our conversion and our faith is upheld by these people we have before us in these coffins. They are messengers of the reality of our people and of the noble aspirations of the Church.

"Look upon this crowd gathered here in your Cathedral, Lord. This is the prayer of a people that moans and weeps, but does not despair, because we know that Christ does not lie."

*(Homily at the burial of Octavio Ortiz and
the four assassinated young men, January 22, 1979.)*

WE WERE STILL GRIEVING. We still hadn't recovered from the murders that had happened here in El Despertar. Monseñor Romero came to visit our community after one month.

"We can't call Octavio's death a failure," he kept telling us, "because Octavio is going to live in you and in the work that you do. Only what is forgotten dies."

Life went on, and we did not forget.

El Despertar is a big complex, really nice. It even has some land with mango trees on it—the ones that give the really big mangos. The space was always used for get-togethers and Christian meetings. But after the big massacre, some other meetings started to happen there—the people's meetings you know—with the goal of continuing the struggle of the people. Some people got scared. Others never knew about it. Since the meetings touched on pretty delicate issues, they were secret. The young people who met there said what they thought:

"They found Octavio with a Bible in his hand, but they're going to find us with something else. We *will* defend ourselves."

The people who were scared decided to go to Monseñor Romero to tell him about the meetings. Since I was always involved in the parish council meetings, I went with them.

"Monseñor," they said during the visit, "the young men are using the parish building for meetings of a different purpose. Do you know what we mean . . ?"

"They say they're going to defend themselves this time."

"It's a danger for us and for the whole neighborhood."

They wanted Monseñor Romero, with all of his authority, to prohibit the meetings, to cut them off. But what he did instead was to cut off their complaints:

"Everyone should contribute according to their ability," he told us, "if those young men are able to defend themselves, let them do it."

"But Monseñor . . !"

"If you can't do that yourself, you should work for the people in some other way. That will also be very valuable."

In that way, he put an end to the objections of the fearful. But he said something else too:

"We are neither blind nor deaf. The army has its barracks. It has its places to meet and make plans to run over people's rights. But poor people have nowhere to congregate. These young people have found a good place to get together and talk, and we're not going to stop them. Where are they going to go if not there?"

(Adela Guerra)

"Monseñor, what if they killed all of us one by one, and they killed all the priests so that there were none left? Then what would we do?"

DARK EVE

THE STRIKE AT *LA CONSTANCIA* and *La Tropical* had all of San Salvador on edge. How could it not? This was the beverage industry monopoly, property of the Meza Ayaus, one of the "14 families."

We had the factory totally paralyzed, occupied by hundreds of workers. There was a menacing line of soldiers all around the factory, and behind them, a ring of people. It was like that for several days. People were burning buses, raising barricades and finding ways to provoke anyone in uniform. All to support us. An action of this magnitude had never happened before. There were seven dead and 14 wounded in the confrontation with the military by the time we managed to get Monseñor Romero to mediate.

He offered us space at the *hospitalito* to have the negotiations, and he was present at all times during the talks. A guy by the name of Muyshondt, who was the legal representative of management, was attending the talks accompanied by his entourage of bodyguards. Since we had to come and go on our own, however, it was dangerous for us . . .

"Stay and sleep at the *hospitalito*," Monseñor invited us, and he found a place for us there.

There were several sessions. We would start when it was already pretty late and argue into the wee hours of the morning. Muyshondt was always very polite with Monseñor, but he was hard-nosed when it came to the demands of the workers.

"You can't resolve conflicts without compromise," Monseñor insisted.

"But you can't dialogue with people who are using violence," Muyshondt.

He wanted us to call off the strike before beginning the negotiations. But our only weapon was labor pressure in the factory and people pressure in the streets.

"What they're doing is violent!" Muyshondt repeated, reproaching the bishop.

"But what they're asking for is fair," he would argue.

Those were tense days. Muyshondt was stubborn, we were determined, and Monseñor Romero was wise in his repeated advice to the management:

"What will it cost you to compromise a little?" he would say. "Give in. Take the rings off your fingers now, so they don't end up cutting your fingers off. If you don't want to let go of your rings for the sake of justice, you risk having them taken away from you violently."

(Julio Flores/Vilma Soto)

"THERE HAS NEVER BEEN A STRIKE in our country that labor authorities have pronounced legal. Since *La Constancia* and *La Tropical* have recently raised the price of beer and soft drinks, to the detriment of consumers' pocketbooks, it's only fair that they offer better wages to their workers . . ."

It was my job to read a lot of these commentaries on the news hour at YSAX, which every one called "the X." So I read the ones about the strike too. That particular strike became famous for the fighting spirit of the workers and for its success. It marked the beginning of the decisive year of 1979.

And since times were particularly tough, my voice might have been tense or emotional.

"That priest speaks with so much hate!"

Some of the conservative priests in the archdiocese were complaining about me to Monseñor Romero. They thought I was a priest. They also thought that what they were hearing was hate. But it wasn't. It was passion.

"Don't personalize your criticisms." That's what Monseñor complained to me about.

At that time, a team of 17 people from the UCA, led by Ellacuría,[1] decided on the commentaries that "the X" would make.

It was something new in journalism. Ours was the first radio station in the country to give commentaries in addition to the news. It was kind of like an editorial. And as the space for media started closing up in the country with censorship and repression, "the X," the archdiocesan radio station, became more and more relevant. Monseñor's homily was, by far and away, the most listened-to program in the whole country. From 1978 on, surveys were showing that 75 percent of the people in the countryside and 50 percent of the people in San Salvador listened to his homily on Sundays. And these were sermons that lasted at least an hour and a half!

The news program, with its accompanying commentary, soon became the program with the second largest audience of our station and the most listened-to news program in the country.

We were making history, setting out our opinions clearly and publicly and creating conflicts in the process. It wasn't just the government that was out to get us, it was also the radio shareholders—one of Duarte's brothers being among them—and also some of the clergy. I used to go to weekly meetings with Monseñor Romero to evaluate the work.

It was during that time when people were threatening to withdraw their advertising in order to pressure us to change our positions that I found him the most worried.

"What do you think? Can we survive without advertisements?" he asked me fearfully.

---

[1] Ignacio Ellacuría was the rector of the Central American University and one of the Jesuit priests murdered by the US-trained Atlacatl Batallion of the Salvadoran Army on November 16, 1989.

"Monseñor, when one door closes, another opens up. You already have a lot of friends overseas . . ."

We decided to turn to international organizations to look for support for the radio station. And since crises give birth to new ideas, we also launched a new set of programs: air space for the *campesino* perspective, time slots for the grassroots organizations, news that didn't come out anywhere else, biting commentary, testimonial music, and the Sunday homily! A bold move!

(Héctor Samour)

A STREAM OF PEOPLE WERE COMING TO YSAX to ask us to air their denunciations of all of the atrocities the government was committing.

"My son . . . three days ago a death squad took him from our house . . ."

"My little grandson was found in a garbage dump all shot up, with his thumbs tied together behind his back, like those guys do when they kill people . . ."

"Tell me his name, and the day he disappeared . . ."

I was just torn apart by the time I left those interviews. I felt so powerless! The only thing we could do was to turn those acts of cruelty into news.

Monseñor Romero would also bring us all of the denunciations that came in to him through the archdiocese.

"Write them up as a news report, and air them for me on the radio."

We had working meetings with him to evaluate how the news show and the commentaries were going. These were the programs with the largest audiences, and the ones that brought the greatest pressures on us. At that time Colonel López Nuila was in charge of the Information Office of the government, and he was filling our mailboxes with letters saying that we were just asking to be shut down.

"Be moderate. Lower the tone of your denunciations. Say the same thing, but in another way so that we don't lose the program."

That was Monseñor's thing. And he would scold me every time: "You, you have such a sweet tone of voice, but you hit them over the head pretty hard!"

We were always socking it to the military and the right wing. But I didn't argue with him. You just didn't argue with Monseñor. He had tremendous authority.

"Don't think for a minute," he would say to me, "that just because you say something softly, it's not heard or that it doesn't have an effect! Be a little more moderate!"

He asked us for moderation. But later, you'd go to hear him at the Cathedral, and he was the one hitting people over the head!

(Margarita Herrera)

HE DIDN'T BEAT AROUND THE BUSH, and he didn't mince words. He was always right on the mark with what he had to say. As a journalist, I attended a lot of press conferences where Monseñor Romero put himself in our hands, so I remember some of the things he used to always say.

"At the very least, you should always say something from both sides so that the Salvadoran people can be well informed about what's going on."

He said that to us many times, kind of calling us to a more objective journalism.

"I'm asking you to tell the truth," he said another time, "although I understand why you might not at times. Who's going to serve the truth for free, when lies are so well paid?"

He would say things like that that would just cut to the quick and eat at your conscience.

Within our profession, we always saw him as a very secure person. For him there was no such thing as an indiscreet question. He always had a good answer for everything. It got to be where it wasn't easy to approach him or to get him aside for an interview. Every Sunday, there would be a bunch of journalists falling all over each other, like hounds after a fox. Our Spanish, French, Dutch and *gringo* colleagues would be there too. He was already famous worldwide.

One thing that was really important in those times of so much repression was that he would always give us something in his homily that would be our foot in the door for confronting the military. Because if a military officer ever dared to show up at a press conference, you could say to him:

"Archbishop Romero said such-and-such in his homily . . . What do you have to say to that?"

And there would be nothing he could say. You'd have him up against the wall.

Monseñor? He was the highest source of information that this country had during those years, and if there's any title that fits him perfectly, it's "the journalist of the poor."

(Armando Contreras)

EVERY MORNING SILVIA AND I received all his mail. We opened it for him, went through it for him and passed it on to him to see what kind of a response he was going to give to each letter.

From early 1979 on, he started to receive anonymous threatening letters on a regular basis. We would pass those on to him as well. They blamed him for everything that was happening in the country: for every strike, every demonstration, every guerrilla action. They called him bad names, and they'd give him until such-and-such a time to change his way of preaching and if not, they'd kill him, they said.

There were insults, nasty comments, complaints—all of them vulgar. "Son of a bitch, we're going to drink your blood!" They'd say things like that. Or "We're going to crush you to pieces," "Your days are numbered," and other things I won't even repeat.

Other letters came without any words—just a Nazi swastika or a white hand over a black piece of paper. It was understood that those were death sentences. There were days when it wasn't just two or three of these anonymous letters, but rather a whole handful of them!

Our duty was to pass the letters on to him. He would read all of them, and we would classify them into different folders. That happened until he got angry one day and threw the folder on top of the desk.

"Don't show me any more of these! Save them, but I don't ever want to see another one!"

But since so many of them were arriving, occasionally we would drop a careful hint:

"Monseñor, those letters that you don't want to see are still coming . . ."

"And I still don't want to see them. It's not for nothing that they say 'Out of sight, out of mind' . . . But keep saving them."

That's what we did. That pile of papers is probably still there somewhere in the files of the archdiocesan offices.

(María Isabel Figueroa)

"TELL POLÍN I WANT TO TALK WITH HIM."

And I'd take him to him. Sometimes it was the other way around:

"Tell Monseñor that I'd like to give him some information," Polín would say to me.

The two of them were both very busy people, but they'd find the time to exchange some ideas, especially about the *campesino* "poor-o-tariats," as Polín would say.

"Things are really screwed up, Monseñor, but at least it doesn't cost us anything to talk to each other!" Polín would say as he arrived in his usual excitable state.

The two of them would laugh out loud. Then they'd start talking. During their encounters at the *hospitalito*, I always noticed one thing. Monseñor never gave up his seat at the head of the dinner table for anyone. No one! Even if it was the nuncio, he'd keep his place at the head. Ungo would arrive, a military man would arrive, a priest or a bishop would arrive, it didn't matter who came, he always presided. With Polín it was different.

When Polín came to talk and eat, Monseñor always gave up his seat at the head of the table for him. Polín was the only one who ever occupied his place.

(Juan Bosco Palacios)

THE RULE WAS: EAT AND REST. In my house Monseñor Romero was not allowed to talk about the problems of the country or about all of the tough situations he was involved in. No, because that's not good for your digestion.

Pork roast with *chismol, tamales pisques,* fried plantains with sour cream . . . He absolutely loved all of these things. Oh, and *torrejas*! And pineapple *pastelitos*. And of course, he'd never go without his beans.

He came here to eat with us for so many years . . .

"Here, I just feel like taking my shoes off and making myself at home!" he'd say when he arrived.

I felt proud of how well he ate at our table. My mother would scold me though.

"*Hija*, for God's sake, you're going to make Monseñor sick!"

But when I saw that he'd eaten too much, I wasn't embarrassed to say: "Open your mouth, Monseñor . . ."

He'd open his mouth obediently, and I'd give him a good spoonful of Maalox, as if he were a little boy. Either Maalox or bismuth tablets so the food wouldn't make him sick!

"This Niña Elvira is a sneaky one. With one hand she gives me the poison, and with the other hand the antidote!"

My father and I used to tell him jokes to make him laugh and help him forget about things, because laughter is the best way to make sure you have good digestion. One day we were telling him that old joke about the bride and groom.

"The story goes that one day at a wedding, after the ceremony was over and they were throwing rice at the couple, the guests were shouting, 'Arriba la novia!' which means 'Hurray for the bride' or 'Up with the bride!' So they were shouting that, and others were shouting, 'Arriba el novio!' or 'Up with the groom!' And they went on like that for a while shouting, 'Arriba la novia!' and 'Arriba el novio!' when a drunk who was passing by decided to let out a shout himself. He says: "Hey! They're married, aren't they? What difference does it make who's on top? Let them do it the way they want to!'"

Monseñor let out a big laugh, and my mother, who was listening in from the kitchen, scolded my father:

"Foncho, please. Show a little respect for Monseñor!"

"Don't worry, Don Foncho," Monseñor told him quietly, "Let's hear another one."

But then my mother came in on tiptoes to impose respect.

"Don Foncho," Monseñor alerted him, "it seems we have a red light."

And we'd change the subject to make it seem like nothing was going on.

"Would you be so kind as to bring me another *tortilla*, Niña Carmen?" Monseñor asked my mother so that she'd go to the kitchen and they could continue with their jokes.

When she was far enough away, Monseñor said to my dad:

"The coast is clear, Don Foncho. Let's hear another one!"

And my father would let loose with another spicy joke. Spicy or mild, we would always laugh. And that's how we spent our time, in good company with good food.

(Elvira Chacón)

San Salvador, April 16, 1979. Interference with the YSAX frequency blocked access to Archbishop Romero's Sunday homily on the Catholic radio station today. This is the third Sunday in a row in which the homily from the Cathedral has met with interference on the radio waves.

So called "airwave pirates," under the protection of the government, are believed to be responsible for the interference, but ANTEL, the government telecommunications company, has yet to issue a statement on the matter. According to reliable sources, this "censorship" of the archdiocese is only one of an escalating number of actions by General Romero's government in response to the growing tide of grassroots organizing—organizing evidenced in these past few weeks by strikes and work stoppages in factories and schools, and by street demonstrations that have left a tragic number of dead and wounded. The archbishop has been referring to these violent events in each of his silenced sermons.

"PLEASE LISTEN TO ME. I need to have an audience with the Holy Father . . ."

"No. You listen to me. You're going to have to wait your turn like everyone else."

Another Vatican door shuts in his face.

Monseñor Romero had asked for a personal audience with Pope John Paul II from San Salvador, and he had done so with sufficient time to get through the various obstacles of the Church bureaucracy. He travelled to Rome feeling sure that when he arrived, everything would be arranged.

Now, all of his planning ahead seems to have gone up in smoke. The Vatican curia officials say they don't know anything about his petition. So he has to go around to the various offices pleading for an audience.

"It can't be," he says again, "I wrote him a long time ago. My letter has to be here!"

"The Italian mail service is a disaster!"

"But I sent it by hand with . . ."

Another closed door. And the next day, another one. The curia officials don't want him to talk with the pope. And his time in Rome, where he has been invited by nuns who are celebrating the beatification of their founder, is coming to an end.

He can't go back to San Salvador without having seen the pope, without having told him everything that is happening there.

"I'm going to keep begging for this audience," says Monseñor Romero mustering some hope.

It's Sunday. After Mass, the pope goes down to the immense meeting hall where the multitudes await him for his traditional general audience. Monseñor Romero has gotten up in the early hours of the morning to be in the first line. And as the pope goes by giving his greetings, he takes his hand and doesn't let go.

"Holy Father," he demands with all of the authority of beggars, "I am the Archbishop of San Salvador, and I beseech you to give me an audience."

The pope agrees. Finally he has achieved his goal. The meeting will be the next day.

It's the first time that the Archbishop of San Salvador is going to meet with Karol Wojtyla, who has only risen to the position of Supreme Pontiff in the last six months. He brings carefully selected reports of everything that is happening in San Salvador, so the pope will be informed. And since so many things have been happening, the packet of reports is quite large.

Monseñor Romero has them in a box. He shows them to the pope anxiously, shortly after the conversation begins.

"Holy Father, you can read here about the entire defamation campaign being organized from the presidential palace itself against the Church and against me . . ."

The pope doesn't touch a single paper. He doesn't even thumb through the files. He doesn't ask any questions, either. He just complains.

"I've already told you not to come weighed down with so many papers! We don't have the time here to be reading so much stuff!"

Monseñor Romero is shaken, but he tries to absorb the blow. And he absorbs it. There must be some misunderstanding.

In a separate envelope, he has also brought the pope a photo of Octavio Ortiz, the priest that the National Guard killed several months ago along with the four young men. The photo is a front-page close-up of Octavio's face. It has been smashed by a tank. You can barely make out his indigenous features, and the blood blurs them even more. A machete mark can be clearly seen on his neck.

"I knew Octavio very well, Holy Father. He was a good priest—the best. I ordained him, and I knew about all the work he was involved in. That day he was giving a Bible class to the young men who lived in the neighborhood . . ."

He tells him everything in detail—his version as archbishop and the version the government spread.

"Look how they crushed his face, Holy Father . . ."

The pope fixes his gaze on the photo and asks nothing. Then he looks at the misty eyes of Archbishop Romero and waves his hand as if to wave away the drama from this story of bloodshed.

"They killed him in such a cruel way. They said he was a guerrilla . . ." the archbishop recalls.

"And wasn't he?" the pontiff answers coldly.

Monseñor Romero puts away the photo which he hoped would invoke compassion. His hand begins to tremble. There must be some misunderstanding.

The audience continues. Seated in front of him, the pope goes over one point again and again.

"You, *Señor Arzobispo*, should make efforts to have a better relationship with your country's government . . ."

Monseñor listens to him, and his thoughts fly to the memories of what his country's government does to his country's people. The pope's voice brings him back to reality . . .

"The most Christian thing you can do in these moments of crisis is to work for harmony with the Salvadoran government."

Monseñor keeps listening. These are the same arguments that other authorities have flung at him on other occasions.

"If you can overcome your differences with the government, you will be able to work in a Christian way for peace . . ."

The pope goes over the same idea so many times that the archbishop decides to stop listening and asks to be listened to instead. He speaks softly, but firmly:

"But, Holy Father, in the Gospel, Christ said that he has not come to bring peace, but rather a sword."

The pope meets Romero's eyes with a look of steel.

"Do not exaggerate, *Señor Arzobispo!*"

The arguments end, and so does the audience.

Monseñor Romero told me all of this, practically in tears, on May 11, 1979 in Madrid when he was hurrying back to his country, wracked with worry about the news of a killing in the Cathedral in San Salvador.

(María López Vigil)

El Salvador, May 8, 1979. Twenty-three people are dead and 70 are wounded after public security forces with machine guns opened fire on protesters on the front steps of the San Salvador Cathedral. The victims, who are young members of the Revolutionary People's Bloc were participating in an occupation of the church when the security forces opened fire on them indiscriminately. Images of bullet-ridden bodies strewn on the bloodied floor near the entrance to the sanctuary were captured on film by several foreign television channels and were seen around the world within hours. These images alone have spoken volumes about the acute nature of the crisis in this country.

"THE ATMOSPHERE HERE IS VERY TENSE. There are many people who have died, who are already standing before God's court to render accounts for their actions on earth. We could almost say that the country has turned into a battlefield. Many families are in mourning . . .

"There is something that I heard back in my seminary days that comes to mind for me today in these circumstances, and I'd like to tell you about it. It's the story of an apprentice sailor who was sent to fix something high up on the mast. From those heights, he looked down at the turbulent sea, became dizzy and was about to fall. The captain realized what was happening and said, "Look upwards, boy!" And that was his salvation. When he looked up, he could no longer see the churning of the sea that was making him so dizzy, and he was able to finish his task calmly.

"This story comes to mind today because the majority of our Salvadoran brothers and sisters are in the same kind of situation now. Looking at the turbulent sea of our history, they are confused, and almost ready to give up hope. And in these circumstances of our history, it seems that our liturgical year is offering us a cry of warning at an opportune time: Look upwards! It's the Feast Day of the Ascension of Our Lord . . ."

(Homily, May 27, 1979)

SOMETIMES I DRESSED UP NICE and went to play with the *gringos* from the American Society and some other groups that were connected with the American Embassy. Sometimes we'd go bowling. They also had "casino nights," where they gave all the money they gathered—thousands of colones—to some work of charity.

One day I gave them a big spiel about the good work that was being done with cancer patients at the Divina Providencia Hospital. I told them that the project survived on donations, and I made them a proposal:

"Why don't you give all the money from the next casino night to the sisters of the *hospitalito*? They're doing magnificent work. You should really go and see for yourselves . . ."

They more or less agreed, so the sisters and I arranged for the *gringos* to come to the hospital, visit the sick people and see the place.

"Bring them at lunchtime," Madre Luz told me. "Maybe they'll even get to meet Monseñor Romero, and he'll encourage them to be generous."

I arrived midday with three North Americans. We were in luck because Monseñor was there that day. He'd already begun to eat, and was absorbed in listening to the news on YSAX. He greeted the fair-skinned visitors with a gesture and went on with what he was doing.

We took them on a quick tour through the various rooms of the hospital, and then the sisters served us lunch next to Monseñor Romero at one of those long tables they have in the dining room. The *gringos*, who couldn't wait to meet Monseñor in person, tried to engage him in conversation. At first they covered general topics: the weather, the cancer patients . . .

but Monseñor was not allowing himself to be engaged. He hardly talked at all. He just kept eating and listening to the news. When the news came on about a robbery, one of them decided to try that topic.

"There is so much crime! Really! There are a lot of thieves in this country!"

And one of the women said, "Yes, there are a lot of thieves and very little respect for private property. Yesterday, my friend's house was broken into, and she was so traumatized because . . ."

"People have every right in the world to steal if they don't have anything to eat." Monseñor cut her off suddenly and looked the three of them in the eye. "The first right of a human being is the right to eat. If they can't eat, then let them steal!"

It was so sudden, so abrupt and so direct that the three Americans' eyes opened wide with shock. No one argued with him. They just turned so pale that they ended up whiter than they already were. An absolute silence followed, and without even finishing their food, they got up from the table, said a cold good-bye to Monseñor and left. I went with them.

They hadn't even gotten as far as the garden when they exploded.

"That man is full of hate and violence!"

"They warned us that he was a troublemaker!"

When they got back to their "society" they voided the check they'd already written. Ten thousand dollars!

Monseñor Romero knew very well that they'd come to give a contribution and that it would be a big one. I don't think the *gringos* understood what happened.

(Margarita Herrera)

San Salvador, June 20, 1979. Today at 8:40 AM, Father Rafael Palacios was murdered as he was walking to the El Calvario Church in Santa Tecla where he has been doing pastoral work over the past year. Two men dressed in civilian clothing got out of an unmarked vehicle and attempted to take him away by force. When the priest resisted, they shot him, leaving him dead on the sidewalk. "I have been moved by the tears of the communities who knew Father Rafael," said Monseñor Romero when he arrived at the scene of the crime to retrieve the body.

A FEW DAYS BEFORE THEY KILLED HIM, Rafael came to tell me:

"Look, they've painted a white hand on my car."

"Be careful then. You'll have to take precautions. Don't use this vehicle anymore. Don't be anyplace where you can be easily seen."

I got worried. He came looking for me the night before too:

"They just killed Major De Paz. They shot him as he was going towards San Salvador."

Armando De Paz was an influential military man in Santa Tecla. He was also a notorious criminal.

"They're going to want to retaliate," Palacios commented. "Who are they going to kill now?"

At that moment I had the strange premonition that the next victim was sitting in front of me.

And that's what happened. They killed Rafael in the middle of the street in broad daylight the next day.

Then a few days later something very interesting happened. A young man who had been a drug addict and who had close ties to the National Guard in Santa Tecla came to see me. He told me what he'd heard a guardsman say a few days before Rafael was killed.

"A priest who's capable of dressing *el Nazareno* in blue jeans is a dangerous priest! He has to be eliminated!"

Two years earlier, Palacios and another priest had taken the statue of Jesus of Nazareth on a Holy Week procession through the streets of Santa Tecla. Instead of dressing him in the purple robe that he wore year after year, they'd dressed him in blue jeans so the young people would feel more of a connection to him. The National Guard, who already had Rafael pegged as a communist for his work in the base communities, sentenced him to death at that point. They were just waiting for a time to do it.

(Javier Aguilar)

WE WERE COMING BACK FROM SAN MIGUEL, where he'd been visiting his family, and he fell asleep in the car. I turned the radio off and let him sleep. When we went by La Paz, I stopped.

"What? What's happening? Are we there?"

"We're at the *quesadilla* place, Monseñor!"

The place was famous for its *quesadillas*—sweet bread made with cheese. We got out and ate a few with hot coffee. This allowed him to wake up completely, and the rest of the way back we talked.

"What do you think about this promise of elections that the President has pulled out of his sleeve?"

"I don't know . . . to promise a cure when the illness is so advanced . . . I don't know if it will help anything. The worst thing is thinking about how many more people we'll have to bury."

When we got back to San Salvador, to the *hospitalito*, we saw that the grounds were overflowing with people and vehicles.

"What could have happened . . ?"

When they saw that it was his car coming in, the sisters ran towards him and just about threw themselves at him.

"Oh, thank God!" they screamed.

"What happened . . ?"

"They said on the radio that you'd had a traffic accident and that you were dead!"

"Me, dead? When did they say that?"

"The news came out around three o'clock this afternoon, Monseñor!"

"Well, what do you know! That was when we were drinking coffee and eating *quesadillas* . . . We were attending our own wake!"

He laughed heartily, and people started to breathe more easily.

"So, do you really pay attention to these kinds of rumors?!" he said loudly, and the crowd started to disperse.

That was the first time. But there were many more. First, there was supposedly an attempt with explosives. Then, you'd hear they were going to poison him, then that they'd get him when he took a trip somewhere . . . There were so many of these kinds of stories that one day when I was driving him, and I stopped at a red light, he yelled at me angrily:

"Haven't you heard they're going to try to get me with a traffic accident? And here you are stopped at a stoplight!"

I took off in a hurry and after that, I never stopped at red lights when I was driving him. Of course I was taking measures to make sure he wasn't going to have his accident with me. I didn't want to serve as his ambulance either. Things were getting worse all over.

(Juan Bosco Palacios)

"WHAT'S UP, HONEY? I thought you'd be in bed reading."

"No, I thought I should wait up for you."

This happened several times, and soon it became the routine for my husband to stay up late, killing time, until he'd see the door open and me coming back home. Finally one night, I insisted he tell me what was happening.

"I can't take it anymore. I just can't take it . . ."

"What? What's happening?"

"We're getting anonymous phone calls every day, threatening you. They say you're Monseñor Romero's adviser."

"Me? That's giving me a lot of credit!"

I was working mornings at the archdiocesan office, doing things like writing letters, filing and clipping newspapers. It was volunteer work. I didn't get paid. After a while, my main job got to be that of transcribing the tapes from Monseñor's homilies.

"Why in the world would they think I was his adviser?"

"Adviser or advised, it's all the same to them. They call me and tell me that if you keep working at the archdiocese, something's going to happen to you. They say they know your license plate numbers, that they know your every move, that they're going to search our house . . . They say I should convince you to leave your work or . . ."

"Or what . . ?"

"María Eugenia, I'm afraid for you and the children. Tell Monseñor you can't work for him anymore. Do it for the kids. Give him some kind of an excuse . . ."

It tore me up to see Eduardo so upset. He had held in his fear for so long.

"All right," I told him finally, "I'll stop working for the archdiocese for the children's sake, but I'm not going to lie to Monseñor."

I didn't sleep at all that night. I felt like I was betraying him. When I got to the office the next day, I mentioned it to one of my workmates. I was looking for a little support from him.

"Well, I guess the rats abandon ship when they smell danger," he said, without a trace of warmth.

That was just what I needed. Now I felt worse than ever. I couldn't concentrate on my work that morning. After a while, when Monseñor asked for some documents, I took advantage of the moment and went in to talk to him. Everything came out at once, and I couldn't even look him in the eye.

"It's because of my children, Monseñor. It's because of them I've decided to quit . . ."

Monseñor was quiet. He closed his eyes and looked down, pensive. He was silent for quite some time. Me, I was dead silent. I could already feel the rat's tail growing on me . . . Then, it was like a light bulb went on. He looked at me smiling:

"Leaving isn't running away, you know. Think of it as a strategy instead . . . Keep doing the work for me without coming in. You can do it from your house. What do you think?"

I saw the heavens open up. I was able to keep helping him, closed up strategically in my house.

(María Eugenia Argüello)

"I BELIEVE I SPEAK FOR ALL OF YOU HERE when I say that our first greeting of the morning should go to our sister republic of Nicaragua. What joy it gives us to know they have begun their liberation![2]

"More than 25,000 human lives were lost to the struggle there. The voices of the people were not heard, and it took a bloodbath to make them heard. That's what happens when power is made absolute, when power is made into a god!

---

[2]On July 19, 1979, the Sandinista National Liberation Front overthrew the government of Anastasio Somoza in Nicaragua. The new government began to redistribute land and dedicate unprecedented levels of resources to literacy, health and new production opportunities for the poor.

"But now they are guaranteeing full respect for human rights, and that gives us great satisfaction . . . 'Legislation will be proposed and measures will be taken to guarantee and promote unrestricted labor, professional and grassroots organizing in the city as well as the countryside.' May God be praised that in our Central America there is at least one place where a person's right to organize is respected, even if that person is a humble *campesino!*"

(Homily, July 22, 1979)

WHAT HAPPENED IN NICARAGUA scared the government. What if something like that were to happen in El Salvador? They were very anxious about it, and they started planning their strategies.

On one hand, President Romero started to promise great miracles: that there would be free elections, that exiles could return and that the paramilitary forces of ORDEN would be dissolved . . . They were trying to feed us a line, as if they thought we were stupid.

On the other hand, the repression kept getting worse, as if the people were just cattle to be led to slaughter.

In La Florencia, in Soyapango, we didn't even have a real church. We just had an old barn-like building with walls about this high. We had all our meetings and Masses there. One afternoon there were a whole bunch of us there beginning a celebration and singing happily: "Let us go now to the banquet/ to the feast of the universe/ the table's set and a place is waiting/ come everyone with your gifts to share . . ." Suddenly, six armed men dressed in civilian clothes came in and spread out to different parts of the room. We were quiet, scared to death, waiting. Bench by bench, the men began to go up to the young men and pull their heads back by their hair, looking at them as if they were trying to identify someone in particular.

"Whoever's got a mole on his forehead is as good as dead!" they shouted.

Some people tried to get out, but they locked the doors and looked us over one by one. Finally they found the one they were looking for, the man who's got a mole.

"Here's the faggot! I found him!"

They grabbed him by his neck as though he were an animal. The boy was putting up a fight and resisting, but they had him outnumbered.

"I haven't done anything!"

"You've been lucky up 'til now, you church-boy son of a bitch!"

They pushed him out of the place, beating him the whole way. Then, they threw him on the ground, and right there in front of everybody, they shot him until he was dead.

"You, finish him off!" shouted one.

And another shot him right in the heart. Then a lot of people left in a stampede, crying and running to their houses. The death squad just stayed right there, thinking about what they might do with those of us who'd stayed.

It was Father Cortés who was celebrating Mass. He was pale and trembling, but he didn't leave. When it was calm again, he told the few of us who were left:

"Life was given to us not for hatred, but for love. One of our brothers has just lost his life. Let us finish this Mass in his memory."

We found the strength to sing again. The death squad finally left, and the boy was still laying there, soaked in his own blood. Then some people in the community walked to the municipal offices so that they'd come and retrieve the body.

Several times, things just as brutal happened. One time there was a drive-by shooting at the same building during Mass. Another time, also during Mass, they shot three boys in front of the building—shot them as they were running away. It was all to terrorize us.

When Monseñor Romero came to a gathering of communities we had in Santa Lucía, I asked him:

"Monseñor, what if they killed all of us one by one, and they killed all the priests so that there were none left? Then what would we do?"

"As long as there is even one Christian, the Church exists. The one who remains is the Church, and he or she will have to forge ahead"

In those days, we wondered every day which of us would be left alive to carry on.

(Teresa Huezo)

San Salvador, August 4, 1979. Father Alirio Napoleon Macías was assassinated today in the parish church of San Esteban Catarina in the Department of San Vicente, approximately 60 kilometers from San Salvador. Macías is the sixth priest to be murdered during the violent and convulsive period of General Romero's presidency.

THE MILITARY CHECKPOINT was at the entrance to Chalatenango. From a distance you could see the silhouettes of the armed soldiers against the background of the burning sun. Monseñor Romero was coming again to visit the communities of Chalatenango.

They increased security around the whole city, but that wasn't enough for them. They also sent spies to listen to Monseñor during Mass. About half of Chalate—or all of Chalate, we never knew how many—came to the celebration. In any case, there were so many of us, we didn't all fit in the church. The chief commander of the department also arrived with several officers. But they didn't come to pray for their souls or anyone else's. They just made themselves comfortable there in the back, and when Monseñor Romero began his sermon, they took out a bunch of recording devices. And, of course, they weren't interested in taping the word of God. They wanted some evidence to accuse him of something. But not even Chalate's church was big enough to allow that kind of intrusion to go unnoticed. And Monseñor's head wasn't in the clouds. He knew what kind of shameless tricks they were up to.

When he was finishing his homily, he pointed them out.

"Before we continue with Mass, I want to ask you something," he said to all of us, "so you can be the judges, and not others. Do you think there was anything subversive about what I said to you today?"

"No!" shouted Lito right away. He was in the first row.

Then the rest of us joined in.

"No, Monseñor, nooooo!!!" The church was shaking with the sound.

"If something was subversive, you tell me and I'll straighten it out right now."

Silence. Even the babies stopped crying.

"Did everything seem correct to you, then?"

"Yes! Everything!!"

Then we gave him an ovation that you could hear all the way to the other side of the park. Even the dogs, who had the habit of wandering in during Masses, barked their approval.

"Well then," said Monseñor, looking to the back of the church, "those of you who have come here as spies with your tape recorders have heard what the people think. Now, don't go around saying things that I didn't say."

And the crowd exploded into another ovation, as if to say: "Yeah! Don't twist his words!"

They left in a hurry. When Monseñor told the whole story during his homily the following Sunday, he got another ovation. And the dogs that go to Mass in the Cathedral barked, too.

(Rosa Amelia García)

WE WERE WAITING FOR MONSEÑOR IN ARCATAO at 7:30 in the morning. But at around 7:00, nine truckloads of soldiers came in from Chalatenango and militarized our whole town.

We had told a lot of people about the party we were going to have, and we'd organized everyone in town to welcome Monseñor. People were lined up on either side of the street all the way from here near the plaza to way, way over there by the entrance to the town near the Sumpul River. But when we'd finally organized in these two long lines, the military came in and stepped in front of us, blocking the path with all of their usual unquestionable authority.

When Monseñor's little car got to the river, they stopped it and made him get out. The priests and nuns travelling with him had to get out, too.

"Get out! We have to search this vehicle!" "Search as much as you want," Monseñor told them, "but you're not going to find what you're looking for."

They went through everything: the floor of the car, the seats, the seat linings. They opened up the hood to look at the motor. They looked at every screw and every spring. Then they looked in the trunk. Finally they took some of his letters out of the glove compartment, opened them up and read them.

"A lot of people write to you!" the officers said to him. "Maybe one day they'll regret wasting their time that way."

Everything they did, they did to bother him. Finally they let him go. We followed along walking beside the car, but when it got to the center of Arcatao, the soldiers stopped him again. This time, they were even worse.

"Everyone out!! Put your hands up on the car!"

There they searched each one of them individually. They touched Monseñor all over his body, without any respect for him. They lifted his cassock. They tried to humiliate him, frisking him as if he were a criminal, and when they were done, one of the guardsmen said mockingly:

"This is all for your protection. We have orders to protect you!"

"You should be protecting the people," he said calmly.

When we finally got Monseñor to ourselves, we gave him a warm welcome to try to help him forget about the insulting way he'd been treated. The soldiers were looking at us enraged.

"If you do anything to Monseñor, you may as well do the same thing to us!"

"Go ahead and kill us now, why don't you? We don't care as long as we're with Monseñor!"

The people were outraged, screaming things in the faces of the soldiers and National Guardsmen. Some of the more fearless people went right ahead and cussed them out. During the Mass, you could tell that Monseñor was feeling bad, and he spoke about what had happened.

"If this is the way they treat me, what won't they do to you *campesinos*? But let us not be afraid of them. Even if they act arrogantly and abusively, let us never kneel before the idols of power and brute force."

(Pedrina Gómez)

HE WAS IN A REAL HURRY when we left Arcatao after that day that had been so full of tension.

He was impatient to get back to San Salvador.

"Drive quickly so we can get there early. I have a lot of important commitments!"

Monseñor was the kind of person who always wanted things done yesterday! When we went through Chalatenango, we stopped a little while to leave a few messages for the Sisters of Assumption.

"From here on," he said to me as he jumped out of the car, "We're going to step on the gas. We're behind schedule!"

"Monseñor," one of the sisters said as she greeted him, "won't you stay with us for a while?"

"I shouldn't and I can't. I've got a lot of things to do in San Salvador."

We left the messages, and he was already rushing to get back into the car when the sister insisted again.

"But Monseñor, you must stay! We've made you some *chilate* with *nuégados* and *buñuelos!*"

He got out of the car immediately.

"May God forgive me, but before idols such as these, I'm afraid I do have to kneel!"

A one-hour delay. He was crazy about these little Salvadoran delicacies.

(Rafael Urrutia)

THE DAY THAT PRESIDENT ROMERO'S BROTHER WAS KILLED, the Vice Minister of Defense and his entourage came to look for him at the archdiocesan offices.

"We are very concerned," the colonel told me, "because something could happen to Monseñor Romero, and we want to make sure he has protection. I want to talk with him right away!"

"But Monseñor isn't here . . ."

"It's urgent that we speak to him, right away!"

"Well you'll have to go look for him at the *hospitalito.*"

"Let's go right away!"

I got into their military truck all equipped with its mounted machine guns. At the *hospitalito*, Monseñor Romero came out reluctantly to talk with him, and the colonel gave him a speech.

"The situation is serious. It's more than serious! We fear for your life, and we'd like to begin providing protection for you. Right away!"

"I appreciate it, but I don't think it's necessary for you to make any special efforts to protect me. Truthfully, I don't think I need it, especially since there are so many other people who need protection . . ."

"All right then. But we should send you some instructions on what measures to take and how to protect yourself, so that you can be familiar with the procedures."

"All right. Send them if you like."

"We'll send them to you right away!"

And he stuck his chest out, gave a military salute and left. But the famed instructions didn't arrive, not "right away," not ever. The offer to protect him was pure theater.

(Ricardo Urioste)

"CÓMO AMANECIÓ?" we'd greet each other when we arrived at the offices of the archdiocese in the mornings. That was like saying, "How'd you feel when you woke up this morning?"

The problem in those days was that one never knew when one woke up how the day was going to end. They were uncertain times. Times of a lot of doubts too. It was a Monday, after a meeting of the clergy council— a tense meeting in which disputes erupted like volcanoes. The situation of the country was just as bad as the atmosphere in our meeting, and the priests weren't even close to being in agreement over what the situation was or how Monseñor Romero should confront it.

Three of us priests stayed that day to eat lunch with him. When we sat down at the table, it was Monseñor who began to speak . . .
"Tell me. Tell me honestly, please . . ."

"Tell you what, Monseñor?"

"Tell me if I'm wrong."

We were totally silent.

"When I pray, I ask the Lord a lot if I'm wrong, and I ask him to illuminate my actions. I'm asking you, too. Tell me. Help me to feel clearer about this."

"But Monseñor . . ."

"Help me. If you can show me that I'm wrong, I will get down on my knees and ask the Salvadoran people for forgiveness."

His eyes were full of tears.

(Rafael Urrutia)

HE DECIDED TO MAKE A TRIP TO MEXICO, but it was kind of hush-hush. He was going to get a checkup.

"Do me a favor," he said to some friends. "Find me a good psychiatrist who can do an evaluation. But I don't want the doctor to know who I am. That's the only way he'll feel free to say what he thinks, and I'll feel better about it that way."

Monseñor Romero was hanging by a thread. He was afraid he was losing his mind, he was apprehensive about losing control over the archdiocese and he felt like different groups of people were trying to manipulate him at different times.

So he went on this trip. The Mexican doctor saw an Oscar Romero in disguise that day.

"My name is Álvaro Herrera. I just came in from El Salvador." Monseñor said to the psychiatrist.

"All right then, Señor Herrera, have a seat and tell me what's on your mind."

He told him a big story that he was married, that his kids were grown and that he had a whole slew of grandchildren. He said that even though there were problems in the family, like there always are, the biggest stress for him was that a few years ago he'd been given a position of great responsibility in a large Salvadoran company.

"It's an enormous business, and it's never been through harder times. Being in the management like I am, at such a high level, I know about all of the problems and all of the disputes. I feel pressured by the interests of the company, the demands of the workers and . . ."

"Álvaro Herrera" talked and talked. He was honest with the doctor about his anxieties and tensions.

"My fear is that I won't be able to meet everyone's needs, and I'm afraid of being subject to undue influence by other people. I'm so exhausted, Doctor, that I don't know anymore if I'm the one making decisions or if I'm being dragged along by other people's desires . . . I need to know if I'm acting freely, based on my own judgement!"

"Good, that's my job—to help you see yourself from the inside . . ."

So in this way, the "president" of that "company"—which, of course, was none other than the Church of San Salvador—was subjected to a complex battery of tests. He spent three days answering questions, filling out questionnaires and absorbed in long patient-doctor conversations.

At the end of this effort, which both of them undertook very conscientiously, the day of the final diagnosis arrived.

"Well, Herrera," the psychiatrist told him, "after all of these explorations, I've come to a conclusion."

"Do you conclude that I'm crazy? Have I lost my mind . . ?"

"Not at all! I was going to say that you've wasted your time by coming, but actually that's not true either because we've even come so far as to become friends in these few days. You, Señor Herrera, are fine. There's nothing wrong with you. You're just tired, and that can be cured with a few days in Acapulco! Surely your business will give you a few days off to do that! You're fine."

"I'm all there?"

"Completely! You can stop worrying. You're on solid ground!"

They joked together, they talked seriously, and finally, it was time to pay the bill and go.

Álvaro Herrera signed a check for the three days of intensive consultations, and after handing it over, his conscience got the best of him, and he decided not to leave without revealing his identity.

"Doctor, perhaps you've heard something about the Archbishop of San Salvador, Oscar Romero . . ." he said to the doctor.

"And who hasn't heard of him? He's a famous man. What about you, Herrera? Do you know Romero back in your country?"

"Sure, I know him. I thought . . . I thought that he . . . that this Bishop Romero was crazy, but now you're telling him not to worry, that he's got all his ducks in a row . . ."

"What are you telling me . . ?"

"That I'm not who I said I was. I'm Oscar Romero, the Archbishop of . . ."

"You're Monseñor Romero?"

"The one and only."

They sat down to talk again—sometimes serious, sometimes joking—and Monseñor explained why he had come in with another name. In the end, the doctor didn't want to accept any payment from him at all, and he gave him back his check.

"With all of the needs you have there! I can't take a penny from you."

"But work should be paid, and I've made you work hard!"

They argued, and finally they reached a compromise. Monseñor Romero gave the doctor the check again, and the doctor gave him another one, for an even greater amount, as a donation to the Church of San Salvador.

Romero told me about this "adventure," half enjoying the story and half doubtful still. Maybe he told me because I'd been his confessor a few years back.

(Francisco Oscoz)

San Salvador, September 29, 1979. Apolinario Serrano, better known as Polín, the legendary leader of the campesino organization, FECCAS, was shot to death today along with three other leaders of the Federation of Rural Workers on Kilometer 27 of the Panamerican Highway.

Polín was travelling with José López, Patricia Puertas and her husband Félix García. When they arrived at the infantry post in Opico, policemen from the checkpoint there opened fire on the vehicle. According to sources in the grassroots movement, the ambush was carefully planned to get rid of these well known leaders, and to do so with impunity.

HE'S CRYING IN HIS ROOM, his face turned toward the wall. He can't lie down. He can't erase him from his memory. He can't even pray.

They killed Polín early this morning. Now he'll never again see him arriving at the *hospitalito* waving his arms and telling those stories like only he could.

"Be careful, Apolinario," he had often told him. "They want to kill you."

"You too, Chespirito!" he would answer. "We're going to have to see who ends up making the big trip first!"

Lately, he'd taken to calling him that—Chespirito. Just like everyone in the Revolutionary Bloc did when they were talking about him in code. And Romero would smile, not understanding all the humor behind the nickname.

"I've already told you, Polín, I've never seen that show on television."

"Well, watch it, and you'll see yourself in that Chespirito. He's someone who always goofs up, but comes out ahead anyway!" And he'd laugh mischievously.

Now he'd never hear Polín's laugh again. Polín had taken the big trip first. They killed him early this morning. They set a trap for him, apparently, and Polín fell for it even though he was such a clever man. He was the most sought-after and the most politically daring leader there was, and in spite of that, he worked in the open—legally.

"I'll die if I have to go underground," Polín had confessed to him. "I'll die if they don't let me be where the people are."

They took him away from the people. And Monseñor Romero is crying for him. He covers his face, and remembers him the way he was when he was alive.

(Juan Bosco Palacios/Antonio Cardenal)

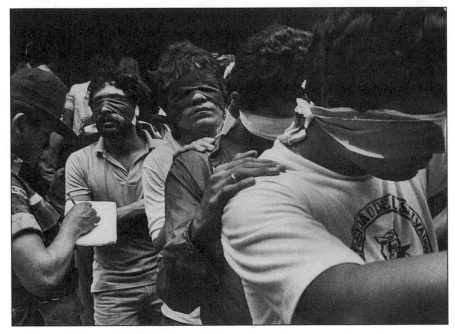

"Monseñor Romero seemed like a pair of enormous hands trying to hold El Salvador together when it was at the point of breaking into a million pieces."

JOIN THE JUNTA?

San Salvador, October 15, 1979. At 8:00 this morning, the Armed Forces of El Salvador staged a successful revolt against the government of General Carlos Humberto Romero. The majority of the army's units participated in the uprising, which ended without bloodshed. General Romero has gone into exile in Guatemala.

Members of a group called the "Young Officers" led the coup d'état. They announced that they will form a five-member junta made up of two military officers and three civilians. The junta will govern the country, making the structural reforms long neglected by the government deposed today.

In their address to the nation, the leaders of the coup recognized that Salvadorans have, for decades, suffered under governments that have employed violence and electoral fraud, and have not respected human rights. They also pointed to the urgent need to carry out an agrarian reform in the country.

According to many analysts, the triumph of the revolution in Nicaragua only three months ago seems to have been determinant in the events that occurred today in El Salvador. The United States Department of State has called the latest turn of events "encouraging."

PEOPLE SAY . . .
that all of the accredited Latin American and European diplomats in El Salvador are saying the same thing.

"Romero beat Romero! The bishop beat the general!"

They're saying that there were so many homilies and cries for change coming from one Romero and so many bullets and so much repression coming from the other, that the stalemate was finally broken.

"Monseñor did what no one else could do! He gave a catechism lesson to the military. His homilies alone turned them into 'revolutionaries!'"

"Well, just the young ones. You can't teach an old dog new tricks!"

The same words are on everyone's lips:

"The coup is the end of the story. And the story is about how Monseñor Romero overthrew General Romero . . ."

But many others know it's not the end of the story.

WITH CIVILIANS OR WITHOUT, with Mayorga or with Ungo,[1] the whole thing smelled like some kind of maneuver. For us, the October 15 coup was nothing more than a smooth move by the *gringos* to put the brakes on the real revolutionary changes happening all over the country. It was pure theater. It was to change a little something so that nothing would really change. The economic elite wasn't going to be touched, and neither was the military. A lot of us shared this analysis. But not Monseñor Romero.

He had been so afraid of an explosion of violence, and he was so happy that no one had been killed in the coup, that he supported it. And he knew a lot of good people that were involved in the whole thing, maybe because of this same fear of violence. I guess they just figured things had gone far enough . . .

A few days after the coup, we threw it in his face. We told him straight out that he was giving his blessing to the military.

---

[1] Román Mayorga and Guillermo Ungo, along with Mario Andino, were the three civilians who held positions on the first "revolutionary" junta along with two colonels in the Salvadoran Army, Adolfo Majano and Jaime Abdul Gutiérrez.

"I haven't given my blessing to anyone! Don't you manipulate what I've said!!"

"You haven't said that you give your blessing, but you did give a favorable review to the coup, and the government has used your words who knows how many times on the national radio station!! So what are people going to think? They're going to think that you're giving your blessing!"

"You guys are seminarians, but you're talking as if you were members of the Revolutionary Bloc!"

"And you're the bishop, but you're talking as if you were a participant in the coup!!"

Man, he scolded us up and down. And the *pupusas* we were eating became knots in our throats as they went down.

(Miguel Vázquez)

HE WAS THE KIND OF GUY WHO was always a team player. But when the young officers' coup happened, it was like he took a step back, and a lot of people in the communities got after him because of it.

On one of those first few days after the junta was installed, it was time for Monseñor Romero to do a series of intensive pastoral visits. He was supposed to go to three parishes. I decided to go with him on the rounds.

We were in San Martín early in the morning, and as soon as we got there, people started looking for opportunities to question him.

"Monseñor, why do you support them? Why are you backing this junta?"

"Because we have to trust the good people who are involved in this . . ."

"But what about the bad people? They're there too, and there are more of the bad ones than the good ones!"

The argument began, and at the end no one was satisfied—not him, not anybody.

On the second stop in San Bartolo, it was the same thing.

"Monseñor, why did you come out on the radio on the side of the government when you've always been on our side before?"

"We have to give an opportunity to the honest civilians who have become part of this project . . ."

"Honest? My uncle was honest, and he's in jail!" said one guy, laughing.

The rest of the folks were all saying the same thing, but they weren't laughing. Everyone was arguing on the other side. They weren't conforming to Monseñor's opinions either.

The third stop was in the Santa Lucía neighborhood. After Mass, Monseñor Romero gave time for questions and answers, and another round of arguments started up! Difficult ones, with people upset on both sides. By the time we headed back, he was angry and at his wits' end.

"You've gotten all of these people to come out against me!"

"Monseñor, how could you possibly believe that? The thing is that people have their own ideas and they want to clarify things. They want you to explain . . ."

"No, the thing is that you people only support me when I speak in favor of your ideas!"

"What do you mean 'you people?' Who are you talking about? Do you think this is a conspiracy?"

"Well if the shoe fits . . ."

But I decided to let the shoe drop right there. I wasn't going to fight with him, and certainly not on that day when we were both so exhausted.

(Francisco Calles)

THE YOUNG OFFICERS' COUP, the promised reform, the junta that called itself "revolutionary" . . . and still, nothing changed. They kept on killing us. That's where people's suspicions were really confirmed, because the killing continued just the same.

When the National Guard came around El Paraiso, that's what we could see—that the new government was just more of the same thing.

They were searching houses, trying to find people who had joined the popular organizations. And there were a lot of people in Zacamil who had.

"Hey, you subversives, the party's over."

That's what they were shouting, putting fear into the hearts of people, especially old women and children. Doors got kicked in, windows were broken, and all of the families' possessions were scattered around the streets from the searches they were doing . . .

Finally they grabbed five young guys who were part of the movement, and they took them out of their houses.

"Let's see if the bishop can save you now!"

They lined them up against the wall in the street.

"Don't kill me, please, please!" said one, who got scared when he saw them pointing their rifles at his chest.

"We're not going to kill just you, shithead. We're going to kill all of you!"

And kablam! They executed them right there in the street in plain view. In my view . . .

But after they finished them all off, we saw that those devils had also come to steal. They spread out all over the neighborhood, to every house—whether it had already been searched or not—and they started to take away everything of value.

"The party's over, you subversive sons of bitches!!"

They took out beds, stoves, sewing machines. The children cried when they saw how they were even taking their toys. They filled up several truckloads with what they'd stolen. That day there were a whole lot of families left without so much as a change of clothes. Truly. The soldiers stole everything. Their party wasn't over. Governing junta and all, the party just kept going!

(Elida Orantes)

THEY'RE STILL KILLING, and they're still stealing, and he's still supporting them? In Zacamil we were really angry with Monseñor Romero because of his sympathy for the junta, and we wanted to make him feel it. We in the community had always bought Orientación—and not just one or two copies, a big stack of them— because there were a lot of people who read Monseñor's messages every week, so we would always sell a lot. But when the coup happened, we stopped buying them for redistribution.

We also asked for a meeting with Monseñor so we could present our views.

"We want it to be a private meeting, and we want you to leave plenty of time for it, Monseñor."

He agreed. A group of us from the community went—some of the oldest members and also us young people. Father Rogelio went, too. Monseñor received us in the parlor of the hospitalito. We started the meeting and went at it.

"You're putting too much trust in those people!"

"And they're the same old military people as always. Look at all of them in the same position they've always been in. Everyone knows the crimes they've committed! They talked about purging people from the military, but who have they purged? No one!"

"You're going to see how the military people are controlling the civilians friends of yours in the government. You'll see, Monseñor . . ."

"You can't let yourself be deceived, Monseñor, and you can't go on deceiving the people!"

He listened to us patiently for a while, but then he got angry and threw all the same tired old arguments in our faces.

"You are all so radical. You're extremist about everything! But you can't build anything with radicalism! Give just a little benefit of the doubt to people who don't think like you do. I'm calling you to moderation . . ."

"And we're calling *you* to listen to those who don't think like *you* do!"

He kept getting angrier.

"You don't understand the need to give things a little time . . . And you're not willing to respect authorities unless they take the exact same position that you do!"

A nun came in and rescued us.

"Wouldn't you like a little coffee?"

We'd been sitting and arguing for so long that we were a little dazed. Standing up, going out of the room and having a little coffee together calmed the tension. We started to talk to Monseñor Romero about other things happening in the community, even though they were sad things. Osmín, one of the catechists, had disappeared and was still missing. We talked to him about Osmín, and about how upset his family was . .

"And did you know, Monseñor, that Marbel was killed?"

"Marbel . . .?"

He knew her. She was 14 years old.

"They killed Elsa, too."

"Who was Elsa? I don't remember . . ."

"That young girl with such pretty long hair who brought up tortillas and coffee as part of the offering in the last Mass that you did there . . . Don't you remember?"

"Sure, I do. Why did they kill her? She was just a little girl?"

After the coffee break, we went back to the parlor and continued our argument. That's when we told him that we'd stopped selling *Orientación* in our community. He kept insisting that we should give the civilians in the junta a little more time . . .

"Samayoa is there. Zamora, Mayorga, Ungo and Enrique Álvarez Cordova are all there . . . [2] They have always defended the people, and they can play an important role where they are. Be patient."

When we said good-bye, he was calmer.

"I want to thank you for coming to tell me what you think. Come back whenever you want, and I promise I'll listen to you."

As I recall, that was the time when the communities of San Salvador had the most conflict with him.

(*Carmen Elena Hernández*)

DURING THE TIME OF THE JUNTA, I argued with him, too. Who didn't? But ours were friendly arguments.

"What do you think about it?" Monseñor was the one who asked me.

"I don't think this junta is the way out of our troubles."

"Why don't you think so?"

---

[2] All civilians. Members of the government of first revolutionary junta. Salvador Samayoa was Minister of Education, Rubén Zamora was Minister of the Presidency and Roman Mayorga and Guillermo Ungo were members of the junta itself. Enrique Álvarez Córdova was Minister of Agriculture during the first junta.

"Monseñor, the army is still the same. The military men are still the same, and they're the ones exercising real power over the civilians. This country needs to be demilitarized, and the bad officers need to be purged from the military. None of this has happened, and I don't see any reason to believe that it will."

"But we have to have hope. We can't put out the fire while the embers are still glowing. We have to fan these flames of peaceful solutions in order to avoid a war . . ."

"Monseñor, whether we like it or not, the stage is already set for a war to break out. Neither the coup nor the junta is going to be able to stop it."

"But we have to try everything to avoid it . . ."

That was what tormented him: the possibility of war. During those months, Monseñor Romero seemed like a pair of enormous hands trying to hold El Salvador together when it was at the point of breaking into a million pieces.

(César Jerez)

San Salvador, October 29, 1979. Some 70 people were killed and more than 100 were injured when security forces used violence to crack down on a demonstration of the People's Leagues of February 28 (LP-28), a revolutionary organization that has not given its support to the civilian-military junta that has been governing the country since the October 15 coup.

RIGHT AFTER THE MASSACRE ON OCTOBER 29, people picked up the bodies of the dead as fast as they could and took them into El Rosario Church. Someone started a collection to pay for coffins and, in the meantime, the corpses were laid out as well as they could be on straw mats on the floor. Marianela García Villas, from the Human Rights Commission, put in some money for the coffins too. But soon the situation got worse: about 600 people were occupying the church. It was all closed up, and the bodies were decomposing . . .

They wanted to have the burial the next day and accompany it with another demonstration, but the National Guard surrounded the church that night so that people couldn't leave. And they didn't just surround the church, they also sent in one of their men, dressed in civilian clothes and armed. Pichinte, Mincho, Odilón and Benito were all in the church.[3] They discovered the guy right away and took him hostage.

Captain Denis Morán, an infamous assassin and death-squad leader, was in charge of the siege of the church. When he realized that one of his men was being held by the LP-28, he decided to go in and rescue him at any cost.

So the National Guard was ready to go in, and the people occupying the church—some of whom were also armed—were ready to fire on them if they tried. Marianela and others from the Commission were the first to arrive and try to negotiate, but the National Guard paid no attention to them. They were already set to go into the church through the atrium.

"We'll get those subversives out of there if it's the last thing we do!"

The air was heavy with the expectation of another massacre. That's when they called Monseñor Romero to mediate.

(Ana Guadalupe Martínez)

"I NEED YOU TO COME OVER HERE! I've been asked to participate in a very delicate mission."

It was 8:00 at night when Monseñor called me at the seminary. We got to El Rosario Church shortly afterwards. The place was crawling with *guardias*. They'd already decided to take the church by assault, and if

---

[3]Pichinte refers to Leoncío Pichinte who was a labor leader. Odilón is Odilón Novoa, the head of the Popular Leagues of February 28 (LP-28). It is unclear who Mincho and Benito are except to say that all four of these were probably leaders in the LP-28, the group that organized this particular church takeover.

they had to kill everyone to do it, they would. If they had to shoot the church to pieces, well, they'd do that too.

Monseñor Romero approached Morán, the one that was leading the operation.

"You!" the man screamed at him. "It's your fault all this is happening! It's because of all your idiotic sermons! So you can just step aside. You don't know shit about what's happening here!"

I'd never seen them so aggressive.

"You leave Monseñor alone!" Marianela García screamed from the place where the *guardias* had her cornered.

"I ought to just blow this bitch away right now!" said one of them, pointing his rifle at her.

They were only interested in rescuing the guardsman who they themselves had sent in as an infiltrator. I stayed close to Monseñor. Four men pointed their rifles straight at him.

"If those subversives do anything to our man, we'll kill the bishop right here!"

"You can stop talking to me like that right now, and try to be reasonable!"

Monseñor was in their faces, and I was pulling on his arm, like a child trying to keep his father from getting into a fistfight. "He's capable of slapping the guy in the face," I thought, "and then all hell will break loose."

"He just wants to talk to you," I said to the *guardias*. "Why don't you let him talk?"

"And who the hell are you? You keep it up, and you're a dead man."

"He's a seminarian. Don't touch him." Monseñor defended me.

"Seminarian, my foot! He's a communist and a damned idiot!"

They didn't care who they were talking to. They just wanted to do away with us all. "They'd kill us in a minute and throw our bodies in the dump," I thought.

Monseñor Romero insisted he wanted to go inside the church, find the hostage and turn him over to Morán, but they wouldn't hear of it. They had called for tanks, which were already arriving. They were ready for action. A well-known torturer they called Baby Face appeared next to Monseñor with a smirk on his face.

"You defend your subversive friends, don't you? Well, we're defending our own people. Isn't that the way it should be *padre* . . ?"

While the guardsmen started to take their positions and make some phone calls, we decided to fall back and think a little more calmly. Monseñor went down a corridor of the convent next to the church, and I followed him. I thought we were going to talk strategy, but no. He took out his rosary and started to walk up and down the hall praying. He didn't say anything to me. I watched him, and followed the count of his prayers as he said them . . . The First Mystery . . . When he got to the second, he said to me:

"What do you think we should do if they start to fire at us?"

"Well, I guess our only option is to drop to the floor if we have enough time."

The Second Mystery, the Third Mystery . . . When he was at his last Ave María, he came back and asked me:

"Why did you say we should drop to the floor?"

"So they don't hit you. They're not going to be firing at your feet. They're going to be shooting to kill."

"Right, right. Look, this is a difficult hour, and I'm more worried about you than me, because you didn't know you were getting into this. Who knows if we'll get out alive . . . And I don't know what they'll say in the papers if we're both found dead tomorrow morning . . ."

He was scared. This was the worst situation he'd ever been in. He kept praying. The Fourth mystery . . . As he was finishing the rosary, he said:

"Look, I think if we hide behind this little wall here, maybe we can avoid the bullets . . . What do you think?"

"Who knows . . ."

"Or, look at that place over there . . . Would that be better?"

"Monseñor, are you praying or planning a defense strategy?"

"Both. I'm doing both."

He was really afraid and it showed. He was praying, trembling and sweating . . . but when we went out onto the street again, he looked calmer. That's when he really started to mediate. He was able to get the National Guard to pull back by the fence and let him into the church to look for the hostage. When the people inside opened the doors for us, the stench of the corpses was unbearable.

"Monseñor," Pichinte begged him, "you're our only hope. We'll turn over the hostage to you, but don't leave us because if you do, we'll all be killed."

We went out to the street again. The siege was continuing. Finally we put together a delegation of three guardsmen and Monseñor Romero, to go inside the church again.

First, they wanted to check all the corpses to see if there were any guardsmen among them. They were saying that the guerrillas had tortured and killed two people. It was quite a picture—those guys poking through the already decomposing bodies. They looked them over one by one and saw that none of them was from the National Guard. They were all members of the LP-28. By the early hours of the morning the hostage had been freed and the siege had been called off. But we had no choice but to bury the 21 dead inside the church. It was still too dangerous to go out with them into the streets.

(Juan Bosco Palacios)

WHEN HE FINISHED HIS SECOND MASS after the coup, Monseñor Romero decided to see what we seminarians had to say. We had a meeting with him.

"What do you think about the junta?"

We knew that he was going to write us off if we spoke frankly, but we did anyway.

"All right. First, as far as what we think of you: we think you're wrong. In terms of the junta: we think it's a farce. Mayorga's not a farce. Ungo isn't. The guys from the UCA aren't. But they're being used by the leaders of the farce. Just look how they're still killing people!"

Monseñor wasn't just angry. He was furious. He refused to continue the meeting, and he threw us out right then and there.

Three days later he sent an invitation to eat *pupusas* to the six of us who were the closest to him. The invitation was to a *pupusa* restaurant in Los Planes. We showed up at 5:00 PM with long faces. We started eating, and at 6:30 he was still trying to get us to talk. He was asking how things were going with such-and-such a professor, how we liked such-and-such a class . . . He couldn't figure out how to bring up the issue, and we didn't feel like helping him. Finally, he gave up and just got to the point:

"I don't understand why you can't agree to give the junta a little time, and I want you to explain all of your reasons to me. I want to get to the bottom of this today!"

"Why don't you tell us first your reasons for being so supportive of the junta?"

"I didn't bring you here to make any confessions to you!"

He was already angry. So we started. The first reason we gave him was that the repression was continuing, and that the same military men were still in the same positions of power. Then we talked about the fact that there were *gringo* fingerprints all over this thing and that it was really suspicious how much the United States was supporting the junta.

"The thing that concerns us most is that *you've* gotten on board!"

At about 8:00 PM, after all kinds of analysis . . .

"Let's go," he decided. "We can continue our talk at the *hospitalito*." He was totally silent on the way back, and when we got there he said:

"Sister Teresa, bring these boys some coffee . . . I'm not offering a stronger drink this evening. It's not the right time for that."

We were there for another couple of hours debating with him. We made our points, and he came back with his counterpoints. He had a response for every one of our arguments! Late into the evening, when we were ready to go, we were still right where we started. No one was convincing anyone.

"Do you think we were too tough on him?" Miguel asked me on our way back to the seminary.

"And what if we were? It's very clear what's happening here. He's being duped, and it's only right for us to set him straight!"

"But he's not being set straight! He doesn't want to be!"

We were left feeling anxious and upset. But the next day, he called for three of us to go see him. We were the "worst" ones, "the socialist ones," as Goyo Rosa, our teacher at the seminary, called us.

"Are you really convinced of everything you said to me yesterday?"

"Yes, Monseñor, we are."

"You're completely convinced and sure?"

"Yes, sir."

He stood up again, thought for a while and sat back down.

"Truly?"

"Truly, Monseñor."

He didn't say anything else. He just asked us with that kind of insistence three times. Our surprise came the following Sunday. In his homily, he criticized the junta strongly for the first time, and he spoke forcefully about the urgent need to purge certain officers from the ranks of the army! After Mass we asked him,

"Monseñor, what happened . . ?"

"There are a lot of people out there who agree with you. They're very disillusioned," he looked away with teary eyes, "and there's too much repression, too much bloodshed."

(Juan Bosco Palacios)

IT WAS A SATURDAY NIGHT in the hospitalito after the 1979 coup. Some of us in the FPL had asked him for an appointment. We wanted to exchange ideas with him because Monseñor Romero had his finger on the pulse of all of the country's problems. On that first visit, Comandante Milton and I went to see him. It was clear he didn't trust us. We didn't trust him either or the fact that the hospitalito was in the isolated location that it was. We took our weapons along in our bags.

"Have a seat. How are you . . ?"

"Fine, and you?"

"I'm fine, and you . . ?

All three of us were nervous. After we exchanged greetings, he was the one that got to the point.

"I was just in the Chalate area, and I have to lodge a complaint with you. Everyone knows that a few days ago you guys—that is people from the FPL—attacked and killed two National Guardsmen with machetes . . ."

"Do you want us to tell you what happened?"

"I do, and it's your responsibility to tell me."

The feeling was tense. I was sweating a little.

"Look, Monseñor, what happened was that those *guardias* came to Las Vueltas at night and took two *campesinos* from their homes. They were going to murder them! But our people—the *campesinos* from FECCAS— found out, and they organized to stop them. In the end, they had to kill them. They killed the *guardias* before the *guardias* could kill them. What do you think about that?"

"I think it's terrible, and I want you to know that I don't approve of using violent means."

"Sometimes there's no alternative, Monseñor. This is the violence of a people who are rising up!"

"No, this is terrorism."

"No, Monseñor, it's legitimate self defense. Isn't it true that Church doctrine allows for the use of violence in situations of self defense?"

"That's true, but the defense has to be proportionate to the offense. If I can defend myself with a punch, it's not legitimate for me to put a bullet into someone."

He was a man of doctrine. He liked to argue, but his thing wasn't really criticism or condemnation. He really just wanted to understand things.

"We're not terrorists, Monseñor, and the FPL is not a terrorist organization. There are a lot of Christians among us, and our *campesino* support base is completely Christian."

He looked at us, still mistrustful.

"You two don't look like *campesinos* to me . . ."

"No. We're university students. But we both come from a Christian back-ground. We had Mass and daily communion at Catholic schools."

Something relaxed in his face and hands, and his mistrust started to turn into curiosity.

"And if there's anything we're grateful for, it's the fact that our Christian formation made us sensitive to issues of injustice. It gave us the desire to struggle for everyone to be equal."

"We haven't come here full of some exotic ideas of international com-munism, Monseñor. We're from the same family!"

He smiled. We smiled. We started to name some of our mutual friends and acquaintances, and after this brief search for the common ground in our past, we felt the remaining tensions fading.

"When I heard that you were guerrillas, I was expecting to see another kind of person. Not such youngsters . . ."

"We're not that young, Monseñor! Maybe this underground life of ours just keeps us looking good . . ."

The conversation took on another tone. He stopped looking at the floor so much, and we started drinking our coffee. Since we knew he'd met recently with some of the women in our organization, we teased him about it.

"Do you mean to tell me that those pretty girls are guerrillas too?"

"They sure are, Monseñor!"

He didn't believe it. He also had a hard time believing that I, being a revolutionary, had gotten married in the Church. You could tell he was intrigued by our lives.

"And you have to be in hiding all the time? Separated from your fami-lies?"

That was hard for him to understand, so we talked about it. "We left our private lives behind to defend what belongs to everyone. We've renounced what we had for ourselves for the benefit of our people as a whole," I told him at one point.

And he could understand that, because he'd done the same thing by becoming a priest. That was the angle from which he understood us the best, and I think he even appreciated it.

We also talked that day about the kidnappings. We'd pulled off several of them, and he'd always been very critical of our using that method.

"Monseñor, the truth is that neither the Soviet Union or international communism is supporting us. You can see that our struggle is just. But where are we going to get money to finance it? By kidnapping rich people! They're the only source of funding we have on hand!"

Our conversation went on for a long time, and we talked about a lot of things. The two of us drank a lot of coffee, but Monseñor hardly touched his. He didn't need coffee to keep him going.

"Well," he said as we were leaving, "they told me you brought some documents . . ." And he pointed to our bags.

"I'd really like to see them."

He kept pointing to the damn bags. God, how embarrassing! How could we open them up and show him we'd come in with a couple of pistols?

"Well, Monseñor, the thing is that . . ."

"No need to hurry. I can be patient, but I *am* interested to see what you've brought."

And he kept looking at our bags.

"Well, go figure, Monseñor . . . We've forgotten to bring the papers! We left them all behind!"

"So what are the bags for?"

He asked us with a smile that Milton and I didn't know how to interpret.

(Atilio Montalvo)

WE MET WITH HIM practically every week. After the first time, we always went without bags and without weapons. We talked to him about a lot of things—everything, practically! Now after so many years, and not having talked about it very much with anyone, I really have to search my memory to come up with some of the things that were said.

I remember that someone from the United States government visited El Salvador during those months. We realized that the *gringo* wanted to manipulate Monseñor Romero to give his blessing to the pact between the politicians and the Armed Forces . . .

"You're a Salvadoran, Monseñor," we said to him, "and no matter what the United States says, we have to be patriotic."

"That's the way it is," he told us. "The interests of the Salvadoran people always come first. I'm going to tell this man about what I've seen on my visits to the countryside and the way the Armed Forces repress the people. I'll tell him that I decide my course of action based on what I see and based on what helps or hurts the Salvadoran people."

We had talked about the army on several occasions. One day he asked us a kind of naive question:

"So your idea is to kill off the entire army?"

"Not at all, Monseñor! We all know there are patriotic and democratic sectors inside the army. We just need to isolate the fascist High Command. We're not interested in killing them. We want to isolate them—purge them from the army!"

He calmed down. We talked to him about the elections, about the Constitution, about the *campesino* organizations, even about Marxism. He had his own criteria, and you could tell that he was in good communication with people, especially the poor.

He did always tug on our sleeve about the lack of unity among the revolutionary organizations:

"Don't you always say that you're all peas from the same pod? Grains of corn from the same ear? But you can't get your act together enough to make a *tortilla* out of that corn! If you were all united, you'd have more strength. I don't understand why some of you pull one way and others another if you all have the same goal. You don't even give each other credit for the things you do! I don't understand it."

We became quite fond of each other, and each time we said good-bye, it became the custom for him to give us a blessing.

"I hope I'll see you again. Be careful, and don't let anything happen to you, all right, boys?"

And he would make the sign of a cross in the air to tell us good-bye.

(Atilio Montalvo)

"IN THE MAGNIFICAT WHEN MARY SINGS about God lifting up the humble and the poor, the political implications resound. She says, 'God has filled the hungry with good things, and the rich, He has sent empty-handed away.' Mary also says a few things that today could be considered downright seditious. 'Throw the mighty from their thrones' when they are a disturbance to the people's well-being! This is the political dimension of our faith. Mary lived it, and Jesus lived it. Jesus was a real patriot in a nation of people who lived under foreign domination. Doubtless, it was his dream that his people would be free!"

(Homily, February 17, 1980)

"COME ON! THE HOMILY'S STARTING!"

I was in the underground as the militia chief of the Paracentral Front. Every Sunday in the FPL collective units where I was placed, we listened to Monseñor Romero's homilies together. It was part of our political education. Not that it was mandatory to listen, but none of us wanted to miss it.

I still remember how all of us would hang on every word the "old man" said. Sometimes we even applauded, hidden there inside the four walls of our safe house, being careful not to make too much noise. When the homily was over, we would have a big discussion about it. Oh, the campesinos among us had tremendous respect for him!

In 1979, the FPL had established ongoing contact with Monseñor Romero, and there were some colleagues of ours that would go and talk about different issues with him. Those were top secret meetings, and not more than 15 of our top leaders knew what was really being said.

When I was elected to the Central Committee, I became one of those who knew. Comandante Milton Méndez came to give us periodic reports about what had been discussed with Monseñor Romero. I don't remember much about those reports now. So many things have happened that the memory gets a little blurred . . . But there is one thing I'll never forget.

"We were talking with Monseñor about the possibility of a war," Milton told us. "We told him that the way things were going, there was no avoiding it . . ."

There hadn't been many big military confrontations yet in El Salvador. It was mostly the struggle of the Masses. But we did, at that time, have the strategic understanding that we were in a process leading to war. It was in its early stages, but it was in progress. Back then, no one knew how much military force we had, or how many armed units we had or anything. That information was all super-top secret.

"We explained to Monseñor that we were already organizing the people's army, because sooner or later we were headed for an armed confrontation, not because we wanted it, but because there was no other way out," Milton said.

We were also counting on a popular uprising as part of this war that was on the horizon. Milton talked about that with Monseñor Romero who listened to all of the analysis with great attention, and came to his conclusions.

"Look," Monseñor said to Milton, "when the uprising happens, I don't want to be separate from or far away from the people. And I *don't* want to be on the other side . . . When the hour comes, I want to be on the side of the people. Of course, I would never take up a weapon. I wouldn't be of any use in that arena. But I can attend to the wounded and the dying, and I can gather up the dead bodies. I can help with that. Right?"

We were dumbstruck.

"So what do you think about how far the 'old man' has come?" Milton asked the 15 of us.

And all 15 of us said:

"Will you look at old 'Chespirito!' The man is something else!"

(Antonio Cardenal)

ONE AFTERNOON, SOME OF US SEMINARIANS went to his house at the *hospitalito* to talk with him.

"What's up, Monseñor? We were just passing by, and decided to come in and see you!"

"Well, at this very moment, I'm waiting for a friend to visit!"

We looked around. A "friend," huh? We thought some well-known political figure was going to drop by at any minute, and we'd get to meet someone important . . .

"A new friend, Monseñor?" we pried.

"A real friend. He always comes by to ask me for advice."

"Ah hah! A real bigwig," we deduced quietly.

"But I'm worried that he's not here yet. These days you just never know."

"Are you going to come by the seminary today, Monseñor?"

"No, I can't after all. My conversations with this friend tend to be long, and I'm not going to have time."

"It's Mayorga or Ungo or one of the other big fish," we whispered among ourselves.

"And does he come to visit you often, Monseñor?"

"Well, you know, when he can. But he always lets me know."

There we were, all ready to see this famous person. We stayed around chatting just to kill time. While we were waiting, the watchman from the *hospitalito* showed up. He was an old man, obviously sick with a cold, and with a towel rolled up around his neck.

"What's the matter, Don Tomás? Are you sick?" Monseñor asked him.

The old man sneezed, pulled up a chair, sat down and made himself comfortable.

"I heard your last homily, Monseñor, and it seemed to me to be right on target. The news on the radio is really different, you know . . ."

"Well, when the so-called friend arrives, this interfering old man is going to slow things up," we thought.

"Tell me about the news you heard, Don Tomás," Monseñor asked him, "I've been waiting for you so we could talk about this . . ."

Could it be? We looked at him. By the look on Monseñor's face we could tell that this Don Tomás was none other than the friend he was so looking forward to seeing. We looked at each other, and we left. On the way back to the seminary, we talked about it.

"Monseñor always one ups us," one guy said.

"Yeah, and even when he doesn't one up us, he's never a step behind!"
I responded.

(Juan José Ramírez)

WHEN MY BOOK, *CLANDESTINE PRISONS,* had just recently come
back from the printers and been presented to the public, Odilón Novoa
took it to Monseñor Romero as a gift. About a month later I was able to
get an appointment with him. Monseñor Romero could have been very
politically compromised by agreeing to see me, but he did.

"I'd very much like to meet her," he told Odilón.

And he received me at the archdiocesan office itself in spite of the fact
that the army was watching the building carefully, and in spite of the fact
that I was considered a "fugitive from justice." Odilón and Pichinte went
with me.

"Monseñor," I said, just to lead off with something, "have you read my
book?"

"Of course! I read it all in one sitting! I was very interested in it."

"In that case, Monseñor, I'd like to give you an even more direct testimony about what the security forces are capable of doing to people
who don't think like they do."

He changed his expression and looked down at the floor. I looked at
him, concerned.

"No, don't do it, don't do it . . ."

He looked at me, and I could see he was nervous.

"Dear child, you've already suffered enough in that hell. Why should
you tell me about it? Talking about it will just be like reliving it. You
shouldn't have to go through it again . . ."

He got teary-eyed, and so did I.

"I already read your book, and I know that everything you say there is true. I believe it all. I know you haven't exaggerated, and I know they're capable of all of that and more . . ."

I didn't bring it up again. There were a thousand other things to talk about. He was the one to bring up the issue that was troubling us so much in those months.

"After all this time, what do you really think about the junta?" he asked me with great interest.

"Monseñor, we know you've supported them. What we don't know is if you're still supporting them. But if you're asking for our opinion, we don't believe in this 'new' government at all."

"Why not? Explain yourself to me."

"The main reason is that they made this change without the participation of the people who have been organizing for a long time . . ."

"Maybe they didn't have enough time to call on the people to support the project, and the idea was to bring them in later . . ."

"But later was already too late, Monseñor. If the organizations aren't involved from the very beginning, it can't work. Not including them made room for the same assassins as always to control the project. Don't you see that that's what they've done?"

"But the intention was a good one. The people I know who are still participating in the junta want to stop the repression . . ."

"But they haven't stopped anything! Every day more people are killed, and they don't care whether they kill ten, a hundred or a thousand."

"It's true that things haven't turned out as planned . . ."

"The thing is, Monseñor, that the people who planned this weren't trying to stop the abuses. They were trying to stop a process of profound change that they saw coming and that they were afraid of. The coup was to stop the people, not to stop the repression."

"But, don't you at least agree that the initial intention was a good one?"

"No. We didn't believe it then, and we believe it even less now. Look at the massacres in the countryside. Look at what happened at El Rosario. You saw them in action there . . ."

He looked down at the floor a lot and held his hands together in front as if trying to listen to me better that way.

"So you're not going to give this junta any breathing space at all?"

"We didn't even on the first day, so why should we give it to them now, when they're completely out of oxygen? The way they are now, they've got nowhere to go. Not a single one of the civilians has any control over what's happening . . ."

"Is that your final position?"

"It is. What about you? Do you still believe in the junta?"

He didn't answer me.

We also talked about the army operations in rural areas like Morazán, La Unión and the northern part of San Miguel. The information we brought him about the massacres that the "new" government was committing in the countryside made a big impression on him. In our entire history, the repression had never been worse.

When it was time to go, he gave me a warm hug.

"Take care of yourself, my child, and don't be seen on the streets. They might capture you again, and now that you've written your book, they won't let you out alive. You can't go through that hell again . . ."

Odilón continued to be our intermediary with Monseñor, and through him we sent Monseñor our reflections on how things were going. Less than a month later, all of the civilians he trusted so much resigned from the governing junta. This clearly confirmed Monseñor's interpretation, and contradicted our black and white analysis. There *had* been people with good intentions behind that effort, and when they couldn't go on anymore, they had the courage to step down.

"In his own way, the 'old man' was right," we said. "The whole coup and junta thing wasn't just a movie about good guys and bad guys."

(Ana Guadalupe Martínez)

"THE VERY DEFINITION OF THE RIGHT is social injustice, and it is never just to align yourself with the right. As for the left, I don't call them leftist forces. I call them the forces of the people. Their violence is likely to be the result of the rage that people feel from having confronted so much social injustice. The so-called 'left' is the people. It's the organization of the people and their demands . . . The people's processes are very creative. We can't say that there is a formula for moving from capitalism to socialism. If you want to call it socialism, well, it's just a name. What we're looking for is social justice, a kinder society, a sharing of resources. That's what people are looking for."

(Interview with Diario de Caracas *[Venezuela],*
March 19, 1980)

"I feel like the Lord on Palm Sunday in Jerusalem."

ON THE EDGE

THAT SPRING WENT BY FAST. The coup, the junta, the young offic-ers promising changes, the hopes . . . But it all came to nothing. Power stayed in the hands of the older officers and the same economic elite as always.

One day during that time, Colonel Majano and Colonel García went to visit Monseñor Romero in the *hospitalito*.

"We need you to express your support for us more clearly," Majano told him.

"For *us*," García repeated.

Monseñor had grown weary of it all, and he'd already gone out on a limb to express support for the civilians in the junta and cabinet, the people whom he did have a lot of faith in.

"The government is going through a crisis, and a word or two from you could help a lot . . ."

After listening to the two military men for a while with his eyes downcast, Romero looked straight at them.

"I understand everything you're telling me and what you want me to do. That's fine, but there's something about this government that I don't like."

"What's that, Monseñor?" Majano asked anxiously.

"That an officer as repressive as Colonel José Guillermo García could have been named Minister of Defense from the beginning and that he's still in that post now after two months."

"Hey!" said the offended party, "I'm Colonel García!"

"I know, and that's exactly why I'm saying it, because I like to be up front about the things I say."

Romero kept looking at him but didn't say anything else. The two officers didn't say anything else either. They just marched out of the *hospitalito* in military step.

(Armando Oliva)

San Salvador, December 10, 1979. The Minister of Agriculture, Enrique Álvarez Córdova, announced the 43ʳᵈ decree of the governing junta today, establishing an agrarian reform to be implemented throughout the country. According to statistics presented by Álvarez Córdoba, less than 2,000 families possess 40% of all land in the country. These families represent 0.7% of all land owners. The land they possess, which is also the best quality land in the country, will be the properties targeted for redistribution under the agrarian reform that is to take effect soon.

MONSEÑOR ROMERO GOT ENTHUSED about the agrarian reform. He was already distancing himself from the junta, but that decree was good news to him.

"It's just an announcement, Monseñor," I told him, peeved about the whole thing. "Let's reserve our judgement. A bird in the hand is worth two in the bush."

"But the Minister of Agriculture is a very honest man . . ."

"He is, but he's not in charge. Only the rich and the military are in charge here. And if there's land to be lost, you can believe they're not going to relinquish any control!"

"Why are you so mistrustful of everything?"

"You're older than I am. You should be more mistrustful, especially with this government! They talk about reforms and beat people over the head at the same time . . . Look how much repression there is in all of the places the agrarian reform is supposed to happen . . ."

He didn't pay much attention to me. He had his doubts, too, but he wanted to look at things with hope. That was his style.

"I like what they said, that the land is going to be for the people who work it, not for people who inherit it . . ."

"They'll say anything, Monseñor!"

"You're such an extremist!"

So we argued. One day he went to Concepción Quetzaltepeque and a bunch of *campesinos* got together for the Mass. It was a big crowd! He took advantage of it to find out what they thought about the agrarian reform.

"It seems to me that it's a law that could benefit you," he started.

"They can say anything on paper, Monseñor," one *campesino* said. "But we can't just trust fancy words or things written on some paper."

"But you have to give the government some benefit of the doubt . . ."

"What about the government? Shouldn't they give *us* some benefit of the doubt, too? All we have to do is open our mouths and lodge some very orderly complaint about all of these reforms they're pushing, and what do they do? They send the National Guard to evict us, shoot at us and kill us! Why should we believe in their reforms, when they're the ones repressing us?"

They told him about the latest atrocities of the army. A massacre of more than 20 people in Joya de Cerén, in Opico. They'd even killed little children there. There were other *campesinos* detained near Chalate and in other places.

"They kill more people every day! The only reform we would believe would be a reform in their hearts, an end to the killing."

"Maybe they're going to distribute land to bury us on!" said a guy named Martín, his broad smile revealing his two remaining teeth.

"But at least there's a law now," Monseñor continued. "Now, we just have to see if they're going to follow through with it."

"A law? Do you really believe in their laws?"

Monseñor looked at them. Did he believe? He *wanted* to believe.

"Monseñor," said one short man with eyes as black as vulture's wings, "don't believe in these laws. Don't believe them! We know it's the same as always. Their laws are like a snake. They only bite people who are barefoot."

Two Sundays later, when more people had died from the repression, and the law was still only on paper, Monseñor mentioned the agrarian reform in his homily. He compared it to a snake.

(Juan Bosco Palacios)

San Salvador, December 30, 1979. Today a majority of the civilian members of the governing junta, members of the cabinet and other high officials made public a letter written to the Permanent Council of the Armed Forces. In it, they expressed their intention to resign if there was no end to the growing wave of repression characterizing this government which came to power by military coup last October 15. Several of the those who signed the letter, which is virtually an ultimatum, called on Archbishop Romero to mediate this conflict as a last measure to hold the government together.

THE FIREWORKS THAT WENT OFF on New Year's Day in 1980 were noisy in San Salvador. Very noisy. And the events occurring in the nation produced a tension greater than the noise.

"Pray for everything to come out all right," Monseñor Romero told the sisters at the *hospitalito* when he left after breakfast. "And just in case your prayers aren't enough, have all the patients pray, too!"

He headed toward the archdiocesan office, praying himself. There was a lot at stake in that January 2 meeting between the civilian and military members of the government, and he knew it. His hands were sweating as he got near the seminary building.

All of the civilians arrived punctually at the agreed time of 9:30 AM.

"Don't allow yourselves to be influenced by the pressures of the moment. Listen to your own consciences, and decide accordingly."

That was the advice that Monseñor Romero was giving to all the civilians as he greeted them. A little later, they went up to the library. Much later, the military officials arrived.

"We've come to talk with you. Only you, the bishop. Not to them!" a man in uniform protested to Monseñor.

"But that wasn't the agreement. As bishop, I promised to mediate a dialogue that you were going to have with the civilians. They're waiting for you upstairs."

They started to argue and kept at it for a while, until finally the military men also went up to the library where the civilians were waiting. Monseñor Romero went with them.

"As a Salvadoran, I ask you in the name of the Church and of the people to find a solution," he begged them as the meeting began. His hands were sweating from nervousness.

The door was closed and the debate began, turning the room into a cauldron of controversy. By the time they left the room at three in the afternoon to eat lunch, the radio was already broadcasting a communique from the Permanent Council of the Armed Forces accusing the civilians of wanting to work outside the Constitution. It was a bucket of cold water that paralyzed the half-finished dialogue.

"What good was all of this? It was pure theater! Here we are wagging our tongues, and those guys had this planned all along!" one of the ministers was practically crying.

A few minutes later, it all fell apart. One by one, all the civilians from that government, which at one time had called itself revolutionary, turned in their resignations.

(Based on Monseñor Romero's Diary,
January 2, 1980)

"WE HAVE TO FIND A WAY OUT."

That's what Monseñor kept saying to me during the last days of my participation as Minister of the Presidency in that government.

I remember I went up to him during a break we had in that emergency meeting in the seminary library and said: "There's no way out, Monseñor."

"Try to find one. If we can't, things are going to get really ugly and the people are going to suffer. Try to find a solution. Try to find something."

Something to avoid war. That's what he was committed to from the bottom of his heart. We spent all afternoon there, hour after hour, in spite of the army radio communique. We tried to find a solution, but . . . Later on that night, I told him: "Monseñor, we can't keep working with this government. It's become a problem of conscience for us."

"If that's the way it is, I respect that. And if you decide to leave the government, you'll have my support."

We left for reasons of conscience, and he supported us. And those without consciences made agreements with the military. The Christian Democratic Party, for instance, joined in with their government. Who knows how much money they got for it.

(Rubén Zamora)

I BEGAN TO WORK WITH THE GOVERNMENT during the second junta along with other colleagues from the Christian Democratic

Party. We were convinced that it was the only way to save the country.

"You decided to join the junta. Now fight from within!"

That's what Monseñor Romero told me every time I went to see him, full of my own doubts.

"Monseñor," I told him, "I give orders and the military men just won't do what I ask. Sometimes I feel like rebelling, too!"

"As long as you're inside, you've got to fight from within."

He always came back at me with the same thing. Still there was something about it that didn't set right with me. He'd give me encouraging words on a Friday, and on Sunday it would be completely the opposite! He used his homily to lash out at us, and he criticized the Christian Democrats really hard! To hear him tell it, everything was our fault. He never recognized the efforts we were making. It was all criticism, and public criticism at that!

How do I interpret this reaction of his? I think that Monseñor Romero was easily influenced by the masses. He was a leader, but the left manipulated him. He had a really romantic conception of social justice, and he was a bit naive when it came to politics. Everything he did was influenced by the idealism of the left and the radicalism of the right, which was killing off his priests and the people in his communities.

I should say that when those of us from the Christian Democratic Party got into this project, we were very clear. I knew there were going to be some deaths. The most optimistic vision was that there would be 20,000. The most realistic vision was that it would be 60,000 to 70,000. And the bloodiest forecast, which we were trying to avoid, was that there would be 200,000 or 300,000 deaths. Monseñor Romero wasn't a politician, and he couldn't accept those kinds of calculations. He didn't want even one person to die! You see? He was a pure idealist! Rubén Zamora and company, they were all the same. They were all purists.

"Look, I've had it up to here! I just can't do this anymore!" they said when they turned in their resignations.

Those were emotional reactions, not political ones. But in a social and political process, how are we going to control whether or not someone's "had it up to here"?

(Antonio Morales Ehrlich)

"I CALL UPON those of you in the Christian Democratic Party to analyze not only your intentions, which doubtless may be very good, but also the real effect of your presence in the government. Your presence is covering up the repressive nature of the current regime, especially at the international level. It's urgent for you, as a political force representing our people, to see where you can most effectively use your strength for the benefit of our nation's poor. Is it by being isolated and impotent in a government controlled by a repressive military? Or is it by joining others in a broad project of popular governance, whose support base comes, not from the current armed forces, which are more corrupt every day, but rather from the consensus of the majority of our people?"

(Homily, February 17, 1980)

PEOPLE SAY . . .
that the ruling class of El Salvador is sharpening its memory and its pencils. They're doing some simple mathematical calculations. And people say they've got regrets.

They're remembering the 1932 massacre of campesinos, with which General Maximiliano Hernández was able to put down the "subversives" of those times. When other people talk about it, they remember it as one of the most chilling massacres in the history of Latin America. But for these rich people, it was a good thing. They remember all that bloodshed, and they feel nostalgic. They move their bejeweled fingers over the keys of the calculator that they always carry in their pocket, and they lament.

They arrive at a conclusion. And they write their complaint in the San Salvador newspapers in a communiqué under disguised names. "In 1932," they declare, "we killed 40,000 and we had 40 years without trouble. If we'd have killed 80,000 we might have had 80 years."

WE WERE SCREWED. Totally screwed. They sent us to kill people in the countryside—people whose names we didn't even know, let alone what they'd done. And they hadn't done anything! More likely, they were Christians like us who were hungry, that's all. And we had to go spray them with bullets, burn their little shacks and steal their pigs and chickens.

Why? Because my captain ordered me to. My lieutenant ordered me to. My colonel ordered me to. And since there are rules even in hell, an order was an order, and it was always to kill.

But our commanders weren't cruel just to the *campesinos*. They were also cruel to us. They beat us, too. It really doesn't matter if you're dressed up like a soldier. If you're poor, you're poor.

"Maybe Monseñor Romero will speak up for us. He looks out for poor people," I said one day to a few of the rank and file who were disgruntled with the lives we had to live.

"Do you think . . ?"

"We can't lose anything by trying. Maybe we'll find a soft spot in his heart."

I had gotten the idea from listening to his homilies. And that's why we wrote him that letter he ended up reading one Sunday. We risked our hides to send it, and he risked his by reading it.

(Ramón Moreno)

"I HAVE A VERY EXPRESSIVE LETTER here from a group of soldiers. It's very revealing! I'm going to read the part that may be of most interest to us. 'We, a group of soldiers, ask you to make public our problems and the demands we are making to our senior officers, the heads of the military and the governing junta. If you can help us, we will be very grateful. What we want are better conditions for the troops of the Armed Forces of El Salvador. We want: 1) better housing, 2) an end to the beatings and threats that we receive, 3) better clothing for the troops, 4) a higher salary. Currently we receive 200 or 300 *colones* a month,[1] but when you count all of the things they deduct from our wages, we are left with nothing. 5) We don't want to be sent to repress the people . . .' [applause]

"Dear soldiers, with this applause, the people are reaching out to you in your anguish."

(Homily, January 20, 1980)

BLOCK AFTER BLOCK was full of people. The demonstration was about eight kilometers long. I had a knot in my throat and in my heart. I'd gone not believing. I went to see if the popular organizations really had all the support they said they had. I didn't believe it. All of it was surprising to me. Such a huge crowd. Such order. Such awareness. Such happiness. It seemed to me more like a celebration. And it was. It was the first show of force by the Revolutionary Coordinating Committee of the Masses, which was the first attempt to unite all of the groups on the left. Damn! I was practically crying, seeing all of it. Two hundred thousand people!

I'd also gone to see the demonstrations that the rich women in the Crusade for Peace and Work were having in those days, and I could see that those old ladies had a pretty big following, too. But, nothing like this! We had many, many more.

The march was so big, it was bound to end in bloodshed. From the very beginning, planes flew overhead spraying some kind of poison on people.

"That stuff stinks!" some yelled as they began to feel the effects.

But everyone went on ahead. Only a few turned back. Maybe just the ones who got the sickest from the stench.

When we got as far as the National Palace, the National Guardsmen, who were all holed up inside their lookout posts, started spraying—not poison, but bullets. I was in the Parque Libertad, and I could see everything. Then the panic started, the screams, the blood, the dead and the

---

[1] In 1980 200-300 *colones* were worth approximately US$100.

wounded hitting the pavement. And people looking for a place to hide. Some fled on side roads, and a whole lot of others sought refuge in the Cathedral or in El Rosario Church.

"These government people just don't understand," an old man next to me said. "The only thing we can do is force them to understand, with a war."

(Jacinto Bustillo)

TWO DOZEN PEOPLE WERE LYING DEAD in the streets, and there were wounded everywhere. Some got taken to hospitals. Hundreds of people sought refuge in the Cathedral or in El Rosario, and more than 40,000 fled to the grounds of the National University where the army, not content to let them leave quietly, surrounded them.

We had to see what we could do to get the as-yet unharmed people back to their houses alive. San Salvador seemed like a battlefield, smoldering after the exchange of fire.

I went running to the archdiocesan headquarters.

"We need to evacuate people. They're in danger!" I said to the first priests I ran into.

"They knew how dangerous it was to organize that demonstration," one of them said to me, cold as ice. "It wasn't very wise of them."

I started to tell them what I'd seen with my own eyes, but it was clear they didn't want to know.

"Where is Monseñor Romero?" I changed the subject.

And without waiting for an answer, I went running to look for him at the *hospitalito*. He was there, glued to the phone, talking to the Red Cross and to Marianela, the one from the human rights office. He was lodging complaints with the government and looking for mediators to help get out the people who were trapped in the university. He was asking, protesting, demanding . . .

"Monseñor, I just came from the plaza. I saw everything!"

When he heard that, he stopped right away to find out more. The official version, now on TV and on the radio, was that the violence had been caused by the demonstrators.

"Tell me everything you saw . . ."

He wanted the details, and I gave them to him. He listened, asked questions and listened some more. Later on in the afternoon, while the phones were still ringing off the hook, he came back and said to me, worried: "All those people in the Cathedral probably haven't eaten anything, have they?"

"I'm sure they haven't, Monseñor. They've been shut up in there since noon . . ."

He made arrangements himself for me to take them something. It was already dark when I started driving all over the place in my car, carrying beans to people. After 10:00 PM, when it looked like things were moving towards a solution to have people evacuated, he invited me to eat supper with him.

Since I worked at YSAX, I knew he had a trip pending to Belgium, where they were going to give him an honorary doctorate.

"Are you going to go, Monseñor?"

"The way things are, I'd better stay. It would be a bad time to leave the country, wouldn't it?"

He was very aware that if there was anyone in El Salvador capable of managing things to avoid more bloodshed, it was he. But he also knew that the Salvadoran voice most likely to be listened to outside the country was his.

"Maybe I should make the trip, after all . . ."

A few days later, he left for Belgium.

(Jacinto Bustillo)

"I COME FROM THE SMALLEST COUNTRY in faraway Latin America, and I bring in this Salvadoran Christian pastor's heart of mine, my greetings, my thanks and the joy I feel to be with you sharing vital experiences . . .

"Our world in El Salvador is not an abstraction. And it's not just one more place in the world, the way people in developed countries like yours tend to think. It's a world in which the immense majority of men and women are poor and oppressed . . .

"We know a little better now what sin is. We know that the death of human beings is an offense to God. We also know that sin is truly 'mortal' sin, not just because of the inner death it causes in those who commit it, but because of the real and objective death it produces. We remember a profound fact from our Christian faith: sin is what killed the Son of God, and sin is still killing the children of God . . .

"The early Christians used to say: 'The glory of God is that man should live.' We could make that even more specific by saying, 'the glory of God is that the poor should live.'"

(Speech at the University of Louvain, Belgium
upon receiving an honorary doctorate in humanities,
February 2, 1980)

THE WITCH-HUNT BEGAN in a terrible way throughout the whole zone of Aguilares. What agrarian reform? It was business as usual. More blood. More repression. The rivers of blood began to flow in February of 1980. The first, most direct case we had that February involved a nurse in the parish clinic and her sister. They were taken from their house during the night, and at dawn, the two were found—raped, tortured and murdered in a sugarcane field in Apopa. After that, they just kept killing people. Between February and December of 1980, we counted 680 people murdered in our area alone. Many of them were leaders— Christians with charisma, capable of organizing communities.

"Of the 250 of us that used to meet with Father Rutilio Grande in those wonderful communities, there are only three of us left," José Obdulio Chacón told me.

They threw dead bodies on the back roads, in the gutters, on the streets. And no one dared retrieve them because the ones who went would be killed the next night. The situation completely overwhelmed us. We couldn't even do all the funeral Masses we needed to do.

(Octavio Cruz)

WE USED FRUIT AND PINE TREE saplings and other greenery to beautify the little street he was going to come down when he visited us. At that time, I was the administrator for San Miguel Arcángel, and it was my job to tell Monseñor Romero about our lives.

"We've had a big movement for unity here, Monseñor, and we are well aware of our poverty and what it means."

That was the message that our *cantón* of San Miguelito, the one in the valley, sent to him. And Monseñor came to visit us and inaugurate the new six-room school we'd built through the efforts of the whole community. It went up to sixth grade, and everyone had helped out by providing free labor. When the news reached us that Monseñor was coming, we sent invitations to everyone in the surrounding *cantones*. Even though the National Guard passed nearby on their way to Ojos de Agua, and even though they'd set up military checkpoints along the way, we all went out to meet him.

"Let's not be like beans that wrinkle up as soon as it starts to get hot!" said one of my *comadres* to encourage us.

And there was enough encouragement for all of us, because everyone was included in the welcome party for the bishop.

We got the children who were 12 and under to go up front with palm leaves and flowers. And we had guitars, violins and fireworks. When he arrived, the applause was deafening, like the sound of a river rising. Monseñor passed between the lines of the children. We walked a little, and then stopped a little, shouting *vivas* to Monseñor. And we went on like that until we reached the church.

"I feel like the Lord on Palm Sunday in Jerusalem," he said, smiling.

When we were ready to sit with him and eat the little *campesino* lunch we'd prepared for him, he said a prayer:

"Lord, please bless the hands of the *campesinos* who grew this corn, so that the corn could feed the chicken and the chicken produce the egg."

When he was ready to go, everyone took him little gifts. From Las Minas, where they make clay jugs, they gave him a jug shaped like a hen—with the beak, the wings and everything—so he could keep his water cool. Other people took him sweet pineapples, beautiful boxes of bananas, coconuts, oranges, eggs from guinea hens, and avocados, too. Everything was arranged all bright and attractive. We put this big load of presents in his little car. It was a cream-colored jeep—not one of the fancy ones, just an old rundown thing. And he was as happy as he could be, because all these gifts were expressions of how much the *campesinos* loved him.

When we got past all the work of getting the first group of students through the school year, we were ready to inaugurate all of the electric posts we'd put in. So, since I was still the administrator, I called him, "Monseñor, we need to know if you would be so kind as to tell us if you can come back to inaugurate our electricity project."

He said that he was at our service, and that he was more than ready to come back.

"Because you're the ones," he said, "who show me around to all of the little corners of El Salvador. This way, I won't die without seeing them."

(César Arce/María Otilia Núñez)

PEOPLE SAY . . .

that Monseñor Romero was in the habit of getting his hair cut every two weeks. One afternoon, the barber got a little carried away. When Monseñor arrived at the meeting with the women of the *Cáritas* team, Elsita said: "Monseñor, they really cut your hair short this time! It looks like a military cut!"

Well, that was the worst thing she could have said. He got so angry! He was about ready to fly off the handle!

"Please, Doña Elsita, don't ever say that to me again!"

He was bristling because he'd been compared with a military man. The women say that they'd never seen him so mad.

I PRACTICALLY FELL OFF THE BENCH when I heard what Monseñor Romero said to us that Sunday at the Cathedral. The usual thing was for him to read on the radio the letters we poor people sent him. But for him to read us a letter that he had written himself, and one to the President of the United States, at that! That was really something!

"Mr. President . . . I am very concerned about the news that the government of the United States is planning to fuel an arms race in El Salvador, by sending military equipment and advisers to train three Salvadoran battalions in logistics, communications and intelligence . . .

As a Salvadoran and as Archbishop of the Archdiocese of San Salvador, it is my obligation to ensure that faith and justice prevail in my country. If you truly want to defend human rights, I ask you to not allow this military aid to go to the Salvadoran government, and to guarantee that your government will not intervene directly or indirectly with military, economic or diplomatic pressure to determine the destiny of the Salvadoran people . . ."

When Monseñor finished reading his letter, the Cathedral just shook with applause. We were applauding as if we'd all signed that letter to the *gringos* ourselves, right alongside Monseñor.

(Víctor Acosta)

THE LETTER TO PRESIDENT JIMMY CARTER was received with a tremendous ovation in the Cathedral of San Salvador. Much farther away, in the Vatican, the reaction was one of consternation and indignation.

"They want an explanation, Monseñor," Father Ellacuría said as he brought him the news. "There's a lot of commotion in Rome about your letter."

They hadn't wasted any time. In less than 24 hours, the Department of State in Washington had already lodged its complaint with the Vatican Secretary of State.

"Father Arrupe thinks that Father Jerez should fly to Rome immediately to explain to all the curia officials in the Vatican why you wrote your letter."

"But aren't my reasons sufficiently clear?"

"For us they are, but not for them."

"But if the United States government begins to give military aid to this repressive government, the repression will have no end! Isn't that clear? We need to put the brakes on in time."

"Apparently the Vatican thinks you're the one they need to put the brakes on . . ."

Monseñor's face grew cloudy. "The eyes of the Vatican are always seeing through different lenses," he thought to himself.

"What can we do . . ."

"You've already written the letter, and the US government has said that it's 'devastating.' That means you've hit them where it hurts," Ellacuría told him.

"Jerez is going to go. We're making arrangements," Estrada added.

"Do you think they'll listen to him in Rome?" Monseñor asked.

"We have to do the possible and the impossible," Ellacuría said. "This is already a crucified people. If there's a war it'll be worse. There will be a lot of suffering."

The two Jesuits, Ellacuría and Estrada, sat down awhile with Monseñor. They talked about what they felt and what they foresaw. War was just around the corner. And it looked like the United States was determined to intervene.

"They've already got a name for the kind of war they're going to wage here," said Ellacuría. "They call it 'low intensity war.' They've already tried it out in Vietnam . . ."

"It's a new concept of war that consists of murdering people to eliminate all of the people's efforts to organize, and justifying it by calling it a fight against communism or terrorism . . ." That's what Monseñor Romero wrote in his diary that same night. His voice comes through in the words with a tremble of anguish.

Before dawn, the telephone rang, awakening him from the deep sleep that had wrapped him up like a blanket and, for a few hours, protected him from dangers and fears.

"Hello . . ?"

"Monseñor, they blew up our broadcasting station. 'The X' is gone. There's nothing left standing. The bomb took everything . . ."

(Based on Monseñor Romero's Diary, February 18, 1980)

THE BOMB TOTALLY DESTROYED the old YSAX station, with its long history and all its problems. A few months earlier, when they bombed us for the first time and threatened our maintenance technician with death, I had gotten involved with the station.

"What are we going to do now?"

When Monseñor came and saw the place in ruins, his face was full of anxiety. He couldn't stand to have the station off the air. It made him feel like he was missing an arm or a leg, or like he'd lost his ability to speak.

"We have to do something, and quick!"

"Monseñor, I know we've had some new equipment in storage for a while. What we have to do is get it out and make it work!" I said, trying to calm him.

Father Pick, a giant *gringo* Jesuit who worked in Honduras, took charge of the hasty rebuilding operation. He had years of experience in radio work, and he came flying into El Salvador with that as his only mission.

It wasn't easy. In those times, nothing was. In addition to having to dig out from under the rubble, and in addition to having to build a new transmitting station in another place, we had the problem of not having the instruction manual for the equipment we had hurriedly taken out of storage.

"Why isn't it working?" Monseñor asked, each time more anxiously.

"This equipment has been in storage too long, Monseñor. And it's not all that new."

It was true. It was a second or third-hand patched together transmitter that Pick had picked up cheap in the States. I guess that's why they say cheap things turn out to be expensive. The amount of time we were putting in was turning out to be expensive! We'd just about have it working when, zzzzt! something would go wrong, and we'd have to start all over.

To top it all off, the Cathedral was under construction, or it was occupied—it always was—and Monseñor had to say Mass in the Basilica. Starting from the first Sunday we were off the air, all the people came with tape recorders to tape the homily and take it back to their communities.

The best we could do for him by the second Sunday was to get him a good telephone connection with *Radio Noticias del Continente* in Costa Rica. That way you could hear the homily by short wave in El Salvador and the rest of Central America. Actually, the signal went all the way to Colombia and Venezuela. So we went international, but it was all very rustic technology. We had to put a telephone on the altar with a long, long wire attached. Then, he would preach by telephone to Costa Rica with an altar boy walking next to him holding the mouthpiece. He had to hold it for so long that his hand went to sleep on him, with those long homilies of Monseñor's . . .

Days went by, and the so-called new equipment still wasn't working.

(Jacinto Bustillo)

"PRESIDENT CARTER HASN'T EVEN RECEIVED the first letter you read in your Sunday sermon," said the official who had taken on the role of Ambassador to El Salvador in those days.

"He hasn't received it? Well, I sent it."

"It's a shame the whole world had to hear about it before it even got into President Carter's hands."

Diplomatic courtesy, bureaucratic scruples. But of course, the man hasn't come just to complain about that.

"I want to clarify something to you, Monseñor. We're not giving new weapons to the Salvadoran army, like you think."

"Then what are you doing?"

"Just refining some things by adding some technical elements to the security forces' equipment."

"Well, it's all the same thing. Colonel García, who you should know is a very repressive man, is the one in charge, and not only of the armed forces but of all the security forces. Unfortunately he gives orders to kill."

"Monseñor, in these times, as you well know, there is violence being used on both sides. The security forces need to be protected, too. Demonstrators can be very violent against those who defend public order."

"I call it public disorder. And isn't it disorder when a few people own everything, and the majority of the people don't have anything? That's what the security forces are defending."

The North American official remains cold and dry, like a bottle of gin straight out of the refrigerator.

"Monseñor, I've come to let you know that the United States government wants the same thing you do—what's best for the Salvadoran people."

"If that's true, then you should let your government know that it shouldn't support the government of El Salvador with a single bullet, a single vest or a single dollar, because the government is against the people."

"Don't you think our mission should be to help this government straighten up?"

"The best way to help right now is not to get involved. The people already know what they want. Pay attention to the process the people are going through—it's already pretty far along—instead of putting obstacles in their way."

The official looks at Monseñor Romero. "If a stick doesn't bend, you have to break it." He tries to remember the exact phrase. And he's thinking about that as Monseñor talks to him about other things. But he recovers quickly, following the thread of the conversation, tying his own knots here and there, diplomatic answers to all of the archbishop's concerns. But he can't get that thing about the stick bending out of his mind.

(Based on Monseñor Romero's Diary, February 21, 1980)

"MONSEÑOR, YOU'RE GOING TO GET KILLED," some of us told him. "Fine, don't accept the protection the government is offering you. But at least be careful and take some security measures like all of the leaders of the grassroots organizations are doing.

"And what would those measures be?" he asked us, a little curious.

"Well, for example: don't do anything at the same time every day. Vary your schedule. Say Masses at different times than the ones you usually say. Only process publicly into the big churches. Don't ever do it at the chapel in the *hospitalito*. It's too open and isolated there. Don't drive your car yourself . . ."

We warned him. But then other priests would come and tell him other things.

"Don't worry, Monseñor, they're never going to kill you. They don't have the courage to do it." The priests spoke for whoever "they" were.

Actually, Monseñor Romero never took a single security measure, not even the simplest ones.

(Rafael Moreno/Rutilio Sánchez)

"MY OTHER FEAR IS ABOUT THE RISKS to my own life. It's hard for me to accept the idea of a violent death, which in these circumstances is very possible. Even the nuncio from Costa Rica warned me about imminent dangers this week . . .

I place my entire life under the loving providence of God, and I accept death, no matter how difficult, with faith in Him. I do not even offer a prayer of intention, as I'd like, for peace in my country and for the flourishing of our Church, because the Heart of Christ will know how to take things to their desired destiny. It's enough for me to be happy and confident, knowing for sure that my life and my death are in His hands, and that in spite of my sins, I have placed my trust in Him. In this I can't be mistaken. Others will continue, with more wisdom and holiness, all of the works of the Church and the country."

(Based on Monseñor Romero's Diary entry from his last spiritual retreat, February 25, 1980)

PEOPLE SAY . . .
that there have been several occasions now when they've seen Monseñor Romero driving his little car alone down the streets of San Salvador, without any chauffeur—without anyone else there to be his driver.

"Why, Monseñor?" they ask him.

"I prefer it this way. When what I'm expecting to happen happens, I want to be alone, so it's only me they get. I don't want anyone else to suffer."

THEY CAME IN AND KILLED MARIO in our own house. We were in a meeting with some of our colleagues from the Christian Democratic Party [PDC] when we heard a loud noise, and a couple of guys with black hoods on—a death squad—kicked in the door.

"Who is Mario Zamora?"

When Mario stepped forward, they pushed him into the bathroom and shot him right there with a machine gun that had a silencer. They went out, leaving Mario in pool of blood.

Someone ran and told Duarte.[2]

"This must be investigated!"

"There's nothing to investigate. Mario was a communist. Just leave it alone."

Mario had been all over the country organizing with the PDC, and he was loved both in and outside the party. But he'd come to the conclusion that the party should withdraw from its participation in that government. And sure enough, when he started to work towards that, they killed him. You know, there really wasn't anything to investigate. It was all too clear.

My husband was a man who taught so many people about their rights. He had defended so many people in the courts . . . I sent a statement to the newspapers condemning the crime and committing myself to educate my children to follow their father's example and struggle for the poor.

Monseñor Romero presided over the ninth day memorial Mass, and he surprised me by referring to my statement in his homily. I wasn't expecting it, and as I was going out I thanked him.

"You've helped me make my commitment even stronger, Monseñor, by publicly telling everyone about what I wrote."

---

[2]Napoleón Duarte was head of the Christian Democratic Party at that time.

"It's time for all of us to help each other make commitments, don't you think?"

He was making a commitment and taking a big risk just by saying that Mass. Definitely! It was for everyone. Because shortly before it began, a priest discovered a bag with 75 sticks of dynamite in it hidden behind the statue of Saint Martha. It was set to go off during Mass and kill all of us, not to mention destroy the whole Basilica and who knows how many houses around it . . .

"It's time for all of us to be taking risks, don't you think?" he had told me.

(Aronette Díaz)

AFTER THE ASSASSINATION OF MARIO ZAMORA, the governing junta did nothing to investigate, but it did announce that it had discovered a list of people who were threatened with death. The first person on that list was Mario Zamora, and the second was Monseñor Romero. Monseñor called some of us to an urgent meeting.

"Did you hear the news? I'm the next one . . ."

We recommended that he be calm, that he be prudent and that he take care of himself. Everyone had the same advice for him: "Don't go anywhere this weekend. Stay here. Prepare your homily. Stay calm. All of this is very new. Let's wait and see what happens . . ."

He listened to us, nodding his agreement. At the end, he finally came out with a "but."

"But I've been invited to visit the community of Sonzacate . . ."

"You're going to have to let that idea go. How can you think of going so far away at a time like this?"

We insisted he should not even consider going and that he should send his regrets.

That same night all of us and a few more came back to have a working dinner at the *hospitalito*. By 8:00 PM he still hadn't shown up. All of us were eating dinner thinking the same thing: the man had gone to Sonzacate.

"Why do we bother to give him advice? He doesn't do anything we say!"

When it was really late and several of the people in the meeting had already gone home, Monseñor arrived, walking with defiant strides and an angry face. He knew that *we* were the angry ones, but he didn't say anything. People turned in their reports for the week and there was hardly any conversation. The whole meeting lasted less than 15 minutes.

Everyone else left, and I was the only one there, chatting with the sisters. Monseñor approached me.

"Are you angry, too?" he said.

"Frankly, Monseñor, we talked about it all this morning, but you refuse to listen to what people tell you."

"It's my work. It's my job . . . They called me from that community of Sonzacate, and how could I tell them no? Besides, don't you argue with me! You're the ones responsible for this . . ."

"We are? Responsible for *what?*"

"For making me afraid. After talking to you, I started to see assassins in places where there were only pigeons!"

It wasn't until then that I realized that he had fear painted all over his face. It wasn't anger, it was fear!

"What happened? Tell me . . ."

We sat down. He wanted to talk.

"Roberto, today I was really at a breaking point!"

"What happened?"

"Well, we were celebrating Mass in an open field in front of the church because there were so many people that I had to take the altar outside. Up until then, everything was fine, but when the offertory started and I was lifting the bread, I saw two men climbing up the bell tower of the church. Step by step, just climbing. I froze! I was thinking, 'what are they doing? They're going up there to kill me. They're going to get their aim just right and . . .' and right away I thought about Moreno and all of you guys. 'They warned me!' I thought. I was praying, and counting the steps my assassins had left to climb . . ."

"What happened when they got to the top?"

"I saw them doing something, but I couldn't tell what, and I started shaking. And believe it or not, Roberto, I even heard a shot being fired!"

He was sweating now, as he talked openly about his fear.

"Later, I asked about it, and they told me that those 'killers' were probably a couple of kids who usually climb the bell towers to get the pigeons out from under the eves . . ."

"So, then . . . it was only a scare!" I said, laughing.

"Only a scare? Only a scare!" he said without a trace of a smile. "You know what bothered me the most? That I would be dead and you guys would be making fun of me, saying 'that old guy deserved it for being so stubborn!' That's what you would have said!"

"Well, you *would* have deserved it, Monseñor!" That's what I told him.

(Roberto Cuéllar)

THEY'RE *GRINGO* SPECIALISTS in agrarian reform, the kind that the United States tries to promote all over Latin America. Now especially in El Salvador. Now they've come to visit Monseñor Romero. They know that if the archbishop criticizes the plan, the people won't support it at all, but that if he supports the plan, the people might accept it. That's why they're visiting.

"The Church applauded when the first junta announced its agrarian reform, but it never got past the drawing board . . ." Monseñor tells them.

"But now with the backing of the Christian Democrats," they reply, "a definitive law of agrarian transformation will be promoted."

They look carefully for signs of approval from the archbishop.

"During those days of the first junta, I said in a homily that agrarian reform is not a gift from the government. It's something the people have achieved. The people have already won this right, and they've lost a lot of lives for it."

The technical experts look at each other.

"You say it's not a gift, it's an achievement," one begins, "but whatever it is, does that mean you're going to support it?"

"It may already be too late . . ."

"Late . . ?"

"When the *campesinos* ask for something, when they say how things should be done and how they want to organize, they get killed. This isn't agrarian reform, it's . . . it's agrarian repression."

"But, Monseñor, some of the lands are already being redistributed . . ."

"They are soaked in blood."

"What? But, Monseñor, the government of the United States . . ."

"Maybe that's the problem." Monseñor cuts them off.

"What problem?"

"That this agrarian reform is coming from the outside. It's coming from up above. It doesn't take into account the way the Salvadoran people are already organizing. It's a plan of the United States government made according to its own interests, not ours. The plan is flawed from its very roots."

In spite of everything, the technical experts don't give up. They start to take out maps and talk about statistics and percentages, perspectives and balances. Monseñor listens to them, and finally sees them out courteously.

(Based on Monseñor Romero's Diary,
March 1 and 14, 1980)

"WHERE IS THIS ALL HEADED?"

That was Monseñor Romero's big worry as he saw the advances the grassroots organizations were making.

"It could be headed toward a people's insurrection, Monseñor. The left could take power and install a revolutionary government. It might be something like what happened in Nicaragua . . ."

"Then maybe we should go and take a look at what's happening in Nicaragua . . ."

"Good idea, Monseñor. Why don't you go ahead and make plans to go yourself, instead of having us tell you about it."

He agreed immediately, and right away we made arrangements for him to visit.

"But I want to be free to go where I want while I'm there," he said to me.

"No problem. The *Nicas* think highly of you. They'll make sure the right doors open so you can see everything you want to."

I talked with people in Nicaragua about the trip—especially with Daniel Ortega and Miguel D'Escoto[3]—in order to put together a good pro-

---

[3]The Sandinista Front for National Liberation held power in Nicaragua from 1979 to 1990. During this time, Daniel Ortega was president and Miguel D'Escoto, a Maryknoll priest, was Foreign Minister.

gram for him and have him see as much as possible. They were eagerly awaiting his arrival and felt very honored that he was coming. The ticket was bought, but never used.

(César Jerez)

"CHRISTIANS AREN'T AFRAID to fight. They know how to fight, but prefer the language of peace. Nevertheless, when a dictatorship works against the human rights and the common good of a nation, when conditions become unbearable and channels of dialogue, understanding and rational exchange are closed . . . When this happens, the Church speaks of a legitimate right to insurrectional violence. It is not the Church's role, however, to determine the time of that insurrection, or to indicate when all of the channels for dialogue have been closed.

"The situation alarms me, but the struggle of the rich to defend the indefensible does not have a future, especially when you take into account the combative spirit of our people. There may be some temporary victory of the forces who serve the interests of the rich, but our people's voice for justice will rise up and be heard again. It will triumph sooner than we think. A new society is coming, and it is coming quickly."

(Interview with Prensa Latina, February 15, 1980)

San Salvador, March 6, 1980. Today a new Agrarian Reform Law was put forth by the governing civilian-military junta. At the same time, the government decreed a state of siege and martial law throughout the entire country. The most conflictive rural areas, where campesino organizations have the most history and strength, were militarized. In recent weeks, Archbishop Oscar Romero has been expressing his opposition to what he calls a government formula of "reform with repression."

"THEY EVEN BROKE THE STONES WE USE to grind our corn, those ingrates!" That's what the poor women from Cinquera said as they came in crying. They arrived with only the clothes they were wearing and their children in their arms. They had come asking for a place to stay in the seminary. They were fleeing the "agrarian reform" . . .

Around that time, we already had two thousand *campesino* refugees in the patios and gardens of the archdiocesan offices. Hundreds more were in other church buildings. There was such a continuous daily influx that there wasn't time to count them all. The only crime those refugees had committed was to be poor and to be part of an organized group.

They were all coming so that Monseñor Romero would protect them from the National Guard, from the repression. They came with so much trust in him. From Chalate, from all over the north, from Cabañas, La Paz, Cuzcatlán and San Vicente.

There were three of us doctors attending to these people, working up to 10 hours a day. A hundred patients a day . . . It wasn't easy! Ninety-five percent of the refugees were women, children and old people. And half were children who were malnourished and full of parasites. We saw more gastrointestinal problems than anything else. And along with that, the neuroses—trauma left like fingerprints of the atrocities of military operations in the countryside.

"The best medicine for this country is going to be demilitarization," Monseñor Romero said to us one day, dreaming.

(Francisco Román)

THE REPRESSION GREW WORSE EVERY DAY. The Human Rights Commission came out with some statistics: an average of 10 assassinations a day in January and 15 a day in February. March started off even worse . . . Our leaders were being killed off everywhere, in the countryside and in the city.

A group of about 200 priests, nuns and lay people from the communities decided to fast for three days in El Rosario Church and end with a Mass on Sunday. It was going to be a resounding denunciation of the whole situation.

Monseñor Romero didn't like the idea. He thought it was too provocative, and he sent some priests to try to dissuade us. When he saw that he wasn't succeeding, he came in person to the planning meeting we were having.

"Monseñor, you're already doing the prophetic work of denunciation," we argued. "That's all fine and good, but you don't have a monopoly on denunciation. We have an obligation to take initiatives, too, don't we? We have the right and responsibility to do something. Besides, we've already decided, and we're going to do it even if you don't like it."

Things got a little uncomfortable, and he just looked at us.

"All right," he swallowed. "If you want to participate in this way, do it, if that's what your conscience tells you to do. Keep in mind that the bishop does not agree with you, but that the bishop cannot oppose what you do according to your conscience."

The next day a group of seminarians joined in the fast, too. They had had a little argument with Monseñor Romero over the same issue, and he had told them the same thing.

They had heard that if you drank a glass of water with a spoonful of honey in it, you could last the whole day without eating anything else. So, Tavo Cruz and Benito Tovar decided to drink a half a bottle of honey at once. That way they were going to be able to fast for a month! They didn't last half an hour. It was a laxative strong enough for horses, and they both had to be taken out of the church quick.

Apart from these two early casualties, the fast was a success, and Monseñor Romero joined us at the end to say our closing Mass.

"This thing has taken on a dynamism all its own," he said. "How could I resist the Holy Spirit?"

(Trinidad Nieto/Miguel Vázquez)

THAT MAN, MY BROTHER, was scheming against Romero. Starting in 1980, he began to say horrible things about him in private and in public. Once, when he called him "a liar" and said other insulting things about him on TV, I got so mad, I decided to write a letter to Monseñor. I wanted to offer him some encouragement and tell him that my faith had been awakened by his words and the things he'd done, and that for the first time in my life I really felt like a part of the Church. I also told him that it pained me to know everything that man was saying. But I didn't want to tell Monseñor that I was his sister. I just wanted him to think I was a relative. I sent him the letter through a friend, and I knew he'd received it. In March, when the Swedish Churches gave him a peace prize, I wrote him again congratulating him. I sent the letter through the same friend.

"What relation is she to D'Aubuisson?" Monseñor asked her curiously.

"She's his sister, but she doesn't think like him at all."

I was told he was surprised.

"Tell her I appreciate her letter and that it's very, *very* special to me."

A few days later he answered me personally. "Testimonies like yours encourage me to keep moving forward," he said.

(Marisa D'Aubisson)

IN THE END, I WAS CONVINCED they would kill him.

All of us bishops had been called to a meeting in Ayagualo. A few days before that, Roberto D'Aubuisson had come out on TV saying terrible things about Monseñor Romero. And when that man opened his mouth, it wasn't long before you had to dig graves for the people he mentioned. That's why I was convinced.

Returning to San Salvador from that meeting, that concern was weighing heavy on my heart. It scared me, too. I was so afraid that I didn't even want to be in the same car with him. I decided to come back on my own in my jeep.

The meeting was to elect the president and vice-president of the Bishops' Conference. There were four of them on one side and the two of us on the other side. Monseñor Romero and I were sure that if we voted for one of them as president, they would vote for one of us as vice-president.

"That would be the most logical thing," he said.

"It would be the fairest thing," I said.

That's how we voted. But we calculated wrong. The four of them voted for their own people for both posts.

Monseñor Romero left Ayagualo very disappointed. Extremely. That was the last battle we fought together. And we lost.

(Arturo Rivera y Damas)

I DIDN'T WANT TO BELIEVE IT: they had murdered Robertico and his wife. He was a close friend of mine. He was like my brother. We'd grown up together and played together. Roberto Castellanos, the son of the General Secretary of the Communist Party of El Salvador, had just returned from abroad to live in his country again. He came with his wife, Annette, a Danish woman, blonde as could be, who didn't even speak any Spanish.

A death squad took the two of them, and after a few days of anguished searching, their bodies were found by sheer accident. A friend of the family went to the Deportivo beach, and the gardener there told him that they'd seen a blonde woman buried over there. It was Annette. Both bodies showed signs of terrible torture, and her breasts had been cut off . . .

Roberto's mother came looking for me: "Hey, you know Monseñor Romero. Ask him if we can have the two bodies present at Mass tomorrow so he can denounce the crime. But I don't want to be dishonest with Monseñor. Robertico was a communist and an atheist . . . Tell him that, and tell him that it's only if he wants to. If he doesn't, we'll understand."

That evening I went running to find Monseñor at the *hospitalito*, and I told him.

" . . . and we preferred to tell you honestly, Monseñor."

"I don't care if he was a communist or not. All people are children of God. Tell Doña Rosita that her son and daughter-in-law will be at the Cathedral tomorrow . . ."

The bodies of Roberto and Annette were at the Mass on March 9, in front of Monseñor and the Salvadoran people.

(Margarita Herrera)

ON WEDNESDAY MARCH 12, Monseñor Romero came to the station to see how it was going.

"When are we going to be on the airwaves again?!"

"We're working on it full time, Monseñor."

We had already built the walls of the structure that would house the new equipment. We just needed to put the roof on. We were doing some special construction work as a security precaution because we were sure that it wouldn't be long before they'd bomb the place again. We set the walls farther apart and made the transmitting room into a kind of labyrinth . . .

"What do you have to do still before you can begin transmitting again?" Monseñor was impatient.

"It won't be long. You'll see . . ."

"But can't you give me a date?"

"Maybe for next Sunday . . ."

Why did we tell him? By Friday the 14th he was there again, anxious for news, and we had more left to do than we thought.

"I don't know, Monseñor. It's hard to tell . . . Tomorrow night I'll come back and let you know where we stand."

On Saturday, Pick and I worked until 9:00 at night. But what could we do? It wasn't ready. The equipment had a lot of quirks. I went to the *hospitalito* with the news of another delay. Monseñor Romero was in the meeting he always had with his advisers to prepare the Sunday homily. I went in and stood in front of him.

All I said was, "No."

All he said was, "Oh well."

He wasn't angry, but he was really discouraged.

Ellacuría was as disappointed as Monseñor Romero, or maybe more so! The next day, he called me into his office: "Look, if you need to, you can go to the United States to get replacement parts or whatever you need to get the radio on the air . . ." he told me.

"No, really. Sooner or later we'll find out what the problem is. You'll see . . ."

"But it can't be later. I'm giving you one week at the most!"

(Jacinto Bustillo)

AFTER WORKING IN NICARAGUA for a few months, I decided to go back to El Salvador on the sly. I wanted to work out a way to stay there. I got in touch with Monseñor Romero right away. He was happy to hear from me.

"That's great that you were able to get in! Why don't you come concelebrate Mass with me tomorrow? We can announce your return publicly."

"All right."

I agreed. A few months earlier I'd been arrested at the airport in San Salvador on my way back from Colombia. Like so many other Salvadoran priests had been, I was expelled from the country. Then Monseñor Romero sent me to Nicaragua to work in Estelí. The Sandinista revolution was already underway, and he was very interested in learning about the latest developments. I was thinking about all of that when the phone rang. It was Monseñor Romero again.

"On second thought, I don't think it's such a good idea for you to come to Mass, but I'll expect you Monday night, and we can chat."

"All right."

On Monday, March 17, I went over to see him.

"You know, Father Astor," he said with great concern, "you really should leave the country. Go back to Nicaragua. You won't be able to do anything here. You won't be able to work or move around. These people in the ruling class are in such a frenzy that you wouldn't last 24 hours. They'd kill you. Me too. Soon, they're going to get rid of me, too . . ."

He moved his hand up to the cross around his neck, held it, let it go and then held on to it again . . .

"But you'll see. There will be other times, better times. We have to create a little reserve with all of you priests that are out of the country right now so that when El Salvador changes, you can come back. Your experience in Nicaragua is going to be important for everybody. For me too. You know, we really have to rethink that word I used to be so afraid of—the word 'revolution.' That word carries a lot of the Gospel in it."

(Astor Ruíz)

ON MONDAY MARCH 17, we started to work even harder on the radio. Monseñor Romero visited on no less than three occasions to see if we were getting anywhere. One afternoon he came by with Pedraz. That day, I needed money to buy some cables and a couple other things.

"Hey," I said to Pedraz as soon as I saw him, "the stores are about to close. Do you have some cash you can lend me? I'll pay you back later."

Rogelio took out his wallet. He had 40 *colones*. I hadn't said anything to

Monseñor. I'd barely even said hello. But he took out his wallet and searched through it . . .

"I've only got three *colones* . . ."

He showed it to me: he had three colones and a driver's license, and that was it.

"Wow, Monseñor, you're broke all right!"

But he still wanted to give what he had. I managed with the 40 I got from Pedraz. But Monseñor stayed around for a while, as if he was hoping the radio would start working by some miracle.

(Jacinto Bustillo)

COLONEL GARCÍA CAME LOOKING FOR HIM at the *hospitalito*.

"Monseñor Romero, there are rumors that you're going to be killed. I've come to offer you an armored car and security guards . . ."

"Colonel García, as long as you don't truly protect the people, I can't accept any protection from you."

García looked at him angrily.

"Why don't you use those armored cars and security guards for the family members of people who have disappeared, been killed or put in jail?"

García stomped out furiously without so much as giving him another look.

(Rafael Moreno)

MUCH TO OUR JOY, the radio transmitter equipment started working on Friday the 21st with a makeshift antennae we built. We still had to connect it to the tower, and there were still a few problems that could come up, but the end was in sight . . .

"We've practically got the thing running," I ran to tell Ellacuría.

On Saturday, we connected the equipment to the antennae, sent out the carrier, made the measurements, asked the studio for the signal . . . And it worked!!! It worked!!!!! Even though some of the protection circuits were still being activated I was sure that by Sunday, March 23 we would be on the air. In the evening, I went to tell Monseñor Romero the good news!

"Now, we're talking!"

His expression was one of great relief and then complete happiness.

(Jacinto Bustillo)

ON ONE OF THOSE DAYS IN MARCH, some journalists from the Mexican newspaper, *Excelsior,* asked Monseñor Romero a question that was on everyone's mind. Everywhere, people had a gut-level feeling that the Archbishop of San Salvador was on the edge of a precipice. He was feeling it too, and he answered:

"Yes. I've been threatened with death many times, but I should say that as a Christian, I don't believe in death. I believe in resurrection. If they kill me, I will rise again in the Salvadoran people. When I say that, I'm not trying to brag. Indeed, I say it with great humility. I hope they will be convinced that it will be a waste of their time. A bishop will die, but the Church of God, which is the people, will never perish."

THERE WAS A FULL MOON. A little breeze gave some relief to the heat of the day's work. We were coming back exhausted from a busy day, a day full of visits to the communities. We were headed back to San Salvador. Barraza was driving, and I was sitting in back with Monseñor Romero. I was leaving the country the next day. This was the last time I would see him, and perhaps that's why I dared to ask him:

"Monseñor, I've heard many people asking you to take care of yourself. Have the threats increased . . ?"

"Yes, they have. Every day there are more, and I take them very seriously . . ."

He was quiet for a few moments. I felt a kind of air of nostalgia come over him. He leaned his head back, half-closed his eyes and said to me:

"I'll tell you the truth, Doctor: I don't want to die. At least not now. I've never had so much love for life! And honestly, I don't think I was meant to be a martyr. I don't feel that calling. Of course, if that's what God asks of me, then there's nothing I can do. I only ask that the circumstances of my death not leave any doubt as to what my true vocation is: to serve God and to serve the people. But I don't want to die now. I want a little more time . . ."

(Jorge Lara-Braud)

ON SUNDAY, MARCH 23, Pick and I went to the radio station. The setup we had was not that reliable yet, and we wanted to be ready for anything that might come up with the equipment. We were going to be there during the whole Mass, at the foot of the transmitter.

The Mass began. Everything was fine. Every once in a while we would disconnect, but since we were right there, we fixed it right away. I kept the earphones on to monitor the signal the whole time.

That Sunday, the Cathedral was brimming with people. I don't know if it was the new equipment or what, but I could hear Monseñor's voice clearer than ever. It was full of energy.

So, the homily begins. He starts to explain Church doctrine on Lent . . . He mentions the Prodigal Son, the adulterous woman, a few spiritual things . . . Every once in a while, *twang!* we have to adjust the equipment . . . The disconnect lasts just a moment, and since Pick and I are acting quickly, no one probably even notices.

I'm still monitoring . . . He talks about Saint Paul, about the need to empower women, about the gardens in Babylonia . . . *"Our history is so full and so varied from one day to the next! If you leave El Salvador and come back the next week, it seems like history has changed completely."*

. . . Twang! A new adjustment. Monseñor is going on and on. He's tireless . . . The equipment is holding up well in its debut. Sometimes it tries to give us a scare, but basically it's behaving well.

Monseñor makes announcements about events in the upcoming Holy Week, news about communities and *cantones* that aren't even on the map . . . Nance Verde, Candelaria de Cuzcatlán, San José la Ceiba . . . He thanks us for our work in repairing the radio . . . Pick and I look at each other, satisfied and proud.

He talks about a humanitarian aid committee, about an Amnesty International report . . . The equipment cuts off for a few seconds, but we don't let it go on long enough for anyone to notice. We get it fixed right away . . . We're still on the air and the reception is as clear as a bell. *"The state of siege and the disinformation campaign to which we've been subjected . . ."* He starts laying out the news of the week: over 140 killed . . . *"This country is, without a doubt, living in a pre-revolutionary period . . ."* The list of the dead continues: in Apulo, in Tacachico, in the UCA . . . The news of the bloodshed ends. You can tell by the tone of his voice that the homily must be just about over . . . *"I'd like to make a special appeal to the men of the army, and especially to the rank and file of the National Guard, the Police, and the various barracks. Brothers, you are part of this same people! You are killing your own campesino brothers and sisters! But above any order that a man might give to kill, the law of God should prevail, the law which says: thou shall not kill . . ."* zzzzzzzzzzzzzzzzzzzzztttttt . . . What's this? He's saying really important stuff! zzzzzzzzzzzzzzzzzzzzzzzztttttt . . . Pick, we lost the signal! Pick, push that button! Now, that one! A couple of buttons get pushed and . . . prrrrrrrrrrrrrrr . . . OK . . .It's back, prrrrrrrrrrrrr. *"No soldier is obligated to obey an order which is against the law of God. No one has to comply with an immoral law. It's time now for you to examine your consciences and obey your conscience instead of a sinful order. The Church, the defender of God-given rights, of human dignity and of the human being, cannot remain silent in the face of such abomination. We want the government to take us seriously when we say that reforms are useless when they come stained with so much blood . . ."* PRRRRrrrrrrrrrrrzzzzzzzzzzzzzzzzz . . . Not again! We can't lose a word of what he's saying! Pick! Pick! We can't lose the signal now! . . . zzzzzzz . . . Go! Go!! Finally . . . *"In the name of God, and in the name of this suffering people, whose cries rise up to heaven more tumultuously every day, I ask you, I beg you, I order you in the name of God: stop the repression!* . . . PRRRRRrr-rrrrzzzzzzzzzzzzzzzzzzzzzzzzzzzzzzzzzzzzzzzzzzzzzzzzzzzzzzzzzzzzzzzzzzzzzzzzzzzzzzz zzzzzzzzzzzzzzzzzzzzzzzzzzzz . . .

The roar was deafening. I had to take off my earphones. I was desperate. Listen to that noise, Pick! We lost the signal! zzzzzzzzzzzz . . . It's messed up! zzzzzzzzzzzzzzzzzz . . . The equipment gave out on us, Pick! It gave out on us . . .RRRRRRzzzzzzzzz . . . What now?

But soon, we heard Monseñor's voice: *"The Church preaches liberation* . . .*"* He kept talking and you could hear his voice clearly. The transmitter was fine, and the Mass continued with all the correct signals.

Pick and I looked at each other and realized what had happened.

"That noise wasn't static, was it?"

"No, it was applause."

They were the most deafening, longest rounds of applause ever heard in the Cathedral of San Salvador.

(Jacinto Bustillo/Felipe Pick)

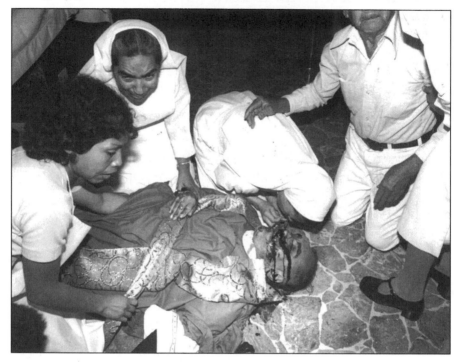

"It's as if we all lost a part of ourselves."

EL SALVADOR'S HEART WAS BEATING TO THE RHYTHM OF MARCH 24

EARLY THAT MORNING on Monday, March 24, someone called him.

"Monseñor, there's a big announcement in the papers saying you're going to celebrate a Mass for the Dead at the *hospitalito* . . ."

"Well, yes, I am."

"But Monseñor, the announcement is really strange. It's so big and pronounced . . ."

"What are you trying to say?"

"It's making a pretty big deal about the fact that you're the one saying this Mass . . . Don't go, Monseñor, don't go . . ."

He excused himself with a few words and hung up. His face showed concern.

"It's not wise, Monseñor," we told him.

"But sisters, it's my duty."

"Your duty is to take care of yourself right now."

"What can I do? I've already made a commitment to the family, and I have to say the Mass. We're in God's hands. Don't you have faith anymore?"

(Teresa Alas)

THE PHONES WERE RINGING OFF THE HOOK at Legal Aid that morning. Newspaper headlines announced the day's news in big bold letters: "Monseñor Romero Asks Soldiers to Disobey Orders," "Archbishop Commits Crime." The colonel in charge of the Armed Forces Information Office was publicly accusing Monseñor. I was a little alarmed by all the commotion.

"Now we're going to have to get involved in another legal mess like the Supreme Court thing to try to save this man," one colleague said to me.

"But this is going to be worse, because now it's the military!" I said.

Truthfully, I was quite worried, but when someone would call, all hysterical, I tried to turn things around and be encouraging.

"Don't worry! We'll get out of this fine. You'll see . . . I love these kinds of entanglements!"

The night before, I'd given Monseñor Romero the first draft of a human rights report we'd been writing so he could use it to back up the call he'd made in his homily to stop the repression. Around noon, I got a message from the sisters of the *hospitalito* that Monseñor wanted to talk with me about the text over lunch.

I got there, but he was running behind, and at 2:00 PM I had another urgent appointment. I decided to eat lunch with Sister Luz and Sister Teresa. The two of them were very nervous.

"Ay, Roberto, we've had five threatening phone calls for him just since Saturday when you had dinner with him. And after the homily yesterday, there were more calls, worse ones. They were talking really ugly . . . They're going to kill him, Roberto . . ."

"No, don't worry," I tried to calm them. "You'll see. He'll still be around to say our funeral Masses. When it's my turn, I've asked him for one of his best homilies—one of those 10-hour ones! I've already told him I'd have to be in my coffin anyway. to put up with those long spiels of his!"

They smiled, but they were still worried. I called him from my office at about 3:30 PM.

"What happened, Monseñor? You stood me up."

"You'll have to forgive me, Roberto. But since you didn't get lunch, come over and have dinner with me. I have a Mass at 6:00 in the *hospitalito*, and I'm free at 7:00. I'll expect you then, and we can go over the report together . . ."

"All right, I'll be there."

(Roberto Cuéllar)

HE DID A LOT OF THINGS ON THE AFTERNOON of March 24. I took him to his ear doctor after lunch because his ears were bothering him. Then we went to Santa Tecla to see Father Azcue, his confessor. It wasn't time for him to go yet, but that day, he told me suddenly that he wanted to go confess.

When we were on our way back to his house, he asked me to have a good, solid platform made to put in front of the Cathedral, so they could have the Holy Week celebrations outside.

"Just a simple one, you know. Find a carpenter who'll do the job for us at a good low price. It needs to be really tall, and it has to be done fast. This Holy Week is going to be one of the best-attended, you'll see. It's going to be Palm Sunday like never before!"

"Monseñor," I scolded him, "you're always making plans, and you don't ever rest. You go way beyond the call of duty. Nightfall comes and you're still at it. It never ends . . . And I'll bet you don't talk about that at confession!"

"Hey, get off my case, will you? Think about the heart that God gave us. It never rests. And it doesn't stop, either! Just imagine, 70 beats a minute, day and night!"

He was laughing. I dropped him off at the *hospitalito* so I could go look for a carpenter. It was already getting to be late in the afternoon. I didn't see anything strange in the gardens.

"Ay! Now I have to go say that Mass!" he said as he was getting out.

It was like he didn't really want to.

(Salvador Barraza)

THE *HOSPITALITO* CHAPEL is full of light, even during the hours when the sun begins its journey to the other side of the earth. It seems like a part of the garden, crystallized in the middle of the lawn and flowers. The sisters who take care of the cancer patients somehow find the time to make its floors shine, and the benches, reflected in the polished floor, have their luster, too. Behind the altar, Christ on the cross is looking upwards to heaven, struggling to escape death.

Today the tidy, happy chapel of Divina Providencia is nearly empty. The Mass to commemorate the anniversary of the death of Doña Sarita de Pinto is scheduled for 6:00 PM. Monseñor arrives punctually, dressed in the purple vestments of the Lenten season. He bows toward the altar and kisses it. The twenty-or-so people who are attending the Mass stand up. They are family members, a few friends and a photographer who has his camera ready to take the picture of the archbishop with Doña Sarita's family after Mass.

"In the name of the Father, the Son and the Holy Spirit . . ."

The answer, though in unison, is tenuous. Barely whispered.

"Lord, have mercy, Christ, have mercy . . ."

The tumultuous, crowded Cathedral of yesterday—Sunday—feels so far away from the scene of this practically empty chapel, white and calm. Monseñor Romero looks at everything around him. His eyes rest for a moment, fascinated, on the light of a candle that flickers stubbornly on the altar, refusing to be extinguished.

"Let us pray: our Lord God, who gave your Son to die . . . "

Monseñor Romero's eyes move from the dying flame toward the rectangle of the door that is in front of him, shutting out the evening. Outside, darkness has taken over. He begins to read. Everyone sits, routinely attentive.

"A reading from the Letter of Saint Paul to the Corinthians . . ."

It's the end of the Lenten season. A warm, but intense, breeze whips through the bougainvillea and the saplings in the garden, trying to tear away the leaves.

The Gospel reading is the parable of the grain of wheat that falls on the ground and multiplies. Afterwards the homily begins. He wants to be brief because he has so many things to do after the Mass. He's going to have to stay up to all hours tonight.

" . . . it's important not to love ourselves so much that we're not willing to take the risks that history demands of us . . ."

His eyes light on his companions from so many liturgies: the white embroidered altar cloths, the red wine in the crystal cruet . . . the earth-colored face of the woman on the third bench who reminds him so much of his mother. His own hands —furrowed with veins and trembling a bit this afternoon—are also earth-colored . . .

" . . . If we nourish ourselves with Christian faith, we will never fail . . ."

The microphone carries the ring of his voice to a distant fence adorned with stubborn *izote* flowers in the back of the garden. This chapel looks like a circus tent, like those circuses that would appear from one day to the next back in Ciudad Barrios . . . The Mass continues; it's almost halfway through now. Behind him, off to one side, Monseñor can hear the familiar sound of pots and pans in the kitchen: the sisters are making supper now. By the windows on the left, he sees a quick movement, like a shadow fighting with the darkness. And he sees a glint of something, almost a spark. It's probably a firefly. Only it's metal.

It's time to put the period on the end of the homily: " . . . justice and peace for our people."

Whispers of "amen" are heard. So be it. So it will be.

He returns to the center of the altar to offer God the bread and wine. His hand isn't shaking now. He's alone. He sees only the white linen of the corporal cloth, unfolding softly. He spreads it out, caressing it, barely brushing the side of the gold plate he is about to lift.

When he looks up, he sees a burst of light from the window on the left. One second of light, sound and gunpowder. Only one shot to the heart. He falls, crumpled at the foot of the crucifix. And in an instant the floor is sowed with seeds of his blood.

I HEARD A SHOT. Just one. Maybe it was because it hit so close to the microphone, but it sounded like a bomb exploding. Then people started screaming. I ran from the second bench to the door, but I didn't see anything. I could only hear the sound of a car hurrying to get away.

(Teresa Alas)

"HE'S BEEN SHOT!"

I couldn't feel my feet flying from the kitchen to the chapel. Monseñor was lying face down on the floor, bleeding. I threw myself on him.

"Monseñor!"

Nothing. I took his pulse. Nothing.

"Let's turn him over," I said to Sister Teresa.

When we did, blood gushed from his mouth. Sister Luz was calling the doctor. I ran over to her.

"It's too late. Monseñor is dead."

(María del Socorro Iraheta)

I WAS COMING BACK HOME, BY CAR at around 6:15, and I saw a light colored Land Rover—one of those longer ones—parked by the entrance of the *hospitalito*. Next to the car, I saw four men, one behind the driver's wheel and three talking to each other outside. They were big guys, wearing *guayaberas*.[1] They looked startled, like they thought I was going to go into the *hospitalito*. But I kept driving towards my house. When I got in, I heard the shot. We used to hear so much gunfire back then, that I didn't pay much attention. Later I put two and two together: the four men were there to provide protection for the assassin as he drove away.

(Regina García)

"MONSEÑOR ROMERO'S BEEN KILLED!!"

"No! It can't be!"

All the phones in San Salvador are ringing at the same time. Everyone who answers hears the same news, and everyone hangs up with the same stupor, the same disbelief, the same tears. The kind of tears you would cry for your father or your mother.

"It's true. Turn on the radio!"

"There's nothing on the radio yet!"

"The news is on the streets. Everyone's saying it's true!"

"Where? How? Who?"

"It was D'Aubuisson!"

El Salvador's heart is beating to the rhythm of March 24, the rhythm of agony.

---

[1] *Guayabera*—Men's dress shirt with decorative stitching.

I STAYED AT THE OFFICES OF THE ARCHDIOCESE a half hour longer than usual because I had to finish some things. Shortly after 6:30, I got a call from the *hospitalito* telling me about his death, but I didn't believe it. In the days before, I'd received so many calls threatening him with death and so many calls telling me that he was already dead, in this place or that place, that I didn't believe it.

"Don't pay any attention to them. Those calls are from people who don't have anything better to do!" Monseñor would tell me when I told him about them.

But, what if . . . I called the *hospitalito* back.

"Yes. It's confirmed. Monseñor's been killed."

I didn't go home that night. Calls kept coming in from all over the world asking the same thing. They couldn't believe it either.

"It's true. Monseñor is dead." I repeated to exhaustion all night long.

(Dina Estrada)

MILA CALLED ALL HER FRIENDS and acquaintances. I know, because she called me, too.

"Did you hear they finally killed that son of a bitch? We're going to have a party tonight to celebrate. You're invited!"

They got together in San Benito that night and had a real carnival, with champagne, fireworks and dancing. Even D'Aubuisson was there. He was the guest of honor.

I couldn't stop crying.

(Flor Fierro)

WHEN WE GOT THE NEWS, it was a chaos of pain and surprise. I left a meeting I was in and ran all the way to the archdiocesan office. When I got to the stairway, I saw two poor, barefoot women sitting on the steps, crying. Their colorful skirts were wet with tears. I sat down to console them, or to console myself . . .

"This is it. This is the end. They've killed our beloved father. What more could they possibly do?"

We felt like orphans.

(José Simán)

JUAN CHACÓN, QUIQUE ÁLVAREZ . . . all of us in the FDR[2] were in a secret meeting. That's where we got the news. I'm not ashamed to say that we all broke down in tears. We couldn't think or analyze anymore. It was inconceivable to us that they could just do away with a man of so much courage. If we had called for it, there would have been a popular uprising that day! But we didn't have the necessary unity to do it.

(Leoncio Pichinte)

I DON'T THINK there was a rebel soldier in all of El Salvador who didn't cry. I did, too. We were all defeated that day.

(Nidia Díaz)

I HEARD WHEN I WAS AT THE UNIVERSITY. When the news arrived, the loudspeakers started announcing that Monseñor Romero had been assassinated. A kind of wave came over all of us. We could only hug each other and cry. Then, we each went looking for our own. I came here to the church. People kept arriving until the church was full. That evening, we all wanted to cry together.

(Miguel Tomás Castro)

---

[2] The Democratic Revolutionary Front, a political group formed to coordinate leftist opposition. It became the political arm of the guerilla movement when the five existing rebel groups united to form the Farabundo Marti National Liberation Front (FMLN) in May 1980. On November 28, 1980 five members of the FDR—including Juan Chacón and Enrique (Quique) Álvarez—were dragged from a meeting, tortured and assassinated.

I'D ALWAYS THOUGHT POLITICALLY about the possibility he'd be killed, but I had never thought about it in a personal way.

"Monseñor," I told him several times, "I'm going to get you a bulletproof jacket."

He would start to laugh and say: "There's no point in that."

The news of his death shook me to my core.

(Rubén Zamora)

WE NEVER THOUGHT those bastards would go so far. Never! And to kill him in the middle of a Holy Mass! When they killed him, do you know what I thought of? "If they do these things in the green wood, what will happen in the dry?" If they can do this to Monseñor Romero, what will happen to us worthless Indians?

(Adela López)

THE NEWS SPREAD in my *cantón*, and immediately afterwards, the sorrow and the rage. All of us *campesinos* felt a terrible grief weighing down on us. We were so discouraged. We gathered together to cry for him, even more than if he'd been a *compadre* or someone from our own family. He was our people's right arm, and they broke it.

(César Arce)

EVERYTHING ABOUT THE CRIME pointed to Roberto. That day I wanted to disappear, to fade away. It's been an ongoing trauma for me to have the same last name and to be from the same family as someone who caused such irreparable harm to the Salvadoran people. From the moment I heard the news until now, I've never had any doubt that that man—my brother—was responsible for the assassination of Monseñor.

(Marisa D'Aubuisson)

WHO KILLED MY BROTHER? D'Aubuisson, of course! Don't you know? From the time I heard the news, I knew it was him. He was the one who threatened him on TV, wasn't he? Showing his photo and saying he was dangerous, that you had to be careful of him because he was the secretary general of the guerrilla organizations? What more do you want?! Someday we'll know the rest of the story. But for now, the last page is still missing.

(Tiberio Arnoldo Romero)

THAT MONDAY, MARCH 24, the renewal of US military aid to the government of El Salvador was being discussed before a committee of the United States House of Representatives. I was in Washington that day, and I was about to make a statement to the committee when I received the news of his death. Remembering Monseñor's enormous desire to live, I spoke in his name. But it was for naught. A few days later, the military aid was approved by a clear majority.

(Jorge Lara-Braud)

THE NEWS RAN through Latin America like a wounded fox. In the Brazilian Amazon, another bishop, Don Pedro Casaldáliga, heard it and expressed the deep sorrow of the whole continent in the first poem written for Saint Romero of the Americas: " . . . Poor, glorious pastor/ murdered for money/ by dollars/ and exchange rates/ like Jesus, by order of the empire . . ."

I WAS EDITING THE HOMILY from Sunday, March 23. That was my task every Monday. The rule in my house was that I was not to be interrupted by anyone for any reason. But my sister came in to tell me. I didn't want to believe it, and I hurried to the Policlínica, where they'd taken him from the *hospitalito*. I went in. There were already a lot of people around, and the journalists had already arrived. He was on a low stretcher, covered up to his chest with a sheet. There was a big needle in his heart, pointing to the place where the bullet had hit. Monseñor looked like he was sleeping. They made me leave when they were going to do the autopsy.

(María Julia Hernández)

SINCE I WAS DRESSED IN WHITE, they thought I was a nurse, and they let me stay.

"Could you hold him please, sister?"

I pulled Monseñor up to me, as if I was cradling him, so they could take the x-rays from underneath. Then I turned him on his side, for the next ones. The sheet was soaked with blood.

(María Teresa Echeverría)

"THE PROJECTILE that took Monseñor Romero's life was a 25 caliber encased explosive. The bullet penetrated the heart and traversed the body, lodging finally in the fifth dorsal rib. Death was due to internal hemorrhaging caused by the bullet wound."

(Autopsy report)

SOON WE STARTED TO HEAR BOMBS exploding all over San Salvador. The plan was to do the autopsy first, then take him to the funeral parlor and from there to the basilica for the wake, but when the bombs started going off, it wasn't clear that was going to be possible. Finally, they embalmed him at the Policlínica, and we went running to the *hospitalito* to get his clothes, his chasuble and his crozier. Bombs were exploding everywhere.

(María Téllez)

THE SISTERS ALL WENT TO SEE HIM at the Policlínica. There was already a really long line of people waiting to pass by his coffin. As they went by, they were crying, crossing themselves, praying the rosary . . . But when I passed in front of him, I thought he looked like he was taking his nap, just like he used to do back when he was a young priest in our convent in San Miguel. I leaned over and kissed him on his forehead. Afterwards, the photo of the nun kissing the bishop came out in newspapers all over the world.

(Germana Portillo)

HIS BLOOD WAS STILL THERE, poured out on the floor around the altar of the *hospitalito* chapel.

"They're going to bring him here for a Mass," I was told.

The bombs were still going off. It was somewhere between 4:00 and 5:00 in the morning. The sun hadn't even come up yet, and it seemed like the whole world was falling down around us. Why were there so many bombs? Was it our boys voicing their protest or the others trying to instill more fear in people? It was still dark when the Mass was held.

"When the sun comes up, we're going to take him to the basilica," Urioste said.

(María Teresa Echeverría)

THE BASILICA WAS FULL OF PEOPLE waiting for him. Someone had put flyers on the walls saying, "Monseñor, talk to God on behalf of El Salvador." As soon as he was brought in, a Mass started, and at 10:00 in the morning, there was another one. There were too many people for them all to fit, and everyone was in tears, sobbing so that it just broke your heart.

"Ay, *padrecito*, ay! What have they done to you, *padrecito*?"[3]

"Why did you leave us? Why?"

From there a procession formed, thousands and thousands of people, 10 abreast, marching toward the Cathedral. There, an even larger crowd awaited him, and another Mass began.

(Teresa Armijo)

THE POPULAR ORGANIZATIONS had the Cathedral occupied during those days, but we got out right away so they could have Monseñor's wake there. We left some banners inside where we'd writ-

---

[3]*padrecito*—An affectionate version of *padre*, or "father."

ten, "Compañero Oscar Romero, Onward to Victory!" and other banners with other messages: "We don't want to see Bishops Revelo or Aparicio or the nuncio here. They are traitors!" and "We repudiate the presence of scribes and pharisees."

(Nicolás López)

URIOSTE HAD THE HOMILY that day in the Cathedral:

" . . . They've murdered our father, they've murdered our pastor, they've murdered our prophet and they've murdered our guide. It's as if we all lost a part of ourselves yesterday . . ."

We were an orphaned people.

They made two rows of benches from where his coffin was in the front all the way to the doors in the back. And that whole area filled up with flowers—some beautiful ornate wreaths, and other more simple arrangements made of handfuls of flowers and palm leaves. Thousands—no, millions—of flowers came in. I don't think there were any flowers left in all of El Salvador that day. They were all there.

(Teodora Puertas)

THE LINE OF PEOPLE passing by to see him didn't diminish day or night. Arrangements were made for buses, and huge numbers of campesinos came to his wake at the Cathedral. Some came on foot. They came from all over the country, from every cantón, from every corner. We men cried the same as the women. Everyone was mourning—workers and campesinos, right alongside some people with money whose hearts had changed because of him. There were children there, too—little kids who already knew what a great loss it was.

(Moisés Calles)

WHEN I WENT BACK TO SEE HIM in his coffin, he was dressed in his white vestments and red stole like he was ready for the eternal Mass. Everything we'd lived through came flooding into my memory, and it all seemed suddenly clear.

"You know?" I said to a friend, "God gave us a prophet for three years. And everything has happened in the period of time between two Eucharists: that single Mass on March 20, 1977 and the Mass that was never finished yesterday, March 24, 1980."

(Inocencio Alas)

San Salvador, March 25, 1980. In the large, unfinished Cathedral of San Salvador, people stood in long lines today for a close-up viewing of "the bishop of the world" as Monseñor Oscar Arnulfo Romero, assassinated yesterday evening, was called. Seven different lines came in through the west doors of the Cathedral from different points in the Barrios plaza. People passed by the coffin, laid down their gifts of flowers, and left by the side doors—visibly shaken and moved to tears.

On this first day, approximately 100 people per minute came into the Cathedral between 10:30 AM and 7:30 PM, making a total of approximately 54,000 Salvadorans who came to say good-bye to their pastor today. Sources from the Archdiocese announced that the body will be open for viewing in the Cathedral until Sunday, March 30, when the funeral service and burial will be held.

IT WAS ALMOST HOLY WEEK, which is always the hottest time of year. During the five days between his assassination and burial, San Salvador became another city. On the streets, in the markets, in the neighborhoods . . . Nobody talked about anything else. All compasses pointed toward the Salvadoran who was lying in the heart of the Cathedral.

"There won't be a homily this Sunday . . ." a lot of us said with nostalgia, dreaming, all the while, that he would somehow get up and speak to us again.

"What will there be without him this Sunday? What will we do?"

Anything could have happened in those days, and the people were ready to go through whatever was necessary. It seemed like the world had stopped. We were all standing and waiting.

(Francisco Calles)

I DECIDED NOT TO GO SEE HIM DEAD. I wanted to remember him alive. I wanted to go far away from San Salvador. I couldn't stand the heaviness I felt, weighing me down with sadness, crushing me. The day of his burial was Palm Sunday, March 30, and at 8:00 in the morning, I was planning to go to the beach with my three girls and some friends. I was trying to get away.

But at 6:00 AM, Father Estrada came running to my house.

"We need a woman's voice on YSAX to narrate the burial. Our usual announcer can't come. You're the best person to do it."

I wouldn't have forgiven myself if I'd said no. I felt like the "old man" himself had asked me to do it—to accompany him to the end. "All right, Monseñor. This will be my last homage to you."

As if it were a festive occasion, then, I put on one of my favorite white dresses, and I went to the plaza. There, they put me on a big stage for the broadcast. It moved me so much to see that sea of people. In the multitude that was growing by the minute, I could feel the same palpable feeling, the same vibrations as I did in the Cathedral when he spoke.

While the plaza was filling up, my job was to read verses from the Gospel, parts of his homilies, testimonies of people that had known him, and parts of his biography. I announced the delegations that were arriving in the plaza, and read condolence letters, cards and telegrams from so many people . . . Paco Estrada and Paco Escobar were reading, too. YSAX was the only station broadcasting the funeral.

(Margarita Herrera)

TWO HUNDRED AND FIFTY THOUSAND PEOPLE were jammed into Plaza Libertad and the nearby streets, all listening to the funeral Mass of Monseñor Romero. Many of them carried pictures of him, pictures of all sizes, adorned with flowers or with palms for Palm Sunday. On the stairs in front of the Cathedral where I was, there was an improvised altar with the archbishop's coffin. Thirty bishops and 300 priests were concelebrating.

Fifteen minutes after the Mass began, an orderly column of 500 people, walking eight abreast, joined the rest of the crowd. They were representatives of the popular organizations who were united in the Revolutionary Coordination of the Masses. Juan Chacón was in front, leading them. They carried their banners as they marched, and when they laid a wreath of flowers by the coffin, the crowd cheered.

The Mass continued. When it was time for the homily, the pope's representative, Cardinal Corripio Ahumada, the Archbishop of Mexico, was paraphrasing one of Monseñor Romero's well-known teachings, "Violence cannot kill truth or justice," when suddenly he was left speechless by the thundering explosion of a bomb.

The explosion came from the farthest side of the National Palace which, like the Cathedral, is located on one of the sides of the plaza. I saw it go off, and kept watching in the direction of the palace with my mouth open. Other booming explosions followed. I saw flames and dense smoke coming from the National Palace. It was as if the pavement were on fire. The crowd started to run, terrified, away from the Palace. Immediately you could hear the sound of gunfire all around. Thousands of people started running towards us like a massive wave. Behind us, there was only the empty Cathedral.

(Jorge Lara-Braud)

I WAS UP IN THE BELLTOWER of the Cathedral, looking out over that huge gathering of people. It was beautiful—solemn—like a field of grass rippling in the wind. But after the bombs went off, it was all terror, like a stampede of cattle. Everyone was running, trying to get away from the sharpshooters that were spraying the people with bullets from the National Palace. People were looking for refuge wherever they could. The Cathedral had always been a welcoming place, and thousands ran toward it. The tragedy was that the gates of the Cathedral open outwards. The more people pushed, the more they closed themselves out. Soon people started to climb the grating and jump over. But all of the iron bars had sharp points on the top. People were falling and pushing each other. They were cutting themselves, tearing open their arms and legs. And many of those who were the farthest back were trampled to death.

(Antonio Fernández Ibáñez)

WHEN THE BOMBS WENT OFF, we were in a building right next to the Cathedral. It was an old shell of a building, made of wood and zinc and full of empty egg cartons. We were there trying to connect the YSAX radio with Radio Sandino in Managua so the Nicaraguans could broadcast the ceremony, too. The mobile radio unit was setup in that old building on Sundays to broadcast the homilies.

Suddenly, when the explosions happened in the plaza, in an instant the tiny little place was flooded with people with terror on their faces. The broadcast was cut off at that point. It was the government who cut us off, but we hadn't seen the avalanche of people in the plaza and we didn't understand what was happening at all. We just heard shooting outside and then found ourselves packed to overflowing in the room. We were running out of oxygen, the building felt like it was going to fall in on us and people were screaming prayers: "Save us, Monseñor!"

(Margarita Herrera)

THE SAN SALVADOR CATHEDRAL can't adequately hold more than 3,000 people standing up. After half an hour of battle in the plaza, more than twice that many were squeezed inside, and there were still many others outside pushing to get in.

People were standing on all the last available spaces, including the main altar. We couldn't move at all, and soon it got to where we could barely breathe. The building shook with the blasts of the bombs, and a terrible echo amplified the noise of the firing guns. All of this was juxtaposed over a background of weeping and prayers rising up from every corner.

I tried to control my panic by looking out for my neighbors, praying with them and trying to keep them calm with comforting words, some of which I'd learned from Monseñor Romero.

I was in the second line of people counting from the wall, and Cardinal Corripio was on my right. On my left, in the line behind me, a woman was praying to God as she was beginning to die. I could barely turn my head toward her, but that's all I could do. I was a Presbyterian lay person, but I improvised the Catholic last rites. "Your sins are forgiven. Go in God's Peace," I prayed. The woman died but she remained standing. There was no place where she could lay to rest on the floor. In some places, people were able to lift those who'd fainted or died over their heads, but no one knew where to put them.

At one point, while we all struggled to survive, I began to hear a shout rise up above the din of the bombs, gunshots and prayers. People were carrying something in their hands over their heads. I was having a hard time making out what it was that was coming towards us. But soon, everyone in the Cathedral had joined in a song announcing its arrival: *"El pueblo unido/ jamás será vencido/ el pueblo unido . . ."*—"A people united/ will never be defeated . . ."

Finally, I could see what the song was announcing: it was Monseñor Romero's coffin. It was coming into the Cathedral transported on everyone's fingertips, opening up a path to his final resting place.

(Jorge Lara-Braud)

IT FELT LIKE THE CATHEDRAL WAS FALLING APART, like it was sand, or water. It was like it was the end of the world, or Judgement Day. I heard a nun shout:

"Let us pray, for this is the final hour!"

You could feel the fervor of that conglomeration of people, each one praying his or her prayers, asking for a peaceful death. And flies swarmed around the dead bodies that were falling around us and that no one could retrieve.

(Alejandro Ortiz)

"AY! FOR THE LOVE OF GOD!" The communion wafers had to be consecrated. "What happened to them?" It was pure chaos! People were trying to climb along the railing to protect themselves. And then there were the high officials of the Church that were visiting. They had to be protected, too. What did we do? We pushed them into the confession booths so that they wouldn't be killed by a stray bullet.

"This is the repression that Monseñor was denouncing!" people shouted loudly, without fear.

"Stop the repression! Stop the repression!" shouted others.

"It doesn't matter! We're prepared to die with him!" most people were saying.

It was the hour of death, and we were embracing Monseñor's coffin.

"They wouldn't even let us bury him in peace!"

There were some who wanted to give more air to the coffin so that he wouldn't get too hot with all the people pressing in around him. There was even a person who died in the squeeze to open a space where no space existed for Monseñor's body.

By the time a decision was made to finish the Mass and bury him, the chalices and hosts had disappeared, and we couldn't figure out how. Maybe people carried them along in the stampede. Julita's mother was trampled to death, and they found her with a little pile of wafers in her lap.

(Juliana Estévez)

AFTER A FEW HOURS, when the Cathedral was full of dead people but there was a little more room, Cardinal Corripio, along with other bishops and priests, were able to get closer to Monseñor's coffin to see if they could finish the liturgy. They were soaked in sweat, and many of them were standing on top of benches.

"Give me the hosts so I can continue the Mass," Corripio said.

"There aren't any, your Excellency."

"Give me the wine."

"There isn't any."

"How about a prayer book, so we can at least do the responsorial prayers . . ."

"There's no book either, your Excellency."

Then Samuel Ruíz, the Bishop of Chiapas, took a little book of prayers out of his pocket, and they used that to say a few prayers before burying him. Everything was done in a hurry. The crypt was already open. They put the coffin in quickly. And even more quickly, the masons started to close it over with cement and bricks, bricks and cement . . . until they were done.

(María Julia Hernández)

I DON'T KNOW HOW MUCH TIME I SPENT in that old building, screaming into a megaphone, trying to calm people down. When it finally emptied out and I was able to go into the Cathedral, it was almost empty. Along the center aisle where Monseñor's body had been set out for viewing earlier, there was line of women who had died asphyxiated inside or trampled outside. Most of the 40 dead and more than 200 wounded that morning were older women.

I went outside to the plaza. It was like an abandoned battlefield. On the pavement there were broken eyeglasses, purses, bags and piles and piles of shoes lost in the stampede.

(Margarita Herrera)

I WAS GOING BACK TO MY HOUSE, crying without tears. Would my mother be dead or alive? She was so old, and I knew she'd been in the plaza . . . I was thinking this when suddenly I saw him, and I was transfixed at the sight . . . A poor man in rags was throwing stones against a big Coca-Cola sign near the Cathedral. He would throw a stone and shout: "It's your fault!"

Then another stone, with even more anger: "It's all your fault!"

He repeated his ritual before the whole world, and before no one in particular. I left him there to take out his anger for all of us.

(Ernesto Martínez)

"THIS COUNTRY IS GIVING BIRTH to a new time. That's why there is pain and anguish, blood and suffering. Christ reminds us that the woman suffers when the time is at hand, but when she gives birth to a new human being, she forgets all of her pain.

"These times of suffering will also pass! Afterwards, we will have the joy of knowing that when the pain of the birth came, we lived as Christians, clinging to our faith in Christ, and that because of it, we did not give in to hopelessness.

"What seems impossible now—what seems a dead-end street—is already being marked by God with hope. This evening we are called to live with the optimism that tells us that, even though we don't know how, God will bring our country out of its troubles, and in the new moment which is to come, the good news of Jesus Christ will still be shining."

(Homily, Christmas Eve, 1979)

YEARS HAVE GONE BY. The plaques of gratitude are piling up around the tomb of Monseñor Romero—on the walls and over the tombstone.

There are little plaques made of varnished wood giving thanks for the miraculous healing of eyes, varicose veins, or the soul. There are marble plaques in square or rectangular shapes, and plastic ones in the shape of a heart or a diamond, giving thanks to the archbishop for a child who was found or for a mother who was healed. They ask for peace. Above all, they ask for peace and for an end to the war. And they name loved ones. There are also little pieces of paper where the thanks are in the form of stories, half-finished novels, letters—even poems and songs. And there are pieces of decorated cardboard, pieces of cloth—embroidered, white, or multi-colored . . . Everything that has caused pain is here, and everything that has brought back happiness, too. Nothing is lost. It all comes back to the arms of Monseñor.

One morning in rainy season when the skies were heavy with the day's rain, a man in rags, with a shirt full of holes and hair made curly by dust, was cleaning the tomb carefully with one of his rags. The sun had just come up, but he was active and awake. And even though the rag was dirty with grease and time, it left the tombstone clean and shiny.

When he was done, he smiled with satisfaction. At that hour in the morning, he hadn't seen anyone, and no one had seen him. Except for me. I saw him.

When he left to go out, I felt like I needed to talk to him.

"Why do you do that?"

"Do what?"

"Clean Monseñor's tomb."

"Because he was my father."

"What do you mean . . ?"

"It's like this. I'm just a poor man, you know? Sometimes I make some money carrying things for people in the market in a little cart. Other times I beg for alms. And sometimes I spend it all on liquor and end up lying hungover on the streets . . . But I never get too discouraged. I had a father! I did! He made me feel like a person. Because he loved people like me, and he didn't act like we made him sick. He talked to us, he touched us, he asked us questions. He had confidence in us. You could see in his eyes that he cared about me. Like parents love their children. That's why I clean off his tomb, because that's what children do.

(Regina García)